❖

THE MYSTERY OF WORK

❖ ❖ ❖

Saints
Popes
Mystics
Seculars

Reflect on **Christ's** Words

"Without Me You Can Do Nothing"

❖

Second Edition

A.M.D.G.

Previously published private revelations included in this book were all originally published with ecclesiastical approval. Previously unpublished private revelations included herein have been reviewed and informally cleared by theologians and priests all of whom are in union with the Magisterium of the Roman Catholic Church. In all cases, the editor and publisher of this work defers to the judgments of that Magisterium regarding the materials printed in this book.
The editor, author and publisher represents and warrants
that he either owns or has the legal right
to publish all material in this book.

❖

CHRIST PANTOCRATOR

ICON ON COVER is a public domain image of a sixth century icon (encaustic on panel) at St. Catherine Monastery in the Sinai, copy of which was obtained by courtesy of the Monastery of
St. Isaac of Syria Skete, Bopscobel, Wisconsin.
The following is quoted from *Wikipedia*: "Pantocrator is a compound word formed from the Greek for 'all' and the verb meaning 'To accomplish something' or 'to sustain something' (κρατεω). This translation speaks more to God's actual power; i.e., God *does* everything (as opposed to God *can do* everything)."

❖

Second Edition
Copyright © 2012 by Logos Institute
ISBN 978-0-9801174-1-7

Editor: Bernard Scott
Logos Institute, Inc. is a Catholic
publishing apostolate

Logos Institute Press.
Tarpon Springs, FL 34689, U.S.A.
logos.institute@gmail.com
www.logosinstitute.org

❖

❖   ❖   ❖   ❖   ❖

I am the vine, you are the branches. Whoever remains in me and I in him will bear much fruit, because without me you can do nothing. Anyone who does not remain in me will be thrown out like a branch and wither; and the branches will be gathered, thrown into the fire and burned.

— John 15: 5-6

❖

"We will say no more,

'Our God,' to the work of our hands."

Hosea 14: 3

❖

"Set me as a seal upon your heart, as a

seal upon your arm."

Canticle of Canticles 8:6

❖ ❖ *Table of Contents* ❖ ❖

MEDITATIONS DIRECTORY………………………………......*v*

INTRODUCTION

Notes Toward a Doctrine of Work……..……….....1

MEDITATIONS

I - Inspiration, Grace, Free Will ………………..23

II - Faith and Understanding about God
and Self……………………………………....47

III - Theology of Primary and
Secondary Causes …………………............81

IV - Work, What We Do………………………... 145

V - Devotion and Virtue in Work…………….....197

VI - The Need for Prayer ………………….......…211

VII - Meditation on The Lord's Prayer…………....229

ADDENDUM

An Unlikely Story: A Case in Point……….............. 249

EPILOGUE…………………………………………..273

ENDNOTES, BIBLIOGRAPHY, ACKNOWLEDGMENTS………277

❖

iv

Meditations Directory

❖

José Luis Acuña R.	III-10
Schema Monk Agapii	III-37, VI-9, VI-10, VI-20, VI-22
St. Annibale di Francia	IV-18, VI-12, p. 275
St. Thomas Aquinas	III-4, III-89, III-93, III-94, IV-80, VI-21
St. Athanasius	III-82
St. Augustine	I-29, I-32, I-34, III-16. III-97
Sts. Barsanouphios and John	IV-66
Venerable Bede	I-34
Blessed Dina Bélanger	IV-59, V-21
Orth. Archb. Anthony Bloom	IV-69, VI-6
Fr. Raniero Cantalamessa	IV-61
St. Catherine of Genoa	III-78, IV-40
St. Catherine of Siena	II-40, II-50, III-55, III-91, IV-87, VI-8
Fr. Jean-Pierre de Caussade	I-4, I-5, II-15, IV-28, IV-29, IV-30, IV-68
Dom Jean-Baptiste Chautard	I-36, III-105, IV-37, IV-75, IV-107, VI-29, VI-33, p. 273
G. K. Chesterton	VI-11
Chrysostom	I-32, III-30,VI-17
St. Claude de La Columbière	II-43
Clement of Rome	IV-83
Sister Mary Consolata (Fr. Lorenzo Sales, IMC)	II-20, II-21, II-22, II-23, III-79
Consuelo	II-57, III-2, III-86, IV-1, IV-103, V-17, V-18, V-19, VI-1, VI-30, VI-31
Cyril of Jerusalem	II-38
Einstein	II-8, IV-84
Bl. Anne Catherine Emmerich	III-63, p. 269
Thomas M. Fahy	I-18
Eileen George	II-47
Pope Gregory the Great	III-51
Romano Guardini	IV-53
Tony Hendra	IV-56
Imitation of Christ	IV-21, IV-43
St. Irenaeus	III-1

Meditations Directory (cont'd)

St. John of the Cross   II-24, II-36, II-54, IV-99

Pope John Paul II   pp. 1-4, IV-10, IV-76, VI-34

Justin Martyr   IV-20

Helen Keller   I-19
  (Anne Sullivan)

St. Maria Faustina Kowalska   III-22, III-31, III-56, IV-71, IV-85

Nicholas Lash   VI-4

Brother Lawrence   II-10, II-11, II-12, II-13, IV-6, IV-82, V-4, V-5,
  (Joseph de Beaufort)   V-6

Pope Leo XIII   VI-5

Peter Lombard   IV-15

Blessed Columba Marmion   I-37

Venerable Mary of Agreda   I-6. I-7, I-9, I-10, II-46, III-87, IV-4, IV-81, IV-92, V-2, V-3, V-14, V-16

Archb. Luis Maria Martinez   IV-73

Sr. Mary of the Holy Trinity   I-31, II-1, II-5, III-39, III-41, III-66, III-69, III-72, IV-74, IV-94, IV-96, IV-97, IV-98, IV-106, V-15, VI-24

H. Monier-Vinard, S.J., ed.   II-32, III-58, IV-17

Origen   II-25

Hugh Owen   III-62, IV-41, IV-42

Luisa Piccarreta   I-2, I-24, I-25, I-26, I-27, I-28, II-2, II-4, II-9, II-26, II-27, II-29, II-35, III-3, III-6, III-9, III-11, III-12, III-13, III-14, III-18, III-33, III-36, III-47, III-50, III-52, III-53, III-57, III-61, III-64, III-65, III-68, III-75, III-77, III-81, III-84, III-99, III-100, III-101, III-102, III-103, IV-7, IV-11, IV-12, IV-13, IV-14, IV-16, IV-18, IV-34, IV-35, IV-64, IV-70, IV-72, IV-77, IV-78, IV-79, IV-89, IV-104, IV-105, V-7, V-8, V-9, V10, V-11, V-22, V-23, VI-14, VI-33, pp.13, 17, 18, 274, 276

Pope Pius XII   IV-9

Joseph Cardinal Ratzinger   I-13, II-53
  (Pope Benedict XVI)

Canon Francis Ripley   VI-13

Fr. Matthias J. Scheeben   IV-33

Meditations Directory (cont'd)

Socrates	II-49
Fr. Raphael Simon, O.C.S.O.	III-92, V-1
Johann Tauler	III-73
Mother Teresa of Calcuta	VI-16
Theodore of Mopseustia	IV-90
Theodoret of Cyr	III-32
Theophan The Recluse	I-14, I-15, II-19, III-38, III-43, III-48, IV-23, IV-24, IV-51, IV-67, IV-86, IV-91, IV-100, V-12, VI-2, VI-19, VI-25, VI-26, VI-27, VI-28
Ste. Thérèse of Lisieux	I-3, IV-36, IV-49, IV-50
Maria Valtorta	VI-15
Second Vatican Council *(Lumen Gentium)*	I-35, II-59
St. Vincent de Paul	IV-22

❖

FOR BY GRACE
you have been saved through faith;
and this is not your own doing,
it is the gift of God—
not because of works, lest any man boast.
For we are his workmanship,
created in Christ Jesus
for good works,
which God prepared beforehand,
that we should walk in them.

Ephesians 2: 8-10

Prologue

Dear reader, as you will see, the set of short meditations contained in this collection all revolve, in one way or another, directly or indirectly, around Christ's mysterious statement: *"Without me you can do nothing"* (John 15:5). Now you may well ask, is there any statement of Our Lord's more opaque to our understanding than this? What can it possibly mean *practically*? What can it mean to a busy secular world to say that we can do nothing without Jesus? In an age where the ideal of personal achievement and the autonomous self holds sway so unquestionably, are we supposed to think that we've got it wrong somehow? Are we who so esteem self-reliance to take Jesus *literally* when it seems so easy not to?

Well, for all our vaunted self-sufficiency, the very air we breathe must be given. And every heartbeat. A little reflection tells us that what brought us into this life and keeps us going in our daily rounds does not come from us.

Dear reader, if you will read even just one or two of these meditations every morning, day after day, and then spend a few moments during the day reflecting on what you have read, taking it to heart, the meaning of Our Lord's statement in *John 15:5* will little by little become very clear to you. And as that happens it will surely change the way you go about doing whatever it is you do in the course of a busy day. Indeed, when that happens, dear reader, many blessings will be yours and those with whom you spend your day.

The *Introduction* to this collection seeks to outline a doctrine of work based on these words of Our Lord. It begins with brief excerpts from John Paul II's papal encyclical on work, *Laborem Exercens,* and then offers a reflection that summarizes what the many voices in this volume have to teach us both about the meaning of work and the way to work. And in the *Addendum* you will read a true and rather remarkable story of what can be done when Our Lord is allowed to enter a work.

— The compiler, for all whose reflections are gathered here

HOW TO APPROACH THIS BOOK

It is recommended that you read the "Introduction" carefully, before anything else. There you will find described four individuals who represent four different ways of going about a task, whatever that task might be. As the "Introduction" explains, only two of the ways of working described there are pleasing to God.

Some readers may then want to begin reading the book, little by little, from front to back. Other may find the book somewhat difficult to get into, given the many, variegated passages in this work. If you should desire a more organized approach, it is highly recommended that you follow the reading guideline suggested in the table below. The recommended readings will help you better understand both the right and wrong ways of working that are cited in the "Introduction." Approaching the book this way will insure a better grasp of the book's purpose, which is to understand how to work in a way that pleases Our Lord.

SUGGESTED READING SELECTIONS

FIRST INDIVIDUAL	SECOND INDIVIDUAL
Caution re first impulses	*God wants to be involved*
I-18 III-64	IV-16 IV-72
IV-43 IV-78	IV-74 IV-77
IV-92 IV-93	IV-79 IV-99
IV-105 V-3	*Why don't we allow God in:*
	Trusting in our own powers
The impulse of grace	III-54 III-55 IV-58 IV-91
I-11 1-14	*Distraction*
II-19 II-21	IV-67 IV-96 VI-9 VI-10
II-22 II-23	*Egoism*
II-28 III-80	II-19 III-63 IV-50
IV-61 IV-72	*Lack of self-knowledge*
	II-29 II-36 II-40 III-61
	III-91 VI-6 VI-20

THIRD INDIVIDUAL	FOURTH INDIVIDUAL
God wants to work with us III-68 III-100 IV-12 IV-16 IV-72 VI-24	*Working in union with Christ* II-21 II-22 II-23 III-15 III-18 III-36 III-53 IV-34 IV-49 IV-59 IV-73 IV-79
Merging work and prayer III-48 IV-56 IV-67 IV-82	*How do we do this?* II-20 II-31 II-50 II-52 II-53 III-31 III-50 IV-75 IV-98 VI-8
Working with God I-13 II-28 III-43 IV-51 IV-61 IV-71 VI-5 VI-11 VI-18 VI-23	*He is the vine, we are the branches* I-36 III-62 III-92 III-98 IV-40 IV-41 VI-29

FREE GROUP STUDY GUIDE AVAILABLE

Since its original publication in 2008, *The Mystery of Work* has been effectively used for group discussions in parish settings. Almost invariably, participants say they experience a life-changing appreciation of the very ordinary things they do in the course of their day, in short a new understanding about work itself, work of any kind. The passages from saints, mystics, theologians, popes—many of these passages Church-approved locutions from Our Lord—all testify directly or indirectly to the deep interest God takes in our ordinary acts. This should not seem strange. After all, Our Lord spent the first thirty years of his life engaged in ordinary acts little different from our own. Once we understand this, these very acts of ours, so similar to Our Lord's, can be seen as a way to deepen our relationship to God.

This experience with parish study groups gave rise to a formal Study Guide for this purpose. This guide is now freely available under the title, *The Mystery of Work Study Guide*. The Guide takes two forms: one for group participants, another for discussion leaders.

The 25-page participant's Guide recommends selected readings from the book along with discussion questions, covering the book in six lessons.

The 10-page group leader's version offers guidance to the discussion of each of the six lessons. This version is also suitable for private individuals who might prefer a more guided reading of the book.

A third aid is also freely available to the discussion leader, a 13-page document called *Discussion Leader's Supplement*. This document is designed to assist the discussion leader in presenting the general topic to the group at their first meeting, presumably before anyone has yet had a chance to become familiar with the book.

All Study Guides can be downloaded free-of-charge from the Logos Institute website:

http://www.logosinstitute.org

Feel free to communicate with Logos Institute regarding any issues concerning the use of this Guide. Contact AJS at:

logos.institute@gmail.com

❖

Introduction

❖

Notes Toward a Doctrine of Work

Pope John Paul II, in his encyclical on work, *Laborem Exercens*, notes that, of all of God's creatures, man alone has the capacity to do work, and that in this he imitates his Creator who worked six days in creating the world, resting on the seventh. And Jesus spoke of his Father as "working still" (*Jn 5:17*). Work therefore has inherent dignity and man, insofar as he is a worker, imitates the creativity of God and finds his own dignity and fulfillment in work.

But work is also, in man's fallen state, "toil," and to that extent a "curse" to which he has been condemned by sin (*Gen 3:19*). But even here, work has no less value for man. Pope John Paul II says that this is so because, in God's Providence, work may also be a cross, a form of sacrifice that can be salvific in its effects. Thus, just as work in its glorious sense is a participation in the creativity of God as Creator, work as "toil" and suffering is able to participate in the salvific work of the Cross.

The Pope also reminds us of the Church's perennial teaching that man must never be treated as though existing for the sake of work, but to the contrary, work must always be for man's sake and benefit. This order is disturbed only at grave price to man's created dignity.

❖

"Elements for a Spirituality of Work"

(Excerpts from the Papal Encyclical Laborem Exercens *of John Paul II)*

The Church sees it as her duty to speak out on work from the viewpoint of its human value... She sees it as her particular duty to form a spirituality of work which will help all people to come closer, through work, to God... *(24.2)*.

❖   ❖   ❖

The word of God's Revelation is profoundly marked by the fundamental truth that man, created in the image of God, shares by his work in the activity of the Creator and that, within the limits of his own human capabilities, man in a sense continues to develop that ability, and perfects it as he advances further and further in the discovery of the resources and values contained in the whole of creation... *(25.2)*.

❖   ❖   ❖

The *Book of Genesis* is in a sense the first "gospel of work." For it shows what the dignity of work consists of: it teaches that man ought to imitate God, his Creator, in working, because man alone has the unique characteristics of likeness to God. Man ought to imitate God both in working and also in resting, since God himself wished to present his own creative activity under the form of work and rest... *(25.3)*.

❖   ❖   ❖

Man's work too requires a rest every "seventh day" but also cannot consist in the mere exercise of human strength in external action: it must leave room for man to prepare himself, by becoming more and more what in the Will of God he ought to be, for the "rest" that the Lord reserves for his servants and friends (*cf Mt 25:21*) ... *(25.3)*.

❖   ❖   ❖

Awareness that man's work is a participation in God's activity ought to permeate, as the [Second Vatican] Council teaches, even "the most ordinary everyday activities... [The faithful] can justly consider that by their labor they are unfolding the Creator's work, consulting the advantages of their brothers and sisters, and contributing by their personal industry to the realization in history of the divine plan"... (25.3).

❖   ❖   ❖

[As] we read in the Constitution *Lumen Gentium*... "Therefore, by their competence in secular fields and by their personal activity, elevated from within by the grace of God, let [the faithful] work vigorously so that by human labor, technical skill, and civil culture created goods may be perfected according to the design of the Creator and the light of his Word"... *(25.6)*.

"Christ, the man of work"

Jesus not only proclaimed but first and foremost fulfilled by his deeds the "gospel," the word of Eternal Wisdom that had been entrusted to him. Therefore this was also "the gospel of work," because *he who proclaimed it was himself a man of work*, a craftsman like Joseph of Nazareth... *(26.1)*.

❖ ❖ ❖

If we do not find in his words a special command to work—but rather on one occasion a prohibition against too much anxiety about work and life—at the same time the eloquence of the life of Christ is unequivocal: he belongs to the "working world," he has appreciation and respect for human work... *(26.1)*.

❖ ❖ ❖

It can indeed be said that *he looks with love upon human work* and the different forms that it takes, seeing in each one of these forms a particular facet of man's likeness with God, the Creator and Father. Is it not he who says, "My Father is the vinedresser," and in various ways puts *into his teaching* the fundamental truth about work which is already expressed in the whole tradition of the Old Testament, beginning with the Book of Genesis?... *(26.1)*.

❖ ❖ ❖

In his parables on the Kingdom of God, Jesus Christ constantly refers to human work: that of the shepherd, the farmer, the doctor, the sower, the householder, the servant, the steward, the fisherman, the merchant, the laborer. He also speaks of the various forms of women's work. He compares the apostolate to the manual work of harvesters, or fishermen. He refers to the work of scholars too... *(26.2)*.

❖ ❖ ❖

This teaching of Christ on work, based on the example of his life during his years in Nazareth, finds a particularly lively echo in the teaching of the Apostle Paul. Paul boasts of working at his trade (he was probably a tentmaker), and thanks to that work he was able even as an Apostle to earn his own bread. "With toil and labor we worked night and day, that we might not burden any of you"… *[2 Thess 3:8].*

Hence his instructions, in the form of *exhortation* and *command*, on the subject of work: "Now such persons we command and exhort in the Lord Jesus Christ to do their work in quietness and to earn their own living," he writes to the Thessalonians. In fact, noting that some "are living in idleness…not doing any work," the Apostle does not hesitate to say in the same context: "If anyone will not work, let him not eat." In another passage *he encourages* his readers: "Whatever your task, work heartily, as serving the Lord and not men, knowing that from the Lord you will receive the inheritance as your reward"… *(26.3).*

❖

Commentary and Notes

So one must work.[1] The obligation is commanded by our Creator, amply fulfilled in the working life of his Son, and pressed home to us in bold language by the Apostle, quoted above. No mortal is exempt from this obligation to work, to meet his or her responsibilities, and also, let us quickly add, to become the person he or she is meant to be, by developing and using talents and means God has given for these very purposes.

Still, the question remains as to how one is to go about one's work. How does one work in a proper way? Are there right ways and wrong ways? Certainly there are many ways one can go about a task, but, as we read in the chapters of this book, not all of them are good. St. Paul admonishes, "Whatever your task, work heartily[2]…" and then adds, "as serving God, not men."

"As serving God, not men." And least of all, not *self.* In taking on a task, one can be so self-absorbed that the thing that really matters in the effort is the benefits or perhaps the costs accruing to the self. That in fact would seem to describe many of us much of the time, but common as this is, and

---

[1] St. Vincent de Paul, IV-22; Theophan, IV-86
[2] *Thess 26:3*; Albert Einstein, IV-84

innocent as it may seem, self-interest as a primary motivation is defective and misguided. Jesus told Luisa Piccarreta that work done "not for him but for self-gratification, however good it may appear, is not pleasing to him." And Our Lord says that He will not bless work done in that spirit; it will fall short of what it would otherwise be when blessed.[3]

Or the work itself might come to mean so much that the worker for one reason or another becomes enslaved to it, either through internal psychological compulsion, as with workaholics, or through external circumstances that reduce the worker to mere means to material ends, as with those enslaved against their will. In either case, internally or externally, the worker is valued only for the sake of the work he performs, as work's slave and not as its master as Christian anthropology would have it.[4]

So how are we to work then? If motives of self-gratification are wrong, and over-attachment to the work itself is disordered, what is the right way? The answers offered in the selections of this book are clear and unmistakable — what makes work right and acceptable is work done, not for self, not for the sake of the work, but for the sake of others, first and foremost of whom must be God who created us, endowed us with gifts, and whose Providence supplies us with means and occasions to serve his purposes. We are to love and serve Him in this life so that we may enjoy Him forever in the next. We are meant to work for God and his good pleasure, and to do so with all our heart because of his goodness to us in the first place.

But still the question remains, does it not, as to how one is to go about this? How does one serve God well? One can have the best intentions, and intentions are certainly fundamental, but what of execution? Does the perfection that Our Lord calls us to not also include the way we go about performing our work?

To try to answer this, let us consider four individual workers each of whom has been given some job to do, and let us examine how each goes about accomplishing the work at hand. The nature of the task is unimportant; it could be anything, physical or mental. What matters is how the work is undertaken, how it is performed. As we shall try to show, four people can work in very different ways.

---

[3] Luisa Piccarreta, II-27, III-36
[4] *Imitation of Christ*, IV-21

In what follows, we employ the masculine convention when referring to the four individuals. We do this entirely for the sake of simplicity, but of course the gender of the individuals is not the issue—what is being said would of course apply to both men and women equally.

First Individual

The first individual is the rather self-absorbed person we have already touched upon whose deepest motivation in any work is self-satisfaction. The key word here is self. The first thing this person does when confronted with a task is to wrap his ego around it and never let anything or anyone else in. Rather than standing back to gain perspective or perhaps ask some advice, he plunges into the work willy-nilly. It may seem that he studies the matter at hand, and of course to some extent he does, and he may appear to listen to others, but he sees and hears very little outside of his own mind.[5] In the end what is most important to him, consciously or otherwise, is that the work reflect him and his ideas, even if this be at the cost of a better idea from someone else.[6]

Least of all does it occur to him to submit his mind to the matter at hand and let the matter itself suggest the way to proceed. A good worker of course would do just that, but our first friend doesn't work that way. For him the motivating undertow is always himself and what the work will say about him personally, which is why, when he looks at the work in progress, he is quick to see what is right and self-affirming, slow to see what is wrong and in need of correction. And this is why, too, he is the sort of person who thinks his work is finished when others see it as still half-done.

It is not that this individual lacks good intentions, or talent, but because he is shut in on himself, he works with preconceived ideas, and being preconceived, more often than not they are ill-conceived for the task at hand. All of this because he has next-to-no misgivings about his ideas and impulses and next-to-no idea what the situation ideally calls for.[7] This may be due to an immature, high opinion of his own abilities, or possibly his blatant self-confidence masks a secret fear of failure. Either case—immaturity or anxiety—could account for his impulsiveness and why it

---

[5] II-28; III-20

[6] Mary of Agreda, I-7 (last para.); Luisa Piccarreta, I-28 (last para.); IV-47

[7] I-11; *Imitation of Christ*, IV-43; Mary of Agreda, V-3

never occurs to him to challenge his own work. If we have any doubt about this, consider how this poor man reacts to criticism. Much like the rest of us, very probably.

Given all that we have seen about this first individual, is it any wonder he is not peaceful? Even his physical movements are brusque, lacking in gracefulness. If the work at hand entailed some physical object and that object could speak, we should not be surprised to hear it complain of manhandling. No wonder his work is often complicated, never quite on the mark and almost always leaving something to be desired.[8] This individual means well, tries hard, and is not a bad person. Truth be told, he is to be found almost everywhere you look, alas with too few exceptions. Most probably, we need only look in the mirror to find some semblance of his type.[9]

Second Individual

This second person, in approaching the task, is open to suggestions and criticism because, more than anything, he wants to get it right, even at the expense of his own ego if that has to be. Workers of this type stand out precisely because their work quality stands out, and it does so just because they do *not* impose ill-conceived ideas on the work. So too our second friend here. Before acting he pauses, considers all angles, listens to the matter, and to others. His tools are all laid out in advance, and he is in no hurry to begin.[10]

This person has a healthy misgiving about first impulses[11] regarding how to proceed, and when he gets an idea, he is inclined to challenge it before embracing it. He is like the sculptor who, before touching the marble, examines it to see what the stone might be telling him. What he winds up doing arises from a dialogue with the stone, wherein he modifies and adjusts his ideas, perhaps even to the extent of doing something quite different from his original intention, just because of what the stone has had to say to him.

He is like Socrates in Plato's dialogue *Crito*, who abruptly stops speaking in the middle of a sentence because an inner voice has told him what he

---

[8] *Psalm 127:1-2*; Theophan, I-14; Luisa Piccareta, IV-78
[9] Luisa Piccarreta, III-100
[10] Thomas M. Fahy, I-18 (Blessed Dina Bélanger)
[11] Luisa Piccarreta, IV-105

was about to say was false. Or like the great pianist Rubinstein, whose fingers, it is said, hesitated an infinitesimal instant before striking the key, as if to defer to a second, more perfect impulse in place of his first.[12]

He is like the scientist who, in attempting to find answers to a quandary, tests and re-tests his ideas, tossing them out one after the other until he gets something that begins to hold water. He is a good scientist precisely in the measure that what is important is not *his* ideas but the truth to be found out in the matter at hand.[13]

Or like that plumber who comes to your house to fix this hard-to-trace leak. He studies the problem, takes his time checking the pipeline above and below the wet spot, goes out to the truck more than once to get the right tool. He works quietly, no fuss, no mess, no noisy tools tossed to the floor, and before you know it the job is done and done well.

Or like the surgeon whose patients recover from the operation twice as fast as normal, with zero complications and hardly any scar.

This second individual takes pride in his abilities and achievements, to be sure. But he has learned how to work in a better way than our first friend. He has learned to have misgivings about first impulses because first impulses are often off the mark. He values truth in the work above his own ego, and for that reason becomes his own best critic, constantly checking his work to see where it might have gone wrong. And for that reason too he is open to criticism and help from others. If perchance he makes a mistake, he does not try to cover it up but is grateful to have found it and fixes it as best he can. And if he can't, he knows that mistakes teach valuable lessons.

It is not that he is humble so much as instinctively wise, wise enough to realize that only in this way can results be good and true. He may be proud but he has the virtue of objectivity[14], and because of that, goes further and achieves more. In sum, his work has a rightness about it, an excellence that our first individual is simply incapable of. As for his physical movements, they tend to be measured as well. It is not likely our second worker would be given to brusque, impulsive gestures, no more

----

[12] IV-93
[13] II-8 (Einstein)
[14] IV-54, 2nd para.

than to impulsive turns of the mind.[15] It might not be quite right to say that this second individual is peaceful, but he is calm and collected as he goes about his work.

But for all its apparent excellence, his work still lacks perfection the way God measures perfection. That is because this second individual works without so much as a thought of God.[16] As our Lord says to Luisa Piccarreta:

> *If you had been more humble and closer to Me you would not have done that work so poorly. But because you thought you could begin, continue and end the work without Me, you succeeded...but not according to my wish. Therefore ask my assistance at the start of everything you undertake. Always have Me present to work with you and it will be completed with perfection.[17]*

Third Individual

Our third individual approaches the work more as Our Lord would have it done, which is to say, doing it for Him and with his help.[18] As such, he stands on the far side of a "bottomless abyss"[19] that separates him from the first two, in the company of those who do what they do for God, not just for themselves, and who, as they go about their work, listen to Him and his holy agents for guidance[20], seeking to do as He tells them.[21] Now, it is true that the first two may also call themselves believers, but they do not work for God, do not think to invite God into their workaday actions, as when, for example, they hammer a nail, or bake a cake, or design a bridge, and as such they work as practicing atheists.

Not so our third friend. He is a true, functioning Christian because, before he begins any task, he prays. He takes to heart Christ's saying

---

[15] Brother Lawrence, IV-82

[16] Theophan, I-14, II-19; St. Catherine of Genoa, III-78; Luisa Piccarreta, IV-7, IV-77; Sister Mary of the Holy Trinity, IV-98; St. John of the Cross, IV-99

[17] Luisa Piccarreta, I-28; IV-72; St. Augustine, III-97; St. Catherine of Genoa, IV-40

[18] Jean-Paul de Caussade, IV-29; Theophan, IV-51; Jean-Baptiste Chautard, O.C.S.O., IV-75; Brother Lawrence, V-5

[19] St. Faustina, III-56

[20] Luisa Piccarreta, IV-16; Our Lady to Maria of Agreda, IV-92, V-3

[21] IV-101; Theophan, VI-25

that without Him we can do nothing. He takes to heart Christ's promise that those who ask shall receive. He is like G. K. Chesterton, who said he prays before doing anything at all.[22] At his best he is like the monks for whom work itself is a prayer (*laborare est orare*).[23]

Though our third friend is a lay person, he resembles the good priest Raniero Cantalamessa who says he asks God, "by the simple means of prayer…whether it is his will that I make that journey, do that job, pay that visit, buy that object, and then I will act or not."[24] Or he is like one wise enough to heed the Orthodox monk, Theophan:

> *When you…busy yourself with secular affairs, do it in such a way that you remember the Lord at the same time. Act and speak always with the same awareness that the Lord is near and directs everything according to his pleasure. Therefore, if there is something that requires your attention, prepare yourself beforehand so that you will not be withdrawn from the Lord in the course of attending to it, but will remain in his presence all the while.[25]*

What he does is not yet perfect; it still lacks the high perfection Christ calls us to, but what matters is that he has begun to let God into the details of his life and work. Yes, he has weaknesses, possibly some of them serious, and knows he must work out his salvation with "fear and trembling," as St. Paul admonishes. But he also takes to heart Paul's reassurance that "it is God who, for his own generous purposes, gives you the intention and the power to act" *(Phil 2:12-16a)*.

Yes, his life is far from perfect. His journey to God is taking him through a minefield of temptations, mistaken notions, distractions, unwise attachments, shortcomings, rebellions of pride, and so on. So yes, *fear and trembling*, for these are all things God will contend with in him.[26] But it is above all a journey into joy and peace as our good friend experiences, over and over again, that he is not alone, that God is with him in all the moments of his life and work, good and bad, big and small. *Joy and peace*

---

[22] G. K. Chesterton, VI-11
[23] Tony Hendra, IV-56
[24] Cantalamessa, IV-61
[25] Theophan, IV-67; Brother Lawrence, IV-82
[26] Jean-Pierre de Caussade, I-4, I-5; Luisa Piccarreta, II-29, III-61; Consuela, V-18; Anthony Bloom, VI-6

because these very shortcomings and weaknesses show up as opportunities for mercy, when mercy is trusted and truth is squarely faced.[27] As our third friend advances along this path of personal truths and divine truths leading both to self-knowledge[28] and the knowledge of God, he learns to say with Paul, *"when I am weak I am strong."* And the cry, *"O happy fault"* takes on ever-deeper meaning.

As this person approaches the assigned task, then, he turns to the One who has promised to help, the One to whom the first two individuals will not turn. He works carefully, confidently, preserving recollection, seeking to do the work as diligently as possible, watchful never to let the work mean too much too him.[29] And because of this faith , and the experiences borne of it, he has come to work peacefully, an inner peace already felt by those around him. And the fruit of this way of working becomes evident in the uncomplicated integrity of what he produces—nothing faked, nothing forced, nothing hurried, everything right and as it should be.[30]

To the world his work might seem ordinary. If a pianist, for example, he is unlikely to sound like Rubinstein; if a scientist, not likely to make great discoveries. Such distinctions are possible, of course, but hardly inherent to this third manner of working. Yet cumulatively, his work will exhibit a quality of rightness that thoughtful people invariably come to appreciate.[31] But what most distinguishes his work, what is most important about it, is the simple, hidden fact that God, being invited into the work, blesses it and accepts it for his purposes.[32] That the world remains clueless about this matters not a whit.

As for his physical movements, these too are apt to be different. Romano Guardini amusingly once suggested you should be able to tell a Christian by the way he climbs a tree. Someday perhaps our third friend may come to make movements like the rabbi Chagall tells us about, a holy teacher to whom disciples would travel from great distances not to hear words of wisdom but to witness how he tied his shoelace. Shortcomings remain,

---

[27] St. Claude de la Columbière, II-43; Jean-Pierre de Caussade, IV-30; Luisa Piccarreta, V-22; 2 *Cor 12: 7-10*

[28] Luisa Piccarreta, II-29; II-40 (St. Catherine of Siena)

[29] Theophan, II-19

[30] I-19 (Anne Sullivan); Hugh Owen, IV-41 (Dina Bélanger); Dina Bélanger, IV-59

[31] III-34

[32] Mary of the Holy Trinity, I-31; St. Faustina, IV-71

surely, but God can write straight with these crooked lines when our failings are brought to him. As the prophet Isaiah reminds us, "It is the Lord who accomplishes all that we have done."[33]

Fourth Individual

The fourth person we describe differs from the others in the most profound and fundamental way (and, of course, the "he" we employ in describing this person could just as easily, if not more likely, be a woman). Let us try to explain this person by way of contrast with the others. The first individual, we saw, places self at center stage and operates that way, producing work that gets by but, like an unseasoned, overweening actor, invariably leaves something to be desired, like less of himself. The second individual also sees himself as principal actor but he restrains upstaging impulses of self for the sake of objectivity and truth and a kind of fidelity to the task, and consequently performs his work in a superior way and with superior results. The third person, through a prayer life stirred by what he has learned about God and about himself,[34] has moved self aside to let God on stage, with the result that, whatever others may think of it, his work is pleasing to God and he is restful in that knowledge.

The difference with our fourth friend may not be noticeable at first. It's not a matter of his going right when the others are going left, or up when the others are going down. Sometimes, yes, but that is not the essence. The essential thing is that this person no longer has a self in the usual sense; it is gone, been given away; it has died and been absorbed back into its Maker who gives it new, divine life.[35] Now, in place of self, God becomes the principal actor, with our friend never more than supporting cast, and even here it is God who animates him. In the words of The Little Flower:

> I believe quite simply that it is Jesus Himself, hidden deep in my poor little heart, who works within me in a mysterious manner and inspires all my daily actions.[36]

So too our fourth friend. This we admit is not easy to grasp. After all, our fourth friend looks little different from anyone else. The fact that when he

---

[33] *Isaiah 26:12*; Jean-Pierre de Caussade, IV-29 (2nd para.), IV-68
[34] III-91 (St. Catherine of Siena) (last 2 paras.)
[35] Lorenzo Sales, II-20 (2nd para.); Luisa Piccarreta, III-53, IV-34
[36] Ste. Thérèse of Lisieux, IV-49

works, God is working, when he does something, God is doing it in him, does not mean these acts are extraordinary, no more than it did in the first thirty years of Our Divine Lord's life as He worked alongside his foster father or helped his mother with household chores. Nothing in Him attracted special notice in the neighborhood. "Is this not the carpenter," they said of Him, "the son of Mary?"[37] But the Father saw the way his Son handled his tools; his unhurried, simple acts had the perfection God wanted for them. And the Father took pleasure in these acts: "This is my beloved Son in whom I am well pleased."[38]

Our fourth friend works this way as well, in the measure that God grants it to him. He understands that Christ is the vine, he but a branch. He knows the branch is meant to bear fruit and knows where branch fruit comes from. He takes Jesus' words in *John 15:5* quite literally. He understands in the depths of his heart, in the very marrow of his bones, that without Christ he can do nothing of worth in God's eyes. It does not mean that he will do great things, only that what he does will please his Lord and accomplish the Lord's purposes, because, whatever the task, whatever the purpose, he looks to Jesus to do it in him, as He said He would.[39]

Listen to what Our Lord had to say about this to Luisa Piccarreta:

> *My dearest daughter, do you see in what close union of life I am with you? Thus, I want you closely united with Me. But do not believe that you should do this only when you pray or when you suffer. No, but rather always and forever. If you move, if you breathe, if you work, if you eat, if you sleep — all of this you must do as if you were doing it in My humanity, as if all of your work came out of Me.*
>
> *In this manner nothing can be yours. Rather, all must be in you only as a shell, and opening this shell of your work there has to be found the fruit of the Divine Work... Hence, by doing everything with this intention of receiving life from Me, even the indifferent and small actions acquire the merits of my Humanity.*

❖

---

[37] *Mk 6:3*
[38] *Mt 3:17*
[39] Sister Maria Consolata, II-23; III-15; St. Catherine of Genoa, IV-40

This volume is filled with reflections and revelations about what goes on in the heart and mind of souls like our fourth worker, describing their relationship to God, and God's relationship to them. To a secular reader these writings must seem incomprehensible, and believers themselves are apt to think them pious exaggerations, if not wholly unbelievable. Yet is this not precisely what we pray for when we utter the words, *"Thy Kingdom come, Thy Will be done"*?

Consider the selections in this volume from the pen of Luisa Piccarreta, the Italian lay mystic (1865-1947) to whom Jesus revealed teachings of a most remarkable kind. (Her cause for canonization is currently being pursued in Rome.) A serious student and disciple of Luisa has this to say about her writings:

> *The doctrine that human acts achieve their true and highest dignity only when they are performed in us by Jesus, or, we might say, by the Divine Will of the Father, Son, and Holy Spirit, is not new… What is new in the recent private revelations [to Luisa] is the understanding that it is possible for souls of good will to participate fully in the divine-human acts of Jesus and Mary and to allow the Divine Will to reign in all of their thoughts, words, and actions during their lives on earth."*[40]

We want to ask, practically speaking, how does this work? Our Lord explains:

> *You must keep one eye on Me and the other on what you are doing… Do not look to see if the task is painful or difficult. You shall close your eyes to all that, and you shall open them to Me, knowing that I am in you to oversee your work.*[41]

This is how our fourth friend, the perfect worker, works. He works as Our Savior worked, of whom it is said, "even when He was working He made of his work a perfect prayer.[42]"As we know from the Gospel, the Son of God did nothing but what he saw the Father doing, said nothing but what he heard his Father say *(Jn 8:28-30)*. No wonder it was said of Him, *"He does all things well" (Mk 7:37)*.

No wonder then that things seem always to go well with this perfect worker, to fall into place just as and when they should. He seems always

---

[40] Hugh Owen, III-62
[41] Luisa Piccarreta, IV-79
[42] Our Lady to Consuelo, VI-31

to have the right touch, know the right word, the right thing to do in a given circumstance. The touches are often small and unnoticeable, always humble in nature, like Jesus' in the carpenter's shop, but cumulatively, the good effect is unmistakable to those with eyes to see. In the end, this person's work has a perfection, an orderliness that sets it apart, a "radiance," (to use Aristotle's description of beautiful things) "beyond the proportioned parts of the matter."

And how can it be otherwise? A perfect worker lets God enter into his work and would not think to work without Him, any more than he can find air to breathe without Him. He has come to believe in the divine order where, in all things and all doings, God is primary and we with our efforts are never more than cooperating causes. This does not mean that secondary causes are not important, or are not free[43], only that the proper order must be preserved. Our friend works within that order and his work reflects it.

Listen to what Our Lord tells Luisa Piccarreta about this:

> *My daughter, all the Divine Science is contained in upright works. This is because uprightness contains all the beauty and good that one can find – order, usefulness, beauty and skill… Where [Divine Science} is lacking in the creature, the creature won't do anything other than dry up amid his disorder.[44]*

And about effectiveness of this *divine order*, listen to Irenaeus:

> *Where there is order, there is also harmony; where there is harmony there is also correct timing; where there is correct timing there is also advantage.[45]*

A perfect worker has come to this felicitous state because, as said, he has died to self and been raised to new life in Christ. This new life is given gratuitously, as a pure gift of grace, but only after a lengthy, not to say easy journey into self-knowledge. As Jesus tells Luisa:

> *The greatest gift that I can grant a soul is to make it know itself. The knowledge of oneself and the knowledge of God go hand in hand. In so far as you shall know yourself, so shall you know God. The soul that has known itself, seeing that of itself it can work no good, transforms the shadow of itself into God; and it comes to pass that it does all its operations*

---

[43] I-20 (3rd para.), I-22, III-42
[44] Luisa Piccarreta, III-64
[45] Irenaeus, II-32

*in God. It happens then, that the soul is in God and walks beside Him,
without looking, without investigating, without speaking. In a word, it
is, as it were, dead; for knowing in depth its nothingness, it does not dare
to do anything of itself but blindly follows the influence of the operations
of the Word.*[46]

And again:

*So that I can pour my graces into your heart, it is necessary for you to
convince yourself that by yourself you are nothing and are capable of
nothing... Souls that consider my gifts and graces – given to them by
my Love – to have been acquired by themselves, are committing many
thefts. Remember that I am generous and pour torrents of graces on
souls that know themselves – souls that do not usurp anything for
themselves and understand that everything is accomplished by means
of my grace...*

*I cannot enter into hearts that stink with pride – souls so puffed up
with themselves that there is no place in their hearts for Me... You
must be like an infant in swaddling bands who, unable to move by
himself, even to walk or move a hand, must rely on its mother for
everything. In that way, I want you to remain near Me – like an
infant – to always ask for my help and assistance, acknowledging your
nothingness and expecting everything from Me.*[47]

Is it any wonder that the perfect worker, in accomplishing his (or her)
given task, exudes peace and tranquility, even if, judging by the world's
standards, he may even fail.[48] Is it any wonder that his movements are
graceful beyond nature.   In the words of an old saying:

> *You can tell a saint*
> *By the way he sits*
> *And the way he stands*
> *By the way he picks up things*
> *And holds them in his hands*

Or, even more, like Our Lady, of whom de Montfort said (in *True
Devotion)* that "she gave more glory to God by the smallest of her actions,

---

[46] Luisa Piccarreta, II-29
[47] Luisa Piccarreta, III-68
[48] St. Faustina, IV-85

say, twirling her distaff, or making a stitch, than did…all the saints together by all their most heroic deeds."

Now, it is true, if someone were to suggest to us that God is the main actor, the principal mover in his or her actions—especially someone the likes of us—this would make us not a little uncomfortable. It would have to strike us as presumptuous in the extreme; and to the secular mind this is bordering on madness. It's hardly something we would ever claim for ourselves. Yet isn't this what St. Paul claimed when he wrote: *"It is no longer I who lives but Christ who lives in me"*?[49] And isn't this the very thing that Jesus claims for us all when he said, *"Abide in me, and I in you. As the branch cannot bear fruit unless it abides in the vine, neither can you, unless you abide in me"*? And then in the very next moment, he pronounces those breathtaking words, *"For without me you can do nothing."*[50] We may think, *OK, sure, the saints are this way;* we are not a bit surprised to hear that The Little Flower felt the hand of God in everything she did.[51] But ordinary folk are not saints, and face it, most people do what they do in their lives without a hint of these remarkable words of Jesus. We seem to get along pretty well on our own, so is it really so? Can we do nothing without Him? Perhaps the voices recorded in this book will persuade us that, truth be told, without *him* we cannot even hold this book in our hands, let alone understand its teaching. But if we open ourselves to this Divine Truth, come to understand and live by it, it is certain things will go well, for us and those around us.

Listen again to what Jesus said to Luisa Piccarreta about this:

> *The Celestial Creator, when He sees the soul in his Will, takes it in his arms and, placing it on his lap, lets it operate with his own hands and, with the power of the "Fiat" with which He made all things, lets all his reflections descend upon the creature in order to give it the likeness of his operation. This is why the operation of the creature becomes light, is united to the single act of its Creator and is constituted in the Eternal Glory and continuous praise of its Creator. Therefore, be attentive, and make sure that the most important thing for you is to live in my*

---

[49] *Gal* 2:20; Dom Jean-Baptiste Chautard, I-36
[50] *Jn* 15:4,5
[51] Ste. Thérèse of Lisieux, IV-36; Blessed Dina Bélanger, IV-58; Archbishop Luis Maria Martinez, IV-73

Volition, so you will never descend from your origin, that is, from the bosom of your Creator.[52]

A doctrine of working in a proper way, as our fourth friend, the perfect worker has learned, is not complicated. All we have to do, whatever the task, is to heed Our Lord's simple request: *"Let me do it!"*[53] Simple but not by any means easy. Doing what Our Lord is asking takes work, a lifetime of work, both on His part and ours[54]. It's called sanctification.

❖   ❖   ❖

While you are working

And while you are working—working because I want to work—look how my fingers are in yours. And, at the same moment I work in you, to how many do my hands bring the light of this world? How many do I call and how many others do I sanctify, correct, chastise, etc. You, then, are also here with Me to create, to call, to correct, and more. And since you are not working alone, neither am I in all my works. Could I have given you a greater honor?

— Our Lord to Luisa Piccarreta (1912)

The purpose I have with you

The purpose I have with respect to you is not to do tremendous things… my purpose is to absorb you into my Will and to make us One alone, and to leave you a perfect model of uniformity of your will with Mine. But that is the most sublime state; it is the greatest prodigy. It is the miracle of miracles, which I intend to make of you.

If there are two objects from which one wants to make only one, it is necessary for one to give up its proper form and take on the other's; otherwise, it would never come to form one single entity. What would be your fortune if destroying yourself in order to make yourself invisible, you would be able to receive a completely divine form! Even by your being absorbed in Me, and I in you, forming one single being, you would

---

[52] Luisa Piccarreta, III-102. *See also* III-75; III-84, IV-34
[53] Sister Mary Consolata, III-79
[54] III-80

come to retain all goods, all gifts, all graces, and you would not have to look for them elsewhere, but within yourself.

– Our Lord to Luisa Piccarreta (1900)

❖

A Practical Note

We still need to ask, if Our Lord wishes to live in us, to act in us, to reproduce his humanity in us, with all the dignity that that implies, why do we not let Him? What holds us back? Is it perversity, ignorance, or is it perhaps a false understanding about what God is asking of us?

As we read this book, we hear the voices of saints, popes, mystics, theologians all telling us that when a soul allows God to act in it, things go well for that soul and that it cannot be otherwise, even when suffering is involved. But is this our experience? Despite our faith, many of us lead mildly discontented lives, unreconciled to what is, wishing for something different, something better. *And we are rarely truly peaceful.* Why is this? Why are we at sixes and sevens when Our Lord offers us a perfect life in him? It cannot be that He is offering something that is simply beyond our reach!

The following may help us with this final question. It is a private instruction from Our Lord to an anonymous soul concerning his own difficulties in this regard, but it is relevant to us all. The instruction speaks to this question of why our lives as men and women of faith may be off-kilter. It tells us there may well be something we do not understand about God, and about ourselves, and must come to understand if we are to become the persons God is calling us to be, and do the things he is calling us to do in the way that He wants—in short, if we are to become his perfect workers. We do well to give what follows a careful reading:

Right and Wrong Ways to Relate to God

THERE ARE TWO EXTREMES, each of which is bad, and which you must learn, therefore, to avoid. One is to seek your peace in Me, as you think, but without striving to conform yourself to Me. And the peace you are seeking, therefore, is not My Peace, but a sensual complacency in yourself which you would like to think is in Me. But it isn't. And that is why My

Love for you cannot allow you to rest in that kind of peace—because it isn't mine.

Then, realizing that something is wrong, you swing to the opposite extreme, now trying [by your *own* efforts alone, without Me] to conform yourself to Me, in order to please Me—and by that motive your act is good, yet it is disordered and so, again, I cannot allow you to find your peace, i.e., My Peace, in it.

What We Do Wrong When Our Failings Come to Light

And here is the very heart of this lesson, that when I show you—through a severe temptation, or sometimes even permitting you to fall—how prone you are to evil, you conclude, rightly, that you are not, in the measure of your evil disposition, conformed to Me. I mean this, not merely in a general way, but in a very particular and precise sense, that you are not conformed to Me *now*. And consequently it is impossible for you to be in peace, My Peace, unless you are actually conforming yourself to Me—not in a general way, but just in the way that I want you to be conforming yourself to Me at this moment.

And here is the mistake you make—you do not understand that the very realization of your inadequacies is My Voice calling you to come to Me in order to get what you need to please Me. *And so the mistake is to seek what you need apart from Me*—and then things go from bad to worse, because then you allow yourself to be separated from Me more and more, and this in the illusion that you are pleasing Me thereby!

The Right Way to Act

Now do you see the lesson I would teach you? *That the more you recognize your lack of conformity to Me the more promptly you must run to Me and the more closely you must cling to Me, to My Heart*—not to remain as you were (that is the other extreme) but to become what I want you to be, realizing that *only as you are united with Me* can you receive the grace necessary to do what I am asking of you at this moment. And then, after this realization, as your soul is in My Peace, you will know, clearly, what you are to do by your own powers—and you will understand that each thing you are doing is pleasing Me—and then your peace will grow as you are actually conforming yourself to Me—

because your every act will be My action in you. You must understand that My Peace which I give you is not something completed in which you can rest as in an end. No! It is My Life, your participation in My Life, which is a constant becoming.

Understanding How Our Own, Distinct Free Will Works within God's Will

You can see, too, in this, how the error comes from your incapacity to understand how the *distinct principle*—your own free will and its operation—is distinct, *not* as it is *separated* from Me, but just as it is *united* with Me. But in your ignorance you are moved to undertake your responsibility in relation to Me by separating yourself from Me, as though it would not be your own act if you were united with Me. Whereas the truth is the very contrary—far from being your own act without Me, *it would not be any act at all.* And so, the natural consequence of your notions of freedom and responsibility is that your act becomes more and more disordered as you remove yourself more and more from the Principle of your acts, your Life. And this increasing disorder, you can see, gradually approaches the state of non-being, or nothingness.

Do you see now? Do you see how true it is that *without Me you can do nothing?* Ponder this lesson very much. It is the secret of My Peace, My Peace which I give to you.

❖

- I -

Inspiration, Grace, Free Will

❖   ❖   ❖

Lord,
may everything we do
begin with your inspiration,
continue with your help,
and reach perfection under your guidance.
We ask this through our Lord Jesus Christ, your Son,
who lives and reigns with you and the Holy Spirit,
one God, for ever and ever, Amen.

— Opening Prayer for Daily Mass during Lent

❖   ❖   ❖
1
I move your will without forcing it

I do not force your will in anything. I move your will without forcing it. Can you understand that? I provide exterior things for you to consider and contemplate, I provide the exterior things that you need in order to grow in grace and understanding, each thing that happens to you, in just the way it happens, when it happens and all the circumstances in which it happens—and every little detail is fashioned with loving care by My Providence.

— Our Lord to a Servant of God

❖   ❖   ❖
2
Steadfastness draws down Grace

My daughter, courage, do not change in anything. Steadfastness is one of the greatest virtues. Firmness produces heroism, and it is almost impossible that man with it will not be a great saint. Rather, as he repeats his acts, so he forms barriers, one to the right and the other to the left, that serve as a support and as a defense to him. Then, repeating his acts, he forms in himself a source of new and growing love. Firmness strengthens Grace, and puts on the seal of final perseverance. Your Jesus does not fear that these graces could remain without effect in firm souls; and, therefore, in constant souls, I pour them out in torrents.

Thus there is not much hope for a soul who today works, and tomorrow doesn't; who now does one good, and now something else. She will not have any support; and then she will be cast to one side, and now to another. She will die of hunger, because she will not have the source of firmness which makes love arise. Grace is afraid to pour itself into this soul because she will misuse it, if not use it to offend Me.

— Luisa Piccarreta

❖   ❖   ❖

3

He guides and inspires me every moment of the day

I know that the Kingdom of God is within us. Jesus has no need of books or doctors of the Church to guide souls. He, the Doctor of doctors, can teach without words. I have never heard Him speak, but I know that He is within me. He guides and inspires me every moment of the day. Just when I need it, a new light shines on my problems. This happens not so much during my hours of prayer as when I'm busy with my daily work.

— Ste. Thérèse of Lisieux

❖   ❖   ❖

4

On readiness to follow the movements of grace

The first duty required of souls is self-discipline; the second is self-surrender and complete passivity; the third requires great humility, a humble and willing disposition and a readiness to follow the movement of grace which motivates everything if they simply respond willingly to all its guidance. And in order that souls should not lose their way, God never fails to provide them with wise directors to show how much freedom and how much restraint will be best for them.

And this third duty truly supersedes every law, every formula and every established custom. It inspires in souls unique and remarkable resolutions and governs their vocal prayers, their inner voice, the perception of their senses and the radiance of their lives. It is what gives them self-denial, their fervor, their prodigal devotion to their neighbor. And, since this is the unique gift of the Holy Spirit, no one should dare to prescribe it for himself, or aspire to it, or lament that he has not the grace to enable him to achieve these rare virtues which are only acquired under God's auspices. Otherwise, as had already been pointed out, there is a danger of being deluded. We must remember that there are souls whom God wishes to keep hidden, humble, and obscure in their own eyes as well as in the eyes of others.

– Jean-Pierre de Caussade

❖   ❖   ❖

5

*There is nothing easier, more ordinary, more available
to all than saintliness*

All must be content with the duties to their state and to God's direction. He clearly demands this. As for the strong impressions and inspirations souls receive, they must not judge them themselves nor exaggerate their importance. Conscious effort is directly contrary to inspired action; this only comes through peace and serenity. For it is the voice of God waking souls who are only able to act when the Spirit moves them and can do nothing on their own. Though they may not be moved by grace to do all those marvels which make saints so admired, they can justly say: "God asks this of saints, but not of me."

I believe if they were so to behave they would spare themselves a great deal of trouble. And the same is true of worldly people. If the former knew what work was to be done each moment, I mean their daily tasks and duties; if the latter could only appreciate the things they disregard and even consider useless and irrelevant to the holiness of which they have formed such exalted ideas; if they knew that those ideas, though perhaps good in themselves, were always harmful because they are limited to our conceptions of what is splendid and marvelous; if all knew that saintliness consists of all the suffering which their state provides each moment; that it is not any exceptional state that leads to the sublime heights of perfection; that the philosopher's stone is surrender to God's will which makes everything they do divine—how happy they would be! How clearly they would see that to be a saint there is no more to do than what they are doing, and no more to suffer than what they are suffering;

that even what they reject and count for nothing would be enough to purchase the most blessed holiness. How I long to be the missionary of your divine will, O God, to teach...that there is nothing easier, more ordinary, more available to all than saintliness.

— Jean-Pierre de Caussade

❖   ❖   ❖

6
Mary as our Model

From the time the Child Jesus was on his feet He commenced to retire and spent certain hours of the day in the oratory of his Mother. As the most prudent Mother was anxious to know his wishes in regard to her intercourse with Him, the Lord responded to her mute appeal, saying: "My Mother, enter and remain with Me always in order that thou mayest imitate Me in my works; for I wish that in thee be modeled and exhibited the high perfection which I desire to see accomplished in the souls. For if they had not resisted my first intentions (*I Tim 2:4*), they would have been endowed with my most abundant and copious gifts; but since the human race has hindered this, I have chosen thee as the vessel of all perfection and of the treasures of my right hand, which the rest of the creatures have abused and lost. Observe me therefore in all my actions for the purpose of imitating Me."

— Our Lady to Venerable Mary of Agreda

❖   ❖   ❖

7
Our Lady on the conversion of St. Paul as a model for all

Many souls the Lord wakes up and urges on by his inspiration and help. Many do respond and justify themselves through the Sacraments of the Church; but not all persevere in their justification and a still fewer number follow it up or strive after perfection: beginning in spirit, they relax, and finish in the flesh. The cause of their want of perseverance in grace and relapse into their sins is their not imitating the spirit of Saint Paul at his conversion, when he exclaimed: "Lord, what it is Thou wishest with me, and what shall I do for Thee?" If some of them proclaim this sentiment with their lips, it is not from their whole heart, and they always retain some love of themselves, of honor, of possessions, of sensual pleasure or of some occasion of sin, and thus they soon again stumble and fall.

But the Apostle was a true and living example of one converted by the light of grace, not only because he passed from an extreme of sin into that of wonderful grace and friendship with God; but also because he cooperated to his utmost with the call of God, departing at once and entirely from all his evil dispositions and self-seeking and placing himself entirely at the disposal of the divine will and pleasure.

This total denigration of self and surrender of the will to God is contained in those words: "Lord, what dost Thou wish to do with me?" and in it consisted, as far as depended upon him, all his salvation. As he pronounced them with all the sincerity of a contrite and humbled heart, he renounced his own will and delivered himself over to that of the Lord's, resolved from that moment to permit none of his faculties of mind or sense to serve the animal or sensual life into which he had strayed. He delivered himself over to the service of the Almighty in whatever manner or direction should become known to him as being the divine will, ready to execute it without delay or questioning…

For as soon as thou beginnest to do anything of thy own choice, it will not be true that thou seekest solely the will of the Lord. The instrument has no motion or action except that imparted to it by the artisan; and if it had its own will, it would be able to resist and act contrary to the will of the one using it. The same holds true between God and the soul: for, if it entertains any desire of its own independently of God, it will militate against the pleasure of the Lord. As He keeps inviolate the liberty of action conceded to man, He will permit it to lead man astray, as soon as he decides for himself, without reference to the direction of his Maker.

– Our Lady to Venerable Mary of Agreda

❖   ❖   ❖

8

Under the very influx of My grace
your will remains your own

Under the very influx of My grace, powerful as it is—really just because it is so powerful—your will remains your own… And therefore you must not wait to be moved by My grace—as though I would do something to you first, and then, as a result, you would begin to love Me. No! Just as in the natural order, it is I who move you to your every act, yet you move yourself to pursue the good you desire, so in your supernatural life, as soon as you are directing your mind to Me in order to be more united with

Me in love, it is I Who am moving you to do this—you are receiving my grace.

— Our Lord to a Servant of God

❖ ❖ ❖
9
Our Lady speaks of the example of St. Joseph

Be ready to obey and fulfill all commands as a willing and careful pupil; let the humility and care and watchfulness of my spouse Saint Joseph, his submission to divine direction and his esteem for heavenly enlightenment, serve thee as an example. For only because his heart had been well disposed and prepared for the execution of the divine will, was he entirely changed and remodeled by the plenitude of grace for the ministry assigned to him by the Most High. Let therefore the consciousness of thy faults serve thee as a motive to submit in all humility to the work of God, not as a pretext to withdraw from the performance of that which the Lord desires of thee.

— Our Lady to Venerable Mary of Agreda

❖ ❖ ❖
10
Be ye perfect as your heavenly Father is perfect (Matt 5: 48)

Thou knowest well, my dearest, that thou hast been incessantly instructed and exhorted by divine enlightenment to forget the terrestrial and visible and to gird thyself with fortitude (*Prov 31:17*), to raise thyself to the imitation of me, copying in thyself, according to thy capacity, the works and virtues manifested to thee in my life… for thou hast in me a perfect model and by it thou canst arrange the converse and conduct of thy life in the same manner as I arranged mine in imitation of my sweetest Son.

The dread with which this command to imitate me has inspired thee as being above thy strength, thou must moderate and thou must encourage thyself by the words of my most holy Son in the Gospel of St. Matthew: "Be ye perfect as your heavenly Father is perfect" (*Matt 5:48*). This command of the Most High imposed upon his holy Church is not impossible of fulfillment, and, if his faithful children on their part dispose themselves properly, He will deny to none of them the grace of attaining this resemblance to the heavenly Father. All of this my most holy Son has merited for them. But the degrading forgetfulness and neglect of men hinder them from maturing within themselves the fruits of his Redemption…

Ponder and scrutinize, by the divine light, the obligation under which I place thee, and labor to correspond with it like a faithful and anxious child. Let no difficulty or hardship disturb thee, nor deter thee from any virtuous exercise no matter how hard it may be. Nor be content with striving after the love of God and salvation of thyself alone; if thou wouldst be perfect in imitating me and fulfilling all that the Gospel teaches, thou must work for the salvation of other souls and the exaltation of the holy name of my Son, making thyself an instrument in his powerful hands for the accomplishment of mighty works to advance his pleasure and glory.

– Our Lady to Venerable Mary of Agreda

❖   ❖   ❖

11
On creativity and inspiration

A famous French sculptor took it upon himself to make a statue of Mary as Bernadette had described her. Being a well-established sculptor, the artist couldn't escape his own artistic impulses and tastes and what he came up with in the end, despite its artistic merit, profoundly disappointed Bernadette. The artist, so used to public acclaim, suffered a deep interior humiliation upon seeing her reaction on the occasion of its unveiling. To Bernadette, the statue had nothing to do with her vision. This illustrates well, I think, the difference between originality and authenticity in any work of art. It also illustrates, does it not, the difference between creativity and inspiration.

There is a difference between creativity and inspiration in art. The former may be thought of as something coming from the artist, something which he originates and which expresses his ideas, imagination, and impulse. In this the creative artist is imitating the creative activity of God, but the artist is not thereby necessarily reflecting God. More likely it reflects the artist himself and his unique genius. Inspiration, on the other hand, is always something which comes to the artist as a gift, something which, in a real sense, surprises the artist precisely because he did not know he had it in him to do this thing. In a real sense the artist becomes an instrument, and the real author of the work is the heavenly source that inspired it. (There can be infernal inspirations too, no doubt.)

Great works of art, it must be said, contain both elements—creative genius and inspiration—and it would be difficult if not impossible to draw the line between them. Everything is always received, as Aristotle said, "according to the mode of the recipient," including inspiration; so even the inspired writings of Scripture have the stamp of their human authors and their unique personality, nature, and genius.

But having said that, there is still a distinction to be made here. We can discern it most of all in iconography where the artist's individual, creative impulse is consciously kept at bay so that inspiration may be everything in the work. The iconographer minimizes his own impulses and opens himself to inspiration by means of prolonged prayer and fasting. The iconographer does not sign the work and thinks of it and speaks of it as something done merely "by the hand of," i.e., under the inspiration of someone else.

Anyone who has spent quiet time before an icon, not just flipping through an art book and admiring the pictures, or even studying them for their artistic value, symbolism, or sheer beauty, but being quiet and letting the image speak to him, allowing it to convey the intended presence, anyone happy enough to have done this in any real sense knows that icons are of a different order than the religious art of the West. For all their greatness as artists, a Michelangelo or a DaVinci cannot convey to us what the icons of orthodoxy convey, icons such as the Theotokos of Vladimir, or the Pantocrator at St. Catherine Monastery in the Sinai, to name but two of the more famous of the many Orthodox icons produced in this fashion. The production of all true icons is closely connected to both the common liturgical experience and to the private prayer life of their creators, or more precisely, the instrumentalists of their creation. And for that reason, these icons are exceptional not as marks of artistic genius, but as portals to a spiritual order, pointing to something beyond the icon itself, and never, we understand at length, to the artist.

It is said that a serious iconographer may fast and pray for as much as thirty days before commencing an icon. And it never enters into his head to innovate or do something that leaves a personal, stylistic mark of his own making. Yes, there are inevitable, inadvertent clues to the individual artist, of his talent and skill, but they are unintentional. And is it not so that the greatness of an icon derives from this very fact, that its iconographer, through prayer and fasting, has allowed an authenticity received through spiritual practice to take the place of creative impulse?

– diarist

❖   ❖   ❖

12
On the benefit of being disliked

God's providence sends us two kinds of souls to help bring us to Him. The first soul reassures us, sees what Jesus intended in us, and makes us believe we are that person or at least are in the process of becoming that person. This first soul builds us up and encourages us on our way. The second soul is quite different. This soul sees what is amiss in us, reacts to it and makes us feel we are far from the person we should be, forcing us to reflect on what we are in and of ourselves, apart from grace, which picture is never consoling. It is always devastating to meet such a person, to experience his or her rejection. But in God's Providence, encounters with both souls are necessary and we should be thankful for what each of them works in that Providence. Children especially seem able to see what's wrong with us and often have the simplicity to say so where others would conceal what they think. I still smart from encounters with certain children. It is easy to like someone who likes us, difficult to even smile at one who does not. But there is value in bowing to truth.

– diarist

❖   ❖   ❖

13
How God guides us

A journalist, Peter Seewald, poses the following question to Cardinal Ratzinger: Is there some particular language that God uses sometimes to say to us, in quite a concrete way, "Yes, do that." Or, again, "Hold on, there—last warning! Just leave it alone!"

Ratzinger's reply: God speaks quietly. But he gives us all kinds of signs. In retrospect, especially, we can see that he has given us a little nudge through a friend, through a book, or through what we see as a failure— even through "accidents." Life is actually full of these silent indications. If I remain alert, then slowly they piece together a consistent whole, and I begin to feel how God is guiding me.

– Joseph Cardinal Ratzinger (Pope Benedict XVI)

❖   ❖   ❖

14

Do Thou perform within me what is pleasing to Thy Will

The first seed of the new life lies in the combination of freedom and grace; and growth and ripening come from the development of the same elements. When making a vow to live according to the Will of God, for His glory, the penitent should say, "Only do Thou strengthen and confirm my resolve;" and from then on he must, as it were, place himself every minute in the hand of God, with the prayer, "Do Thou Thyself perform within me what is pleasing to Thy Will." In this way, alike in consciousness and will and in actual fact, it is God who will be acting in us, both in what we desire, and in what we do according to His good pleasure. But as soon as man himself expects to achieve something in virtue of his own power and self-mastery, then immediately true spiritual life, full of grace, is extinguished. In this state, in spite of immeasurable efforts, true fruit cannot come into being.

— Theophan The Recluse

❖   ❖   ❖

15

Christ stands at the door and knocks

St. Makarios of Egypt says (*First Treatise on Guarding of the Heart, Chap. xii*) that the grace which comes to man "does not bind his will by force of necessity, nor does it make him unchangeably good, willy-nilly. On the contrary, the power of God which exists in the man gives way before his free will, in order to reveal whether the man's will is in accordance with grace or not. From this moment on the union of freedom with grace begins. At first grace stands outside, and acts from the outside. Then it enters within and begins to take possession of parts of the spirit: but it only does this when man by his own desire opens the door for it, or opens his mouth to receive it. Grace is ready to help, if man desires.

"By himself man cannot do or establish within himself that which is good, but he longs and strives for it. Because of this longing, grace consolidates within him the good for which he yearns. And so it goes on, until man acquires final mastery over himself, and thus is able to fulfill that which is good and pleasing to God."

— Theophan The Recluse

❖　❖　❖
16

Sing to God, ye kingdoms of the earth: sing ye to the Lord:
Sing ye to God, who mounteth above the heaven of heavens,
　　to the east.
Behold he will give to his voice the voice of power:
　　give ye glory to God for Israel,
　　his magnificence, and his power is in the clouds.
God is wonderful in his saints:
　　the God of Israel is he who will give power and strength
　　to his people.
Blessed be God.

— Psalm 67:34-36 (Douay Rheims)

❖　❖　❖
17

What advantage has the worker from his toil?

What advantage has the worker from his toil? I have considered the task which God has appointed for men to be busied about. He has made everything appropriate to its time, and has put the timeless into their hearts, without men's ever discovering, from beginning to end, the work which God has done.

— Ecclesiastes 3:9-11 (NAB)

❖　❖　❖
18

The first impulse is usually the wrong thing to do

Blessed Dina Bélanger remarked that the first impulse of nature was usually wrong thing to do. She would take a moment to reflect and try to follow the impulse of grace.

— Thomas M. Fahy

❖　❖　❖
19

*I cannot explain it; but when difficulties arise, I am not perplexed or doubtful.
I know how to meet them… It is wonderful*

The remarkable story of Helen Keller is famous, how an inspired teacher by the name of Anne Sullivan took this blind, deaf, and dumb child, so intelligent and yet so cruelly shut out from the world about her, and through a combination of unfailing effort and uncanny inspiration, led her into the world of knowledge and understanding until, in the end, Helen Keller became a personage of great learning and truly remarkable nobility of spirit. From Anne Sullivan's account, it was an almost impossible task she set out for herself. Before she came into Helen's life at the age of seven, Helen was literally uncontrollable, willful, fitful, and virtually animal-like in her behavior. At the dinner table, she would reach into other people's dishes and just take what she liked, and should they attempt to discipline her, her family could not endure Helen's wild tantrums. This was the situation Helen's father asked Anne Sullivan to address.

Anne described her new charge in a letter written at the time. "She is very quick-tempered and willful, and nobody, except her brother James, has attempted to control her. The greatest problem I shall have to solve is how to discipline and control her without breaking her spirit… Don't worry. I'll do my best and leave the rest to whatever power manages that which we cannot."

A bit later, Anne Sullivan would write to this same correspondent, "As I wrote you, I meant to go slowly at first. I had an idea that I could win the love and confidence of my little pupil by the same means that I should use if she could see and hear. But I soon found that I was cut off from all the usual approaches to the child's heart. She accepted everything that I did for her as a matter of course, and refused to be caressed, and there was no way of appealing to her affection or sympathy or childish love of approbation… Thus it is, we study, plan and prepare ourselves for a task, and when the hour for action arrives, we find that the system we have followed with such labor and pride does not fit the occasion; and then there's nothing for us to do but rely on something within us, some innate capacity for knowing and doing, which we did not know we possessed until the hour of our great need brought it to light."

In a letter to a friend, Miss Sullivan wrote: "I am glad Mr. Anagnos [her own teacher] thinks so highly of me as a teacher. But 'genius' and 'originality' are words we should not use lightly. If, indeed, they apply to me even remotely, I do not see that I deserve any laudation on that account." She goes on to say, "And right here I want to say something which is for your ears alone. Something within me tells me that I shall succeed beyond my dreams. I know that she [Helen] has remarkable powers, and I believe that I shall be able to develop and mould them. I cannot tell how I know these things. I had no idea a short time ago how to go to work; I was feeling about in the dark; but somehow I know now, and I know that I know. I cannot explain it; but when difficulties arise, I am not perplexed or doubtful. I know how to meet them; I seem to divine Helen's peculiar needs. It is wonderful."

And succeed she did, and with almost lightening speed managing to tame this wild creature and open up her mind to language, ideas, culture and things of the spirit, as we know from Helen Keller's own remarkable auto-biography. Word of Anne Sullivan's accomplishments spread rapidly and she was quickly recognized as having done something no one ever thought possible. That Miss Sullivan resisted adulation and refused to take credit says much about this woman and indeed helps explain why she was able to do what she did.

— diarist

❖ ❖ ❖
20
There is nothing that any creature, natural or supernatural, can do which does not come utterly and totally from Me

Do you think that you depend on Me less because you are living the life of grace? The truth is the very contrary: the closer you are to Me, the more you depend on Me. In your supernatural life you must receive everything from Me, even as I receive everything from the Father.

No, there is nothing that any creature, natural or supernatural, can do which does not come utterly and totally from Me. *"Which one of you by taking thought can grow a single hair?"* You must meditate ceaselessly on this truth, so that it will penetrate to the very core of your being: you must be overwhelmingly convinced that there is nothing, absolutely nothing, that you can do without Me, that everything, absolutely everything, comes totally from Me.

But I move each thing according to the nature I gave it—it could not be moved in any other way. And since you have a rational nature, what you do as I move you to operate, is to operate rationally, that is to say, freely. And because what you do is free, even as I move you to do it, it is merito-rious. Yes, you must understand that what I reward is your merit—other-wise it would not be just. But you must remember that your merit is not the same kind of thing as My Merit. Yours is the merit of a creature, created merit, whose very being is to be caused by Me. My Merit alone is Uncreated, Uncaused. How many times have My children misunderstood this, and in the name of freedom usurped the Uncreated Merit which belongs to Me alone. And not only have they usurped My Merit to themselves, but they have taught others to do the same thing, not realizing that in doing this they were burdening My children with a load and a responsibility which they could not possibly carry. And how many times have My children fallen into the opposite error, making their dependence upon Me an excuse for sloth, and pretending to glorify Me as they buried the talent I had given them in the ground! And they too, not content with the error in their own hearts, have led so many others into their same error!

You see, then, that you must learn to depend totally on Me, for everything — *you must penetrate always more deeply into the truth that you can do absolutely nothing without Me* — you cannot depend on Me too much. But then what you must understand is that you depend on Me to move you, not violently, as one would kick a stone, but according to the rational nature I have given you. I move you to move yourself, freely, and the more perfectly everything you do is subject to your rational and free dominion, the more perfectly will you be totally subject to Me — and the more perfectly you are subject to Me, the more perfectly free will you be in all your actions.

The secret of perfect freedom is to be My slave, and those who are the slaves of their own passions make freedom a cloak for malice — of My omnipotence an excuse for sloth. That is why I tell you I never refuse you anything — yet I wait. I neither force you to take what I would give; neither do I withdraw and refuse you the things you need when you ask. All that I would teach you is hidden in My few, simple words, "*Ask, and you shall receive.*" Yes, I always give you what is necessary for you to do My Will, but because I do not move you violently, the very reality of my moving your will is the reality of your loving Me, of your asking Me, therefore, for what you need in order to love Me more.

When I tell you, "*Ask, and you shall receive,*" it seems to you as though your asking would come from yourself alone, and what you receive from Me. But that is not the way it is. No, your very asking, just as it is your asking, is the effect of my loving you, I, hidden within your soul. As you ask, you do not see it, but it is My love that is moving you to ask. And that is why when you ask you shall receive, because only what comes from Me is acceptable to Me, and therefore your asking procures for you what you need, because it is My asking within you.

– A Servant of God

❖   ❖   ❖

21

It is clear now that there are two extremes
each of which is bad

It is clear now that there are two extremes, each of which is bad, and which you must learn, therefore, to avoid. One is to seek your peace, in Me, as you think, but without striving to conform yourself to Me. And the peace you are seeking, therefore, is not My peace, but a sensual complacency in yourself which you would like to think is in Me. But it isn't. And that is why My Love for you cannot allow you to rest in that kind of peace – because it isn't Mine.

Then, realizing that something in wrong, you swing to the opposite extreme, now trying [by your *own* efforts, *without* Me] to conform yourself to Me, in order to please Me – and by that motive your act is good, yet it is disordered and so, again, I cannot allow you to find your peace, i.e., My Peace, in it.

And here is the very heart of the lesson, that when I show you, through a severe temptation, or sometimes even by permitting you to fall, how prone you are to evil, you conclude, rightly, that you are not, in the measure of your evil disposition, conformed to me. I mean this, not merely in a general way, but in a very particular and precise sense, that you are not conformed to me *now*. And consequently it is impossible for you to be in peace, My Peace, unless you are actually conforming yourself to Me – not in a general way, but just in the way that I want you to be confirming yourself to Me at this moment. And here is the mistake you make: *you fail to recognize that the very realization of your inadequacy is My Voice calling you to come to Me in order to get what you need to please Me.* And so the mistake is to seek what you need apart from Me – and then things go from bad to worse, because then you allow yourself to be separated from Me more and more, and this in the illusion that you re pleasing Me thereby!

Now do you see the lesson I would teach you?   That the more you recognize your lack of conformity to Me the more promptly you must run to Me and the more closely you must cleave to Me, to My Heart—not to remain as you were (that is the other extreme) but to become what I want you to be, realizing only as you are united with Me can you receive the grace necessary to do what I am asking of you at this moment. And then, after this realization, as your soul is in My Peace, you will know, clearly, what you are to do by your own powers—and you will understand that each thing you are doing is pleasing to Me—because your every act will be My action in you. You must understand that My Peace which I give you is not something completed in which you can rest as in an end. No! It is My life, your participation in My life, which is a constant becoming.

You can see too, in this, how the error comes from your incapacity to understand how the distinct principle, your own free will and its operation, is distinct, *not* as it is *separated* from Me, but just as it is united with Me. But in your ignorance you are moved to undertake your responsibility in relation to Me by separating yourself from Me—as though it would not be your own act if you were united with Me. Whereas the truth is the very contrary—far from being your own act without Me, it would not be any act at all.

And so, the natural consequence of your freedom and responsibility is that your acts become more and more disordered as you remove yourself from the Principle of your acts, your Life—and this increasing disorder, you can see, gradually approaches the state of non-being, of nothingness. Do you see now? Do you see how true it is that without Me you can do nothing? Ponder this lesson very much. It is the secret of My Peace, My Peace which I give to you.

— Anonymous

❖ ❖ ❖

22

My one desire in loving souls is to rejoice in their goodness, their perfection

I do not force My Will on souls, respecting their freedom, so you must be careful to imitate Me in this. Have confidence that I am working all the time in each soul, and cooperate with Me as I work there. Do not try to win souls for Me by violating their freedom, but let them be attracted to Me in you by loving them as I love them, by letting Me, in you, love them.

Do you see how I love souls? I love them by wanting nothing for Myself. My one desire in loving souls is to rejoice in their goodness, their perfection. (How could anything be added to Mine?) And that is how I want you to love souls with Me, to desire their goodness so that you may rejoice in them with Me—wanting nothing except for them to love Me—that is their perfection—and to be loved by them in Me—that is your happiness with them.

— A Servant of God

❖ ❖ ❖

23

The Lord has something to tell us about how to do our work

Peter and his brothers were out fishing all night and came in without a single fish. Jesus tells them to go back out and lower their nets. "Master we have toiled all night and took nothing. But at your word I will let down the nets" (*Lk 5:1-11*). And of course Peter and his brethren catch so many fish they fill two boats almost to the point of sinking. So here we have two lessons: (1) that the Lord has something to tell us about how to do our work, and (2) that when we do so we enjoy unimaginable results.

And is there not this further point? The Lord blesses our work, our efforts, but always to a higher end. In the case of Peter, so that he might become a fisher of men. This seems to me to be terribly important, that the Lord in perfecting the work of our hands, always does so for purposes that are beyond our original intention. Is it not so then that he not only elevates the work but also the purpose or ends to which it will lead?

— diarist

❖ ❖ ❖

24

Use the things of this world as though you use them not (St. Paul)

My daughter, in order for grace to freely enter, the soul must be in the world as if there were nothing other than God and the soul. This is because any other thought or thing that comes between the soul and God prevents grace from entering the soul, and the soul from receiving grace.

— Luisa Piccarreta

❖   ❖   ❖
25
I go in search of souls who want to live in my Volition

Imagine a wheel: the center is my humanity; the spokes are everything I did and suffered. The circle where all the spokes unite is the human family which revolves around the center. If the circumference is revolving and doesn't receive the support of the spokes, the wheel cannot receive the good the center has. Oh, how much I suffer seeing all my goods suspended and that the ungrateful human family not only does not receive them but despises and tramples them! It is with such eagerness, then, that I go in search of souls who want to live in my Volition to fasten in them the spokes of my wheel. My Volition will give them the grace to form the circumference of the wheel, and they will receive the goods that have been rejected and despised by the others.

— Luisa Piccarreta

❖   ❖   ❖
26
I want to enrich your soul with new merits

Say to me often, "Lord, give me the grace to do well, from beginning to end, all that I want to undertake solely for You. I no longer want to be a slave to creatures." Do this so that when you walk, speak, work, or do any other thing, you will do it solely for my satisfaction and pleasure. When you experience mortifications, hurts and contradictions, I want you to have your eyes fixed on Me and believe that it all comes from Me and not from creatures. I want you to know that it is from my mouth that you hear, "Daughter, I want you to suffer a little. By these sufferings, I will make you beautiful. I want to enrich your soul with new merits. I want to work on your soul so that you may be like Me." And while enduring these sufferings for my Love, I want you to offer them to Me in thanksgiving for having made you work with merit. In doing so, you will compensate, with some benefit, for those that wronged you and made you suffer. Thus you will walk directly in front of Me. Things will no longer bother you and you will enjoy perfect peace.

— Luisa Piccarreta

❖ ❖ ❖
27

The Lord in his Justice gives us what we desire, be it good or evil

My daughter, when man disposes himself to receive grace, then he receives grace; when he disposes himself to evil, it is evil that he receives. All these voices that you hear reach my throne, and not once, but repeatedly. So, when my Justice sees that man not only wants evil but repeatedly demands it, then evil is what my Justice is forced to grant to make them understand the evil that they desire. You truly know what evil is when you find yourself in that very evil. That is the reason my Justice is seeking to punish man… It will serve to humble man, who has become so proud.

— Luisa Piccarreta

❖ ❖ ❖
28

On God's action and human freedom

Jesus to Luisa, at a time when she was plagued with doubts about whether it was He or the deceiver who came to her. In the midst of this, Jesus suddenly appears to her and holds her, saying: Quiet down, quiet down. Would it be right for someone who has seen the sun to say that it wasn't the sun he saw, merely because at that particular moment he doesn't see it?

Then later Jesus said to her: While it is true that I do everything in the soul so that without Me she could do nothing, it's also true that I always leave a thread of free will in the soul. So, she is capable of saying, "I'll do everything according to my own will." By being upset, you disrupt your union with Me. So, I have to hold you in my arms, being unable to work anything in you. I have to wait until you are once again at peace and your will is in union with Mine, before I can continue my work.

— Luisa Piccarreta

❖ ❖ ❖
29

It is God who grants efficacy to our labors

Writing of the Apostle Paul and his incredible accomplishments, St. Augustine says that "all in the City of God look up to…this athlete of Christ." "This man was a spectacle to the world, to angels and to men. He lawfully carried on a great conflict in the theater of this world and strained forward to the prize of his heavenly calling."

St. Basil, commenting on this marvel of Paul and all that he accomplished, states that "it is God who grants efficacy to our labors."

And St. Augustine, using the example of Paul, explains how this works: "Paul did not labor in order to receive grace," he wrote, "but he received grace so that he might labor."

– Commentary on I Cor 15: 8-11

❖   ❖   ❖
30
The Holy Spirit is in charge and will not fail to accomplish
the Lord's work in us, if we let him

"And when they bring you to trial and deliver you up, do not be anxious beforehand, what you are to say; but say whatever is given you in that hour, for it is not you who speak, but the Holy Spirit" *(Mk 13:11ff)*.

Jesus is speaking here of the trials that his disciples must undergo as they spread the gospel and preach "to all nations." But is not this for us as well, for are we not on trial, in a sense, at every moment of our life, at each branch point as we decide to do this or that, not do this or not do that? Our Lord is telling us that insofar as we do all things in His Name, we need have no anxiety, for we are not alone in what we do and are asked to do. The Holy Spirit is in charge and will not fail to accomplish the Lord's work in us if we let him.

– diarist

❖   ❖   ❖
31
I long for [souls] to surrender themselves to Me
so that I may work in the world!

You are nothing—a nonentity. Be pure like a drop of dew, that My Face may be reflected in you. It is because you are nothing that I can take possession of you, substitute Myself for you. Oh, how I thirst for souls— how I long for them to surrender themselves to Me so that I may transform them, for them to surrender their humanity to Me so that I may work in the world! Why do you not hear My call? Have I not exhausted every means to beg for your attention and your gratitude...?

"My Jesus, what ought I to do?"

Do not resist grace. Do not resist love. My love is exacting: efforts and weariness, sacrifice and disappointments count for little in comparison with what it gives. You must not dwell on them; love rules them and passes over them to draw strength and life from eternal realities. Act quickly, with precision. Let all your material work be regulated by order, method, and promptitude, so that you may be free to give yourself more to the life of the Spirit.

I await you in material work in which I have such need to be served with perfection—but I also await you in stillness and freedom of mind, in order to surrender Myself to your gaze.

— Sister Mary of the Holy Trinity

❖ ❖ ❖
32
God chose what is foolish in the world to shame the wise

But God chose what is foolish in the world to shame the wise, God chose what is weak in the world to shame the strong, God chose what is low and despised in the world, even things that are not, to bring to nothing things that are *(I Cor 1:27 – 28 RSV).*

Chrysostom, commenting on this writes: "In human terms, it is not possible for fishers to get the better of philosophers, but that is what happened by the power of God's grace."

And elsewhere, in his homily, the commentator says: "A little learning is a dangerous thing, because it makes those who have it unwilling to learn more. The unlearned are more open to conviction, because they are not so foolish as to think that they are wise"

— Chrysostom

❖ ❖ ❖
33
A voice shall sound in your ears: "This is the way; walk in it."

The Lord will give you the bread you need and the water for which you thirst. No longer will your Teacher hide himself, but with your own eyes you shall see your Teacher, while from behind, a voice shall sound in your ears: "This is the way; walk in it," when you would turn to the right or to the left.

— Isaiah 30:20-21 (NAB)

❖   ❖   ❖
34
God alone is good

Augustine's commentary deals with Jesus' statement in Mark to the rich young man who addressed Jesus as "good master," and to whom Jesus replied, "Why do you call me good? No one is good but God alone" (Mk 10:18).

When a finite being is good, his goodness derives from God, because he cannot be his own good. All who become good do so through his Spirit. Our nature has been created to attain to him through acts of its own will. If we are to become good, it is important for us to receive and hold what he gives, who is good in himself.

– St. Augustine

Commenting on this Gospel, The Venerable Bede says "It is only by participation in the divine goodness that a rational creature is capable of becoming good." Being good means to act with goodness—as a thing is, St. Thomas said, so does it act. And we understand by goodness *here not just moral actions, but good actions of any kind, for all actions no matter whether spiritual, moral, intellectual, physical, or some combinations of these, can be spoken of as well done or badly done. Insofar as they are well done, is it not so that they are well done only by virtue of their participation in God's perfect Goodness?*

– diarist

❖   ❖   ❖
35
We have access to the Father through the Spirit, who enables us to do the work the Father gives us

When the Son completed the work with which the Father had entrusted him on earth, the Holy Spirit was sent on the day of Pentecost to sanctify the Church unceasingly, and thus enable believers to have access to the Father through Christ in the one Spirit. He is the Spirit of life, the fountain of water welling up to give eternal life. Through him the Father gives life to men, dead because of sin, until he raises up their mortal bodies in Christ…

Moreover, the Holy Spirit not only sanctifies and guides God's people by the sacraments and the ministries, and enriches it with virtues, he also distributes special graces among the faithful of every state of life, assigning his gifts to each as he chooses. By means of these special gifts he equips them and makes them eager for various activities and responsibili-

ties that benefit the Church in its renewal or its increase, in accordance with the text: *To each is given the manifestation of the Spirit for a good purpose.*
— *Lumen Gentium*

❖ ❖ ❖

36

Everyone is obliged to accept the following principles as absolutely certain, and base his inner life upon them

Supernatural life is the life of Jesus Christ himself *in my soul*, by Faith, Hope, and Charity, for Jesus is the meritorious, exemplary, and final cause of sanctifying grace, and, as Word, with the Father and the Holy Ghost, He is its *efficient* cause in our souls.

The presence of Our Lord by this supernatural life is not the real presence proper to Holy Communion, but a presence of *vital action* like that of the action of the head or heart upon the members of the body. This action lies deep within us, and God ordinarily hides it from the soul in order to increase the merit of our faith. And so, as a rule, my natural faculties have no feeling of this action going on within me, which, however, I am formally obliged to believe by faith. This action is divine, yet it does not interfere with my free will, and makes use of all secondary causes, *events*, *persons*, and *things*, to teach me the will of God and to offer me an opportunity of acquiring or increasing my share in the divine life.

This life, begun in Baptism by the *state of grace*, perfected at Confirmation, recovered by Penance, and enriched by the Holy Eucharist, is *my Christian life*. By this life, Jesus Christ imparts to me His Spirit. In this way, He becomes the principle of a superior activity which raises me up, provided I do not obstruct it, to think, judge, love, will, suffer, labor with Him, by Him, in Him and like Him. My outward acts become the manifestations of this life of Jesus in me. And thus I tend to realize the ideal of the interior life that was formulated by St. Paul when he said: *"I live, now not I, but Christ liveth in me."*
— *Dom Jean-Baptiste Chautard, O.C.S.O.*

❖ ❖ ❖

37

Grace becomes in us the cause of actions and operations that are super-natural and tend towards a divine end

Grace is an *interior quality* produced in us by God, inhering in the soul, adorning the soul and making it pleasing to God—just as, in the natural domain, beauty and strength are qualities of the body; genius and learning, qualities of the mind; loyalty and courage, qualities of the heart. According to St. Thomas Aquinas, this grace is a "likeness to the Divine nature, by participation": *participata similitudo divinae naturae*. Grace, in a manner the uttermost depths of which elude us, makes us sharers of God's nature. By grace, we are raised above our nature, we become, in a way, gods. We become, not equal to, but *like* God; that is why Our Lord said to the Jews: "Is it not written in your law: 'I said, you are gods'?"

For us, then, participation in this Divine life is effected through grace, in virtue of which our soul becomes capable of knowing God as God knows Himself; of loving God as God loves Himself; of joying in God as God is filled with His own beatitude, and thus of living the life of God Himself… And as participation in the Divine life constitutes our holiness, this grace is called sanctifying…

In relation to us, as in relation to every [human] creature, the life to which God raises us is super-natural, that is to say, exceeding the dimensions and the strength, the rights and the exigencies of our nature. That being so, it is no longer as simply human creatures that we must be holy; but *as children of God, by acts inspired and animated by grace.*

Grace becomes in us the mainspring of a divine life. What is *to live*? For us, to live is to move by virtue of an inner mainspring that is the source of actions which tend to the perfection of our being. Upon our natural life is grafted, so to speak, another life of which the basis is grace. Grace becomes in us the cause of actions and operations that are super-natural and tend towards a divine end, namely possessing God one day and joying in Him, as He knows Himself and joys in His perfections.

— Blessed Columba Marmion

❖ ❖ ❖

38

You receive not a human word but the word of God
which is now at work in you who believe

That is why we thank God constantly that in receiving his message from us you took it, not as the word of men, but as it truly is, the word of God at work within you who believe.

— I Thessalonians 2:13 (N

-II-

Faith and Understanding about God and Self

❖   ❖   ❖
1
What My Love is capable of devising for you

It is not what you give Me that glorifies Me, it is when, by your confidence, you give Me the opportunity of showing you what My love is capable of devising for you.

— *Sister Mary of the Holy Trinity*

❖   ❖   ❖
2
He who approaches me and prays while uniting himself with Me receives the graft of my prayers and the goods they contain

My dear daughter, all that my Humanity did—prayers, words, works, steps, pains—are in act to be given to man; but who receives them? Who receives the graft of my work? He who approaches me and prays while uniting himself with Me receives the graft of my prayers and the goods they contain. He who speaks and teaches while united with Me receives the graft and fruits of my words. And, in the same manner, he who prays and suffers while united to Me receives the graft and the goods that my works and pains contain. And if it were not so, then all the goods which I acquired for the creature would remain suspended. And, not being grafted with Me, the creature would not be nourished by the goods of my Humanity which I wish to give with so much love. If there is no union, the goods of one remain as though dead to the other.

— *Luisa Piccarreta*

❖   ❖   ❖
3
If you had faith the size of a mustard seed (Luke 17:5-6 NAB)

The apostles said to the Lord, "Increase our faith," and he answered: "If you had faith the size of a mustard seed, you could say to this sycamore, 'Be uprooted and transplanted into the sea,' and it would obey you."

❖   ❖   ❖

4

The best way to make Me be born in your heart

The best way to make Me be born in one's own heart is to empty oneself of everything. Therefore, finding this void, I can put all my goods within you…

The second way which makes Me be born and increases my happiness is that everything the soul is and does, interior and exterior, all is and must be done for Me. All must serve to honor Me, to carry out my commands. If even one single thing—a thought, a word—is not for Me, I feel unhappy. Moreover, when things are done apart from their Master, such souls render Me a slave. How can I tolerate this?

The third way is heroic love, ever-increasing love, and love of sacrifice. These three loves make my happiness grow in a marvelous manner. This is because they render the soul superior to the other forces, having it love with my strength alone. This soul will increase my happiness by making not only herself but others love Me. Hence such a soul will come to suffer anything, even its own death, to be able to triumph in everything. Moreover, it allows that soul to say to Me, "I don't have anything more. Everything is only love for You." This way, not only will that soul make Me be born and make Me grow, but it will form a beautiful Heaven for Me in its own heart.

— Luisa Piccarreta

❖   ❖   ❖

5

Do what I tell you

Do you understand, My little daughter, that in the majority of souls I find tumult? Conflicting desires in opposition to the prayers which the lips pronounce…

- Tumult of ambitions, of personal interests which are permissible to lay-persons—which are a theft in religious souls who have vowed themselves to accept My interests, while abandoning theirs to Me.

  - Tumult of exclusive affections, of judgments, of comparisons with others, that distract you from your duty.

  - Tumult of anxieties, of material preoccupations, which stifle the spirit of faith.

My little daughter, be watchful to banish all that. I wish to find in your souls an all-embracing silence, which, like the ocean, engulfs all passing things, a silence immense as the Majesty of God. Then, within the depths of your soul, you will hear a very gentle voice rising: it is I …

It is I who desire to live again in you…
Lend me your human nature…
Do what I tell you…

— Spiritual Legacy of Sister Mary of the Holy Trinity

❖   ❖   ❖
6
We know not what we do

Our Lord said that *"Without me you can do nothing,"* yet we see it is in the nature of Divine Providence that the sun shines on both those who hear Our Lord and those who do not, and in some measure the light of truth is given to people who do not even believe in truth's possibility and yet do some degree of good in the world. Such people, among them scientists, road builders, homemakers, accountants, taxicab drivers, all use the measure of truth they have to do that good and in that measure serve the common good. Only God knows the greater good we would effect in this world if our minds and hearts would pause and listen to his words: *"Without me you can do nothing."* But he also said, *"Father, forgive them for they know not what they do."*

— diarist

❖   ❖   ❖
7
The obedience of faith must be given to God
who reveals himself (John Paul II)

From this notion of *obedience* we learn that faith is not so much a "leap," as the Danish philosopher Kierkegaard suggests, as it is a "response." Not a leap in the dark to someone we cannot tell is really there, but a response we make to light that has shined in that darkness, illuminating the one who beckons us. It is not blind faith that animates us then, but a signal, one we have received and responded to in a hidden place within us. This means that faith is not our doing so much as a right response to something God is doing in, to, and for us, and yes, with us, for nothing happens if we do not make our response.

Secular minds cannot understand a lively faith as something not engendered by ourselves, by dint of will borne of ignorance, or simple psychological need, a calculated leap to someone who for all we know is not there. But if faith is a leap of the will, it is a leap into arms that have invited us. No secular mind can understand this because what takes place takes place as a gift placed deep within the soul, unobservable and unfathomable to the unbeliever and the merely curious.

Faith is our yes to one who has made us aware of him. And to what he wants to give us and what he wants to ask of us, both in myriad ways, through Scripture, through the witness of those who surround us, through the things that happen to us in the course of our day, and most particularly through the quiet stirrings someplace deep within us. We can pay attention to these signals or ignore them, but whatever the case, they are not our doing.

This is why the Council and the Pope speak of faith as *obedience*. An obedient soul is a soul disposed to receive what is being given, and to do what is being asked, both in the order of belief and in the order of doing. An obedient soul is an attentive soul. *The eyes of the handmaid are on the hands of the master.* When the Master beckons, such a soul will answer.

— diarist

❖ ❖ ❖

8

On the limits of the human mind to ponder the mysteries of creation

Just hours before his death, Albert Einstein asked for pen and paper and began writing down some mathematical formulas on a problem that had seized his mind for most of his life. It was a final attempt to solve what in the end he could not solve, no matter how deeply he thought about it. It concerned the physicist's quest to account for all the forces of nature in a single explanation, what those who picked up the quest after him would call a "theory of everything." Einstein sought this unified theory virtually all his life.

Einstein never succeeded, though he would not stop trying virtually to his dying breath. Yet, like any good scientist, he was a realist and he had a realist's instinct that the goal he sought was probably unattainable. Unattainable, in his own words, "due to human inadequacy of thought and inability to comprehend nature, so that every abstract formulation of it was inconsistent somewhere." All one could do, his biographer would paraphrase, was to "test each idea to destruction, replace it, and repeat the process, and so on, thought without end." Which is exactly how this great mind of his functioned, until his demise put an end to thought in this life altogether.

Einstein before God

Einstein: Now that I have a chance to ask you directly about the great physics problem, would you tell me if the four forces of nature are unified?

God: They are.

Einstein: Ah good! I always thought so. Can you tell me what the unifying principle is?

God: My Will.

Einstein: That is not too helpful. How, may I ask, can one know your Will?

God: Only those who do my Will can fathom my Will.

Einstein: Hmm, I don't think it likely physicists will buy into that very well

God: If you are right, then they will only get so far in their physics. Let me tell you how they can get started on the right track, when they realize that the first problem that must be solved has to do not with the physics but the physicists.

— diarist

❖   ❖   ❖

9

Physics and a holy unschooled woman

A holy, unschooled woman (Luisa Piccarreta) records an experience in 1923, shortly after Einstein was honored with the Nobel Prize and just as he was starting to apply his mind in his lifelong quest for a unified theory of nature. She kept a diary; here are some of her entries. They form a remarkable counterpoint to Einstein and his famous quest, and to the difficulties he faced in attaining what he sought.

May 2, 1923: I was feeling as if my poor mind was lost in the immensity of the Eternal Will.

April 20, 1923: I was completely immersed in the Divine Will, and I said to my Jesus, Ah, I beg You never to allow me to depart from your most Holy Will. Let me always think, talk, act, and love in your Will.

While I was saying this, I felt myself surrounded by a most pure light. Then, I saw my Love, and He said to me: "My beloved daughter, I so love those acts that have been done in my Will that, as soon as the soul enters into It to act, my light surrounds it, and I run to ensure that my Act and the soul's act are as one. Since I am the first Act of all creation, without Me as the First Mover all created things would remain paralyzed, impotent, and incapable of the slightest motion. Life consists in motion; without it every thing is dead. I am, therefore, the First Mover who makes all other motion possible. So, it is my first Act that sets the creature in motion. It's like a machine; after the first gear starts to move, all the other gears move. You see, therefore, how it is almost natural that whoever acts in my Will also acts in my own first Act and, therefore, in the action of all creatures…

To act in my Will is the wonders of wonders, but it is without human accolades or honors. It is my triumph over all creation. Since this triumph of my Supreme Will is wholly divine, there are no human words with which to express it."

– Luisa Piccarreta

❖   ❖   ❖
10
The times of activity are not all that different from the
times of prayer (Brother Lawrence)

Brother Lawrence began by faithfully cultivating this exalted awareness of God's presence, contemplating by faith, in his heart. He fostered this awareness by continuous acts of adoration and love, invoking Our Lord's help in what he had to do, and then thanking him after doing it. He asked pardon for his sins, admitting them, as he said, without bargaining with God. Since his occupations were bound up with these acts [of adoration and love] and provided material for them, he accomplished them with greater ease, and far from distracting him from his work, they helped him do it well.

He admitted, however, that there were considerable periods of time when he was not mindful of this practice, but after humbly confessing his fault, he would take it up again without difficulty. Sometimes a host of inappropriate thoughts would violently seize the place of his God, but he was satisfied to put them aside gently and return to his ordinary conversation. Thus his fidelity was rewarded with a continuous awareness of God. His various, multiple acts were changed into a simple view, an enlightened love, an uninterrupted joy.

"The times of activity are not at all different from the hours of prayer," he said, "for I possess God as peacefully in the commotion of my kitchen, where often enough several people are asking me for different things at the same time, as I do when kneeling before the Blessed Sacrament. My faith sometimes becomes so enlightened I think I've lost it, for it seems to me that the curtain of obscurity has been drawn aside, and the endless, clear day of the next life has begun to dawn."

This is where his determination to reject all other thoughts in order to devote himself to a continual conversation with God led Brother Lawrence. Eventually it became so familiar that he said it had become almost impossible for him to turn away from God to deal with anything else.

— Joseph de Beaufort

❖   ❖   ❖

11

"Come what may, at least I will do everything for the love of God."

Brother Lawrence said he never swayed from his initial determination in spite of the terrible sufferings he had for four years, so terrible that he was certain he was damned... Without thinking about what would become of him, and without concerning himself with his sufferings (as troubled souls would do) he consoled himself by saying, "Come what may, at least I will do everything for the love of God for the rest of my life." Therefore, by forgetting himself he resolved to love himself for God, and this worked to his advantage.

In him the love of God's will had taken the place of the attachment we ordinarily have to our own. He saw only God's plan in what happened to him, and this kept him in continual peace. When he learned of some evil, he was not astonished by it; he was, on the contrary, surprised that things were not worse, given the malice of which the sinner is capable. Brother Lawrence would immediately turn to God who, he realized, could remedy the situation, and who permitted these evils for just reasons, beneficial to the general order of his action in the world. Once he prayed for sinners, he no longer worried about them and returned to his state of peace.

— Joseph de Beaufort

❖   ❖   ❖

12
It is enough to love God and offer him our works

"We look for methods [Brother Lawrence said] to learn how to love God. We want to get there by I don't know how many practices. A multitude of methods makes it more difficult for us to remain in God's presence. Isn't it much shorter and more direct to do everything for the love of God, to use all the works of our state in life to manifest our love to him, and to foster the awareness of his presence in us by this exchange of our hearts with him? Finesse is not necessary. We need only approach him directly and straightforwardly."

We must not conclude, however, that it is enough to love God and offer him our works, to invoke his help and perform acts of love. Brother Lawrence did not attain the perfection of love by these means alone, but because he was most careful from the very beginning to do nothing that might displease God. He had renounced everything but God, and he had forgotten himself completely.

This is how Brother Lawrence began, by the more perfect way, thus leaving everything for God and doing everything for love of him. He forgot himself entirely. He no longer thought about heaven or hell, nor about his past or present sins, once he asked pardon of God.

— *Joseph de Beaufort*

❖   ❖   ❖

13
Leaving the choice to God

A very important man went to see Brother Lawrence, who was seriously ill, and asked him which he would choose: if God permitted, to remain alive longer to increase his merits, or to receive them now in heaven. Without deliberating, Brother Lawrence answered that he would leave the choice to God, and that, as far as he was concerned, he had only to wait peacefully until God revealed his will.

— *Joseph de Beaufort*

❖   ❖   ❖

14
"He leads me besides the still waters…" (23rd Psalm)

The Psalm is a hymn to the Lord who provides in every way, whose rod and staff are always, unfailingly with us. In the smallest details of our lives we need fear no evil, no failure, no mishap. The waters are still because he is leading us. Without him, there is turbulence, as when the disciples were in the boat during the storm, before turning to the Lord and the waters were stilled.

— diarist

❖ ❖ ❖
15
His ways are not our ways, nor are our plans his plans

The doctrine of perfect love comes to us through God's action alone, and not through our own efforts. God instructs the heart, not through ideas but through suffering and adversity. To know this is to understand that God is our only good. To achieve it, it is necessary to be indifferent to all material blessings, and to arrive at this point one must be deprived of them all. Thus it is only through continual affliction, misfortune and a long succession of mortifications of every kind to our feelings and affections that we are established in perfect love. The point must be reached when the whole of creation counts for nothing and God for everything. This is the reason why God opposes all our personal inclinations and ideas. No sooner do we form our own ideas or notions of piety or means to perfection or whatever designs we may have, or advice we may take, God disconcerts all our plans and instead permits us to find in them only confusion, trouble, vanity and folly. Scarcely do we tell ourselves "This is the way, this is who to ask, what to do!", then no sooner does God say exactly the opposite and withdraws his virtue from the decisions we have made. And so, discovering in everything only mortality and consequently nothingness, we are forced to turn to God himself to find our happiness in him.

— Jean-Pierre de Caussade

❖ ❖ ❖
16
Salt and pepper Christians

Jesus said of the disciples, the first saints, that they were "the salt of the earth." Thinking of salt, apart from its use in cooking and preserving, what strikes you is its whiteness, in fact the brilliance of its whiteness. Salt has an unusual purity in that regard. What else in the natural order, among common things, is naturally white in the way salt is white? Only sugar perhaps after it is refined. The interesting thing about the whiteness of salt is that the slightest particle of something foreign stands out immediately, like an offensive presence seeming to vitiate the whole. Yet, speaking for myself, I am a salt and pepper Christian, given to black specks in my nature.

But we can take consolation, can we not, from Our Lord's parable about the wheat and the tares. According to Our Lord, tares and pepper serve a mysterious purpose in God's Providence, for in the case of sinners it is often these very things that drive us to seek Him who came to save sinners. The Good News is that the negative things in us are ordained not to defeat us but to bring us to our senses as it did the Prodigal Son, and bring us to make our way back to the Father. And to do what is the most natural thing in the world to do when we see a black speck in a teaspoon of salt or a bowl of sugar.

– diarist

❖   ❖   ❖

17

Our Lord heals the wrong and multiplies the good

They came laying the sick at Jesus' feet and He cured them. Then afterwards, when the disciples complained that people were getting hungry and that there were no means to feed them, suggesting that He send them away to fare for themselves, Jesus asked what they had—just seven loaves and a few fish. But it was adequate to feed five thousand with baskets of food left over.

We are confronted by a dire situation beyond our means and we bring our inadequacies to the Lord full of doubt and tribulation, and he takes the little we have and brings about the ends he desires. Things are made right in unexpected ways; what is beyond us is suddenly within reach, or in one way or another the problem goes away. And indeed the Lord may respond in ways hard to understand. But however he deals with it, his merciful purposes are being achieved, as they always are in everything that happens save sin. And this extends to the most ordinary things. He feeds us, as if to make us understand that his Providence relates not only to the Last Things but to everything in our lives, even to the food on our table. It is a miracle that every moment of our day will re-enact, as we bring to him the little we have to somehow make it do. And He does, more than enough to suffice and something left over.

— diarist

❖   ❖   ❖

18
Our Lord's work in us

For we are his workmanship, created in Christ Jesus for good works, which God prepared beforehand, that we should walk in them.

— Eph 2:10 (RSV)

❖   ❖   ❖

19

However painstaking our work, so long as we omit to surrender ourselves to God while performing it, we fail to attract God's grace

When you undertake some special endeavor, do not concentrate your attention and heart on it, but look upon it as something secondary; and by entire surrender to God open yourself up to God's grace, like a vessel laid out ready to receive it. Whoever finds grace finds it by means of faith and zeal, says St. Gregory of Sinai, and not by zeal alone.

However painstaking our work, so long as we omit to surrender ourselves to God while performing it, we fail to attract God's grace, and our efforts build up within us not so much a true spirit of grace but the spirit of the Pharisee. Grace is the soul of the struggle.

Our efforts will be rightly directed so long as we preserve self-abasement, contrition, fear of God, devotion to Him, and the realization of our dependence upon divine help. If we are self-satisfied and contented with our efforts, it is a sign that they are not performed in the right way, or that we lack wisdom.

— Theophan The Recluse

❖   ❖   ❖

20
The unceasing act of love

The act of love ought to be so unceasing that not one act would be willingly lost throughout the day; it ought to be so virginally pure that no other thought could enter. To attain this, it is necessary for the soul to carry her faith in Love so high as to abandon herself to Love like a feather to the breeze.

In other words, it is necessary to abandon herself so irrevocably to Love as to renounce not only every thought of other creatures, but even every thought of herself. It means to obliterate herself, to die to herself—a difficult matter, and one which is little understood by the majority of souls—but it is, therefore, no less necessary if Jesus is to have freedom of action within the soul.
— *Fr. Lorenzo Sales, I.M.C., commenting on Sister Maria Consolata*

❖ ❖ ❖
21
Allow Me to do it

When speaking of the life of love in general, we already pointed out that to forget oneself and to abandon oneself to God does not imply that the soul should neglect her own spiritual development and relax into blameworthy indifference; the soul should avoid proceeding according to her own whims and preferences; instead, she should comply with the workings of Jesus in the soul with simplicity and docility. Our Lord's watchword to all souls whom He calls to high perfection in the path of love is simply this: *Allow Me to do it!*
— *Fr. Lorenzo Sales, I.M.C., commenting on Sister Maria Consolata*

Commentary: It is not that God does everything and we do nothing—rather, we do everything in our power to allow God to act in us, as perfectly as we give up our self-generated thoughts and ideas.
— *A Servant of God*

❖ ❖ ❖
22
Let Jesus do it!

Yes, let Jesus do it! And why not? Has anyone else the sanctification of the soul more at heart than He? Is anyone else able to sanctify her? Who can perceive her real needs as well as He? To Him alone are known the designs which God has for the soul. Being omnipotent, He can do everything; being faithfulness itself, He will keep all His promises!... Why then should one not entrust oneself to Him and give Him a free hand so that He can work in the soul as absolute and uncontested Master? Why not submit to Him one's own opinions, one's thoughts, aspirations, desires, preoccupations? Why not adapt oneself trustingly at each moment to His actions which alone are always sanctifying?

— Fr. Lorenzo Sales, I.M.C., commenting on Sister Maria Consolata

❖ ❖ ❖

23

I will do everything, but you must let Me do it.

Jesus to Sister Consolata on September 22nd, 1935: "You see, Consolata, sanctity means self-forgetfulness in everything, in thoughts, desires, words… Allow Me to do it all! I will do everything; but you should, at every moment, give Me what I ask for with much love!"

Love of abandonment resolves itself in practice into docile love. In speaking to the multitude, Jesus reminded them that it was written by the Prophet: "They shall all be taught of God." Jesus is the sole teacher of all souls: "Neither be ye called masters; for one is your Master, Christ." He is the Master who possesses the knowledge of sanctity in an infinite degree, and He wants to and is able to communicate it to the soul. But the soul must lend herself to being instructed and must execute with promptness every divine command or wish, no matter whether it be pleasant or painful, and without regard to the manner in which it is manifested.

September 24th, 1935: "Consolata, I have every claim upon you, but you have only one duty: to obey Me. I require a docile will which permits Me to act, which lends itself to everything, which trusts in Me and serves Me always in peace and joy, no matter what the situation is."

Nov. 18th, 1935: "Let Me do everything! You will see that I will do everything, and do it well, and that My little victim will become fruitful in love and in souls."

Aug. 22nd, 1934: "Think no longer about yourself, about your perfection, on how to attain to sanctity, or about your defects, your present and future troubles. No, I will see to your sanctification, to your sanctity. You must henceforth think only of Me and of souls; of Me to love Me, and of souls to save them!"

Oct. 15th, 1935: "Let Me do everything! Act as though only I existed. Of yourself there should remain only the continual act of love and an extreme docility to do simply and always whatever I desire directly or indirectly through your superior or your Sisters."

— Fr. Lorenzo Sales, I.M.C.

❖   ❖   ❖
24
Prayer of St. John of the Cross

Father of mercies, come to our aid, for without you, Lord, we can do nothing.

— St. John of the Cross

❖   ❖   ❖
25
If we are lacking something in our faith

To the extent that we are lacking something in our faith, then we are missing out on what the power of God has to offer us.

— Origen

❖   ❖   ❖
26
The good we lack on earth we receive in Heaven

My daughter, for however many things the soul is deprived of here, that much more wealth will it have in Heaven. The poorer one is on earth, so much richer will that one be in Heaven. The more one is deprived of tastes, of pleasures, of entertainments, of trips, and of walks on earth, so much more tastes and delights will such a one find in God. Oh, how many walks in the space of the Heavens—especially in the immeasurable Heavens of the attributes of God! This is because each attribute of God is another Heaven!

Moreover, for the Blessed who enter there, heaven could be likened to a door to the attributes of God. Thus whoever walks through this door has greater enjoyments. Additionally, the more they continue walking, the more they will relish—and the more they will rejoice and enjoy themselves. Therefore, whoever leaves behind the earth takes hold of Heaven, even in the least little thing.

Thus it follows that whoever is more despised, will be more honored; whoever is smaller will be greater; whoever more submissive, will have greater dominion; and so forth with all the rest. Yet, of mortals, who is the one who thinks of depriving himself on earth, in order to possess it eternally in heaven? Almost no one!

— Luisa Piccarreta

❖　❖　❖

27

The intention purifies the action

My daughter, all human actions — even though holy — if done without any special intention for Me, come out of the soul full of darkness. However, when they are done with rectitude and with the special intention of pleasing Me, then they come out full of light because the intention purifies the action.

— Luisa Piccarreta

❖　❖　❖

28

Right intention grows in the soil of right attention

The intention of doing all things to please God is a disposition of the soul to do all things *for* Him, *in* Him and *through* Him — which disposition is the fruit of proper recollection. Recollection is proper when it is informed by a proper understanding, for a soul may be good and even holy and yet be deficient in its understanding of what Jesus is saying to us through someone like Luisa Piccarreta (immediately above). But a soul that is quiet understands this and goes about its day doing what it does with purity. Jesus calls such actions pure because He is in them. And He is in them because such a soul, in its intention, invites Him and allows Him to be present in the least actions of the day, like picking up a stamp and placing it on the envelope, for no act is too small but that it can reflect the light of God.

Thus, right intention grows in the soil of right attention. We exhibit right attention when we listen to Christ more than to our own thoughts when wondering what to do in a given circumstance. And from that right attention will come right intention born of God's movement in our soul. What does our faith amount to if we do not believe this? And do not act this way.

A soul whose intentions are only for itself, its own benefit and interests Jesus tells Luisa is a "soul full of darkness." We call such a soul selfish, self-centered, self-absorbed, familiar traits that characterize us all far more than we care to see. We can see them in others however. We readily see them in the Pharisees who were preoccupied with their own goodness and so could not see the good that stood before them, the good that the

Father was accomplishing in Christ. Their attention was only for their own advantage, to be seen, to be honored, to be called Rabbi, and so on.

But if we would re-focus our self-interest on Him, He would take care of our interests far better than we could ourselves. A wise man once said that the son who wants what his father wants, moves the father to want what the son wants. That is the two-way reciprocity of familial love. So if we do what we do with the right intention, with the intention of pleasing God, however small the act, will not Our Lord, as it were, feel obliged by love to reciprocate, to lend his hand, his power, his authority, his wisdom to this act, whatever it be, and thereby to free us? Isn't this the hidden meaning of St. Augustine's words, "Love God and do what you want"?

– diarist

❖   ❖   ❖

29

Insofar as you know yourself, you shall know God

Jesus to Luisa: "The greatest favor that I can grant to a soul is to make it know itself. The knowledge of oneself and the knowledge of God go hand in hand. In so far as you shall know yourself, so shall you know God. The soul that has known itself, seeing that of itself it can work no good, transforms the shadow of itself into God; and it comes to pass that it does all its operations in God. It happens then, that the soul is in God and walks beside Him, without looking, without investigating, without speaking. In a word, it is, as it were, dead; for knowing in depth its nothingness, it does not dare to do anything of itself but blindly follows the influence of the operations of the Word."

Luisa: It seems to me that to the soul that knows itself, it happens as with those persons who go by train: while they pass from one point to another without themselves taking a step, they make long trips, but all in virtue of the train that transports them. Such is the soul: putting itself in God, as the person on the train, it makes sublime flights in the way of perfection, knowing well that it is not of itself, but in virtue of that blessed God who carries it in Himself. Oh, how the Lord favors, enriches and concedes the greatest graces to the soul that, not to itself, but to Him attributes all! Oh soul that knows yourself, how fortunate you are! . . .

Jesus: "My daughter, only the little ones let themselves be handled as one wants—not these who are little in human reason, but those who are full of Divine Reason. I alone can say that I am humble. In man, on the contrary, that which is called humility should instead be called knowledge of oneself, and he who does not know himself already walks in falsehood."

— Luisa Piccarreta

❖   ❖   ❖

30

Faith gives us the promise of peace
And makes known the demands of love

Father in heaven, God of power and Lord of mercy,
  from whose fullness we have received,
  direct our steps in our everyday efforts.
May the changing moods of the human heart
  and the limits which our failings impose on hope
  never blind us to you, source of every good.
Faith gives us the promise of peace
  and makes known the demands of love.
Remove the selfishness that blurs the vision of faith.
Grant this through Christ our Lord.

— Opening prayer, Mass, 31st Sunday of Ordinary Time

❖   ❖   ❖

31

The act of faith is an act of reason

You must not believe that the way you think has nothing to do with the way you love! It has everything to do with it. Try to understand this: your faith exists in your reason. That means that the operation of faith, your act of faith, is an act of reason. "As a thing is, so does it operate." And therefore you "live by faith" as you live by your enlightened reason, your reason enlightened by faith.

You must pray and work, therefore, to rectify your reason—in order to love. You must understand that as your understanding becomes more pure, so does your love!

— Our Lord to a Servant of God

❖   ❖   ❖

32
I want to take your place

"I so hunger for you that I want to enter you to the point of taking your place so that my Father and my brothers see only Me in you. So that you take my place, continuing Me, prolonging Me close to them. Coming and exchanging places means to give up one's place in order to take one's place. And in order to make place for Me, must I not banish and drive away all the rest, substituting my thoughts, my Heart, my volition for yours, so that there is no longer anything left of yourself, only of Me.   *– Our Lord to an anonymous French nun*

❖   ❖   ❖

33
What the Psalmist and a Prophet say when things go wrong

We are all inclined to think that Scripture, and the Old Testament especially, teaches that in this life the good are blessed and the wicked are punished. In *Isaiah 26:7* we read: *"The way of the just is smooth; the path of the just you make level."* And indeed, did not the calamities in the Old Testament occur because of Jewish perfidy? Yahweh rescued the Jews from Egypt and gave them the promised land but then, isn't it the case, before long the Jews forgot Yahweh, with exile and other dire consequences, just as the prophets forewarned? The answers of course are all affirmative, so it is tempting to conclude that when we are good, God blesses us and things go well, and when we are bad, He chastises us and things turn sour. That seems to be the lesson from Scripture.

But this of course is not exactly the case. God's action in history is not like a schoolmarm, who favors the good and punishes the bad. It doesn't quite work that way. Indeed, we can't say how it works: the fate of peoples, and of ourselves, is woven by a Providence simply beyond our grasp. This we see in Psalm 43 (44), when the psalmist goes on to lament: *"Yet now you have rejected us, disgraced us, you no longer go forth with our armies… This befell us though we had not forgotten you; though we had not been false to your covenant; though we had not withdrawn our hearts; though our feet had not strayed from your path. Yet you have crushed us in a place of sorrows and covered us with the shadow of death"* (vv. 10,18-20 Grail).

The psalmist cannot understand this. All the psalmist can do is plead: *"Awake, O Lord, why do you sleep? Arise, do not reject us forever. Why do you hide your face and forget our oppression and misery?… Stand up and come to* our help! Redeem us because of your love!"(vv. 24-25, 27). Nor can we neglect the laments of psalmist and prophets over the prosperity of the wicked. In *Isaiah*, we read: "*The wicked man, spared, does not learn justice*" (26:10 NAB).

But then Isaiah announces a great mystery, that even the good that we do comes from God, even our disposition to turn to Him: "*Oh Lord, you mete out peace to us, for it is you who have accomplished all we have done…it is from you only that we can call upon your name*" (vv. 12, 13b).

Yes, in the end the Lord will "*punish the wickedness of the earth's inhabitants*" (v. 21b.) But punishments are of two kinds—chastisements for those who are to be ultimately redeemed: "*Oh Lord, oppressed by your punishment, we cried out in anguish under your chastising…but your dead shall live, their corpses shall rise*" (vv. 16, 19a)—and punishment of an ultimate kind for those who are unredeemable. "*Let the fire prepared for your enemies consume them*" (v. 11b).

For the Chosen People, the Prophet advises: "*Go my people, enter your chambers and close your doors behind you; hide yourselves for a brief moment until the wrath is past*" (v. 20).

— diarist

❖   ❖   ❖
34
Deeds wrought in God

And this is the judgment, that the light has come into the world, and men loved darkness rather than light, because their deeds were evil. For every one who does evil hates the light…lest his deeds should be exposed. But he who does what is true comes to the light, that it may be clearly seen that his deeds have been wrought in God.

— John 3:19-21 (RSV)

Deeds done outside of God's will darken the mind to truth. This is axiomatic: an evil man cannot see the truth of his evil because truth is light and what is evil resists the light and thus darkened cannot see itself. But the man who welcomes the light of truth is the man whose deeds are "wrought in God." In the end, only the person who welcomes this light can be doing God's Will, which is to say can accomplish anything good.

— diarist

❖   ❖   ❖
35
Get to work!

This morning I saw my confessor completely humiliated. There with him were both Blessed Jesus and St. Joseph, who said to him, "Get to work; the Lord is ready to give you the grace you want." Afterwards, seeing my dear Jesus suffering as during the time of the Passion, I said to Him, "Lord, don't you feel tired from suffering so many different sufferings?"

And Jesus: "No. One suffering merely inflames my heart to suffer another. That is the way of Divine suffering: in suffering and in acting, to look at nothing else other than the fruit to be gained. In my wounds and in my Blood, I see nations being saved and creatures receiving graces. Rather than experience fatigue, my Heart feels joy and an ardent desire to suffer more. So, this is the sign whether what one is enduring is a participation in my own sufferings: if it unites suffering and the joy of suffering more; and if, in his actions, he acts with Me; if he looks not at what he does, but at the glory that he gives God and at the fruit he will receive."

– Luisa Piccarreta

❖   ❖   ❖
36
God's power is made perfect in weakness

It is better to be burdened and in company with the strong than to be unburdened and with the weak. When you are burdened you are close to God, your strength, who abides with the afflicted. When you are relieved of the burden you are close to yourself, your own weakness, for virtue and strength of soul grow and are confirmed in the trials of patience.

Whoever wants to stand alone without the support of a master and guide will be like the tree that stands alone in a field without a proprietor. No matter how much the tree bears, passers-by will pick the fruit before it ripens… God desires the smallest degree of purity of conscience in you more than all the works you can perform.

– St. John of the Cross

❖   ❖   ❖
37
Each man's work will become manifest

Each man's work will become manifest; for the Day will disclose it, because it will be revealed with fire, and the fire will test what sort of work each one has done. If the work which any man has built on the foundation [of Christ] survives, he will receive a reward. If any man's work is burned up, he will suffer loss, though he himself will be saved, but only as through fire.

— I Cor 3:13-15 (RSV)

❖ ❖ ❖

38

Faith which empowers activities surpassing human nature

This faith which is given by the Spirit as a grace is not just doctrinal faith but a faith which empowers activities surpassing human nature, a faith which moves mountains… For just as a grain of mustard seed is of little bulk but of explosive energy, taking a trifling space for its planting and then sending out great branches all around, so that when it is grown it can give shelter to the birds, so in like manner the faith present in one's soul achieves the greatest things by the most summary decision. For such a one places the thought of God before his mind and as enlightenment of faith permits it, beholds God. His mind also ranges through the world from end to end, and with the end of this age not yet come, beholds the judgment already, and the bestowal of the promised rewards.

— Cyril of Jerusalem

❖ ❖ ❖

39

I can do all things in him who strengthens me.

— Phil 4:13 (RSV)

❖ ❖ ❖

40

On self-knowledge

A man not very close to God and with little self-knowledge walks down the street and thinks in his heart, "He (God) is a nice guy and I'm a nice guy. We're both fine men." A holy man, knowing himself, walks down the street and thinks of all the things in him that must offend the One whom he has come to adore. They say a saint is someone who believes all the world's evils can be traced to his heart, so well does he know himself, what he is like apart from his God. G. K. Chesterton, once asked for his observations about what was wrong with the world, answered, "I am."

The Father told St. Catherine in *The Dialogue* that the spiritual life is perfected in the cell of self-knowledge.

— diarist

❖   ❖   ❖

41

Judgments about others that oppose God's intentions for them

Each person in the world exists as an intention of God, who only intends that person's good, who never brings anyone into being but for a good end. So when we decide someone is a bad person and leave it at that, are we not contravening God's intentions? When we see the defects in another person, perhaps a misguided political leader or a nasty boss, and just want to write him off, are we not contending with God over that person? If we see these negative things and let it go at that, are we not adding to the distance that may already separate that soul from God? These judgments have their consequences, we may be sure.

It is true we cannot help judging people, calling a spade a spade. Truth is of God. But what we need to do, and I must learn to do, is never to stop at truth, but use it as a springboard to mercy, as Our Lord has done for us. Seeing what is wrong in a person is an occasion for merciful prayer. Then instead of employing truth to oppose God, we cooperate with him.

And the person we have prayed for will benefit, for God, given his intention for that individual in the first place, will surely hear our prayer. Then our seeing the truth about another's faults will have served a divine purpose. For truth is our friend, and nothing draws down mercy where mercy is needed more than truth. Then we will be like the good Samaritan helping a man who is down, not the Pharisee who keeps to the other side of the road for his own comfort's sake.

When I see what is wrong in others and do not extend a hand, a prayer, I am that Pharisee. Merciful Father, help me change my ways. Truth mixed with charity can save a man. Truth without it can ruin him.

— diarist

❖   ❖   ❖

42

God is to be experienced in love for the divine image in human beings

A young college student wrote Flannery O'Conner that he was in the process of losing his faith. Flannery O'Conner replied that Bridges once wrote Gerard Manley Hopkins with a similar complaint, and Hopkins wrote back, not with a long treatise on faith as Bridges expected, but with the simple advice, "Give alms." Says Flannery O'Conner: "He was trying to say to Bridges that God is to be experienced in Charity (in the sense of love for the divine image in human beings)."

— diarist

❖ ❖ ❖

43

But for this [trial] you would not have perhaps become less good than you are, but you would not have become holy

When I see a Christian grief-stricken at the trials God sends him I say to myself: Here is a man who is grieved at his own happiness. He is asking God to be delivered from something he ought to be thanking him for. I am quite sure that nothing more advantageous could happen to him than what causes him so much grief. I have a hundred unanswerable reasons for saying so. But if I could read into the future and see the happy outcome of his present misfortune, how greatly strengthened I would be in my judgment! If we could discover the designs of Providence it is certain we would ardently long for the evils we are now so unwilling to suffer. We would rush forward to accept them with the utmost gratitude if we had a little faith and realized how much God loves us and has our interests at heart.

What profit can come to me from this illness which ties me down and obliges me to give up all the good I was doing, you may ask. What advantage can I expect from this ruin of my life which leaves me desperate and hopeless? It is true that sudden great misfortune at the moment it comes may appear to overwhelm you and not allow you the opportunity there and then of profiting by it. But wait a while and you will see that by it God is preparing you to receive the greatest marks of his favor. But for this accident you would not have perhaps become less good than you are, but you would not have become holy. Isn't it true that since you have been trying to lead a good Christian life there has been something you have been unwilling to surrender to God? Some worldly ambition, some pride in your attainments, some indulgence of the body, some blameworthy habit, some company that is the occasion of sin for you? It was only this final step that prevented you from attaining the perfect freedom of the love of God. It wasn't really very much, but you could not bring yourself to make this last sacrifice. It wasn't very much, but there is nothing harder for a Christian than to break the last tie that binds him to the world or to his own self. He knows he ought to do it, and until he does there is something wrong with his life… The misfortune which has befallen you will soon do what all your exercises of piety would never have been able to do.

— St. Claude de La Columbière

❖   ❖   ❖

44

On limping along with ambivalent minds

A good illustration of God's action in the lives of those who have complete faith in Him may be seen in the story of Elijah confronting the prophets of Baal. The Israelites were surrounded by worshipers of Baal— as many as 450 prophets of Baal were active in their midst—and the Israelites had become ambivalent in their worship, accommodating both the Lord and Baal, "limping with two different opinions" as Elijah put it. The word "limping" is interesting here because ambivalence in faith left the people ineffective.

Elijah would show them the power of faith in the one true God. So Elijah challenged the prophets of Baal to a contest. Build a pyre of wood for a sacrifice, he said. Place the sacrificial bull upon the wood and call upon your god to ignite the fire. The pagan priests did just that, calling upon their god from morning to night. It's interesting to note that these prophets clearly had faith in what they were doing—they prayed long and hard and even beat themselves. As we know, all to no avail. Then it was Elijah's turn. He poured water on the wood just to make his case, and then poured even more water. When he called upon the Lord, the wood ignited instantly. The pagan priests had faith in their god, so it isn't faith but *proper* faith that matters. It isn't faith *per se* but the true God in whom we have this faith that makes the difference.

Here is the point. We today are rather like the Israelites. In great unthinking patches of our lives, we too are of two minds in what we do and believe. We are surrounded by legions of spokesmen arguing for a false god, whatever it may be—self-sufficiency, wealth, comfort, ambition, reputation, possessions, whatever. And more often than not, perhaps, we heed the cultural voices. Like the Israelites in Elijah's time, we make room for competing points of view. What, after all, distinguishes us from the confirmed secularist in huge areas of our lives? If no one notices our faith, how real can it be? Are we too not limping?

The Lord God is just as capable of manifesting his power and goodness today as back in Elijah's time. After all, He is the primary cause of all good that is done anywhere in the world. Think of the good that would be done if all men turned to him, as Elijah did, and asked him to show forth that goodness and power and put the false gods to shame. The place to start is in our own lives, and if many did this, would not the world begin to be a different place? Yes, it would take heroic faith like Elijah's, believing in God without the least shadow of doubt. And then we would have to take this belief and call upon him as the prophet did in the areas of our lives where false gods held sway. God will surely manifest himself. He will ignite something in us and the way we *are* will change, the way we *act* and *work* will reflect his hand. Faith teaches us that this has to be the case. For it is unthinkable that the Lord of history would fail to manifest himself in us when we turn to him in faith. In the measure we do not, we limp along, as the prophet said.

— diarist

❖ ❖ ❖
45
If anyone loves the world, the love of the Father is not in him

Do not love the world or the things in the world. If anyone loves the world, love for the Father is not in him. For all that is in the world, the lust of the flesh, and the lust of the eyes, and the pride of life, is not of the Father but is of the world. And the world passes away, and the lust of it; but he who does the will of God abides forever.

— I John 2:15-17 (RSV)

❖ ❖ ❖
46
The Blessed Mother, on how the soul that is privileged to suffer the cross with Christ also receives the gifts of Christ's joys and consolations

Each of these gifts [joys and consolations] are correspondingly augmented in him who in the state of grace performs the least meritorious work, even if it be no more than receiving a straw or giving a cup of water for the love of God (*Matt 10:42*). For each of the most insignificant works of the creature gains an increase of these gifts; an increase of clearness exceeding many times the sunlight and added to its state of blessedness; an increase of impassibility, by which man recedes from human and earthly corruption farther than what all created efforts and strength could ever effect in resisting or separating itself from such infirmity or changefulness; an increase of subtlety, by which he advances beyond all that could offer it resistance and gains new power of penetration; an increase of ability, surpassing all the activity of birds, of winds, and all other active creatures, such as fire and the elements tending to their centre.

From this increase of the gifts of the body merited by good works, thou wilt understand the augmentation of the gifts of the soul; for those of the body are derived from that of the soul and correspond with them. In the beatific vision each merit secures greater clearness and insight into the divine attributes and perfections than that acquired by all the doctors and enlightened members of the Church. Likewise the gift of apprehension, or possession of the divine Object, is augmented; for the security of the possession of the highest and infinite Good makes the tranquility and rest of its enjoyment more estimable than if the soul possessed all that is precious and rich, desirable and worthy of attainment in all creation, even if possessed all at one time.

Fruition, the third gift of the soul, on account of the love with which man performs the smallest acts, so exalts the degrees of functional love, that the greatest love of men here on earth can never be compared thereto; nor can the delight resulting therefrom ever be compared with all the delights of this mortal life.

– Our Lady to Venerable Mary of Agreda

❖   ❖   ❖
47
God never gives us a failure

God never gives us a failure. We [make] it a failure by not accepting the grace and cooperating with grace.

– Eileen George

❖   ❖   ❖
48
The spiritual journey begins with desire, and this desire, we learn, must be
fed…and the food that feeds holy desire…is self-knowledge

According to what the Father reveals to St. Catherine of Siena in *The Dialogue*, the spiritual life begins with "holy desire, the ardent longing for God and for the salvation of souls, first for one's own salvation, then for others."

The Dialogue opens with this sentence: "A soul rises up, restless with tremendous desire for God's honor and the salvation of souls. She has for some time exercised herself in virtue and has become accustomed to dwelling in the cell of self-knowledge in order to know better God's goodness toward her, since upon knowledge follows love. And loving, she seeks to pursue truth and clothe herself in it.

"But there is no way she can so savor and be enlightened by this truth as in continual humble prayer, grounded in the knowledge of herself and of God. For by such prayer the soul is united with God, following in the footsteps of Christ crucified, and through desire and affection and the union of love he makes of her another himself."

The spiritual journey begins with desire, and this desire, we learn, must be fed, nurtured, and the food that feeds holy desire, according to this doctor of the Church, is self-knowledge.

It is through self-knowledge that the soul learns to know God and God's goodness to her, and from this knowledge of God's goodness there then arises holy desire and love. And loving, she seeks to pursue truth and clothe herself in it. But there is no way she can so savor and be enlightened by this truth as in continual, humble prayer, grounded in the knowledge of herself and of God. This we learn directly from the Father, through this saint.

— diarist

❖   ❖   ❖
49
Know thyself

The unexamined life is not worth living

— Socrates

❖   ❖   ❖
50
The Father to St. Catherine of Siena: You are rewarded not according to your work or your time spent but according to your love

I have sent all of you into the vineyard of obedience to work in different ways. Each of you will be rewarded according to the measure of your love, not according to your work or the time spent. In other words, those who come early will not get more than those who come late, as it was said in the holy Gospel…. My Truth was showing you that you are rewarded not according to your work or your time but according to your love."

— Dialogue of St. Catherine of Siena

❖ ❖ ❖
51
How shall this be done?

Pope John Paul II, in his encyclical *Fides et Ratio*, speaks of *wonder* as the source from which springs all inquiry and knowledge. This wonder is our response as we contemplate the mystery of creation and our life within this order. He says that the modern mind has turned from wonder and concentrated instead on issues of truth and knowledge, focusing not on our capacity to know truth but rather upon how greatly that capacity is limited and conditioned, to the point where truth is no longer felt to be knowable.

Mary responded to the angel's announcement with a very simple question, "How shall this be done, since I do not have relations with a man?" Contrast this with Zachariah whose response to the angel is one of skepticism: "How shall I know this?" Zachariah, poor fellow, was struck dumb as a consequence. Mary, full of grace, does not question the angel, only wonders as to the means, since to her the means are not available. The angel explains that the Most High will come upon her. God himself will accomplish this. To which Mary utters her holy and salvific *Fiat*.

— diarist

❖ ❖ ❖
52
This is how you will love Me more…by the loving solicitude which moves you to understand my Goodness more and more

Yes, you have so many false ideas of Me—but do not think that they are unimportant practically, do not think that they do not hurt you. That is another great and terrible error which so many of My children make—as though loving Me had nothing to do with the way you thought, nothing to do with the truth. No! Your act of love is an act of your reason, and it is the very effect of your love to purify your understanding more and more, and the purer your understanding becomes, the more purely, the more perfectly will you love Me. No! that is a dreadful error so many of My children fall into. They must learn to use their minds to know Me, to understand Me, to penetrate more and more into My Love for them, My Father's Love.

When you understand Our Love for you, you will see that your love for Us is the resonance of Ours for you, the response of your heart to Our Love as your heart is moved by your understanding, your understanding of Our Goodness. When you have realized this, you will strive unceasingly to understand Our Goodness more and more. That is what love is—a force that moves you without rest to know Us, more and more. That is why those who love Us more in this life will know Us more perfectly in the next life.

We give each soul exactly what it wants. We are perfectly simple. Those who love Us more want to be united with Us more—and since you are united with Us in knowledge, those who love Us more will, in the end, know Us more. But not only in the end. For in this life, as you are growing in love, you seek more and more to be united with Us in understanding, and so you grow in wisdom—until it is almost as though there were only a thin veil between Us, between Our very Essence and your understanding.

And so, My beloved children, do not permit yourselves to be led astray, but use the mind I have given you to understand Me always more. This is how you will love Me more, and that, too, is how you will make a perfect use of your freedom—and that too, is how you will know that I am loving you, by the loving solicitude which moves you to understand my Goodness more and more.

— *A Servant of God*

❖   ❖   ❖

53

What is really important in the life of a man

The temptation story [of Christ in the wilderness] summarizes the entire struggle of Jesus: it is about the nature of his mission, but at the same time it is also, in general, about the right ordering of human life, about the way to be human, about the way of history. Finally, it is about what is really important in the life of a man. This ultimate thing, this decisive thing, is the primacy of God. The germ of all temptation is setting God aside, so that he seems to be a secondary concern when compared with all the urgent priorities of our lives. To consider ourselves, the needs and desires of the moment to be more important than he is—that is the temptation that always besets us. For in doing so we deny God his divinity, and make ourselves, or rather, the powers that threaten us, into our god.

– Cardinal Joseph Ratzinger (Pope Benedict XVI)

❖   ❖   ❖

54

One should not wonder that the soul is capable of so sublime an activity

The soul united to God and transformed by him draws from within God a divine breath, much like the most high God himself. And God, abiding in the soul, breathes forth the life of the soul as its exemplar. This I take to be what Paul meant when he said: "Because you are children of God, God has sent the Spirit of his Son into your hearts, crying, 'Abba, Father'"; this is what takes place in those who have achieved perfection.

One should not wonder that the soul is capable of so sublime an activity. For if God so favors her that she is made God-like by union with the most Holy Trinity, I ask you then, why it should seem so incredible that the soul, at one with the Trinity and in the greatest possible likeness to it, should share the understanding, knowledge and love which God achieves in himself…

The Father thus gives them the same love he shares with the Son, though not by nature as with the Son, but through the unity and transformation of love… Accordingly, souls possess the same goods by participation that the Son possesses by nature. As a result, they are truly divine by participation, equals and companions of God…

So the soul, in this union which God has ordained, joins in the work of the Trinity, not yet fully as in the life to come, but nonetheless even now in a real and perceptible way. O my soul, created to enjoy such exquisite gifts, what are you doing, where is your life going? How wretched is the blindness of Adam's children, if indeed we are blind to such a brilliant light and deaf to so insistent a voice.

– St. John of the Cross

❖ ❖ ❖

55
May he enlighten your innermost vision

May he enlighten your innermost vision that you may know the great hope to which he has called you, the wealth of his glorious heritage to be distributed among the members of the church, and the immeasurable scope of his power in us who believe. It is like the strength he showed in raising Christ from the dead and seating him at his right hand in heaven, high above every principality, power, virtue, and domination, and every name that can be given in this age or in the age to come.

— Ephesians 1:18-20 (NAB)

❖ ❖ ❖

56
Take courage, it is I. Do not be afraid!

In the Gospel of *Mark*, Jesus, after feeding the five thousand, tells his disciples to get into a boat and proceed to the other side of the lake towards Bethsaida, while he goes off into the mountains to pray. Later that evening, on the high seas, those in the boat encounter stiff winds and rough going. Jesus appears, walking on the water, as if to pass them by. They are terrified at this sight, thinking him to be a ghost. But he speaks to them, *"Take courage, it is I, do not be afraid!"* He then gets into the boat and the wind dies down. Then the Gospel writer comments, "They were completely astounded. They had not understood the incident of the loaves. On the contrary, their hearts were hardened" *(Mk 6:45-52)*.

In the Gospel of *John*, after feeding the multitude Jesus withdraws to pray. When it grows dark the disciples decide to return to Capernaum on the other side of the sea, without Jesus. They encounter a storm on the way that terrifies them. Then Jesus appears to them on the water and they are frightened. He draws near to them and says, *"It is I, do not be afraid."* Then scripture tells us, "They were glad to take him into the boat and *immediately* the boat was at the land to which they were going" *(Jn 6:21)*.

Jesus had no need of a boat to cross the lake, but got into the boat to comfort his disciples, taking on their limitations (a tiny reflection of the Incarnation where Christ emptied himself to come into our world to be with us) and at the same time transforming it since now the going would be smooth. In *Mark* we see the disciples' lack of comprehension because as yet their hearts remained hardened despite the miracle of the feeding.

When these hearts became softened, by grace, they too would in effect walk on water, performing great miracles and showing no fear of anything, not even martyrdom.

In *John's* account, the disciples' *instantaneous* transition to their destination when the Lord is with them—contrasting their labors with the sea and elements when he is not—is instructive. It tells us, does it not, how the trials of daily labor will go when the Lord is with us: *"Take courage, it is I, do not be afraid!"*

— diarist

❖ ❖ ❖
57
Everything, even the most minute detail, is directed to one
single purpose: the salvation of souls

It is no longer possible to live in ignorance. For everything that the Lord has created and permitted man to know has as its sole purpose that man might become holy, might set aright his steps, that he might live in communion with God, and that he might understand that everything, even the most minute detail, is directed to one single purpose: the salvation of his soul.

— Our Lady to Consuelo

❖ ❖ ❖
58
"I am a Father who gives Himself…"

My little children, you must understand that I am a Father who gives Himself and in giving Himself, gives everything—just as I communicate My Being to My Only Begotten Son eternally, so that even as He is true God, He has nothing in Himself but everything from Me—that is why He is the Littlest of the little. *And so I would be a Father to you, communicating Myself totally to you as you are in My Son.* O My little children, see, then, how necessary it is for you to be so small that you are nothing in yourself, nothing outside of Me—like My Son—*so that you may receive everything from Me."*

— Anonymous

❖ ❖ ❖
59
"Upon all the laity, therefore, rests the noble duty of working to extend the divine plan of salvation to all men of each epoch and in every land." (Lumen Gentium)

34. The supreme and eternal Priest, Christ Jesus, since he wills to continue his witness and service also through the laity, vivifies them in this Spirit and increasingly urges them on to every good and perfect work. He also gives them a sharing in His priestly function of offering spiritual worship for the glory of God and the salvation of men. For this reason, the laity, dedicated to Christ and anointed by the Holy Spirit, are marvelously called and wonderfully prepared so that ever more abundant fruits of the Spirit may be produced in them. *For all their works, prayers and apostolic endeavors, their ordinary married and family life, their daily occupations, their hardships of life, if patiently borne — all these become "spiritual sacrifices acceptable to God through Jesus Christ."* Together with the offering of the Lord's body, they are most fittingly offered in the celebration of the Eucharist. Thus, as those everywhere who adore in holy activity, the laity consecrate the world itself to God. (*Italics added.*)

— Lumen Gentium

❖ ❖ ❖

60

How could a thing remain unless You willed it?

Before the LORD the whole universe is as a grain from a balance
    or a drop of morning dew come down upon the earth.
But you have mercy on all, because you can do all things,
    and you overlook people's sins that they may repent.
But you love all things that are
    and loathe nothing that you have made;
    for what you have hated, you would not have fashioned.
And how could a thing remain unless you willed it;
    or be preserved, had it not been called forth by you?
But you spare all things, because they are yours,
    O LORD and lover of souls,
    for your imperishable spirit is in all things!
Therefore you rebuke offenders little by little,
    warn them and remind them of the sins they are committing,
    that they may abandon their wickedness
    and believe in you, O LORD!

— Wisdom 11:22-12:2 (NAB)

❖

- III -

Theology of Primary and Secondary Causes

Father of mercies, come to our aid,
for without you, Lord, we can do nothing.
— St. John of the Cross

❖ ❖ ❖

1

God is the source of all activity throughout creation

God is the source of all activity throughout creation. He cannot be seen or described in his own nature and in all his greatness by any of his creatures. Yet he is certainly not unknown. Through his Word the whole creation learns that there is one God the Father, *who holds all things together and gives them their being....*

From the beginning the Son is the one who teaches us about the Father; he is with the Father from the beginning. He was to reveal to the human race visions of prophecy, the diversity of spiritual gifts, his own ways of ministry, the glorification of the Father, all in due order and harmony, at the appointed time and for our instruction. Where there is order, there is also harmony; where there is harmony, there is also correct timing; where there is correct timing, there is also advantage.

— St. Irenaeus

❖ ❖ ❖

2

See how good the Lord is. He does what is great
without neglecting what is little

My children, see how good the Lord is! He begins all his works with divine mastery, and He does not neglect the least detail until He has fulfilled his designs. In an efficacious and astonishing way, without leaving anything to chance or unaided by his grace, He brings to completion everything that He begins. He does what is great, without neglecting what is little. He is the Lord of all, and He governs all with wisdom and goodness.

— Our Lady to Consuelo

❖ ❖ ❖

3

My Will is always working in created things
in order to benefit the creature

My daughter, my Will is always working in created things in order to benefit the creature; but who fulfills it? Who brings to an end the work of my Will? The creature who takes all created things as fulfillment of my Will.

My Will makes Its way in the seed that the earth receives, giving it the virtue of germinating and multiplying itself. My Will does Its constant work in calling the water to sprinkle it, the Sun to make it fertile, the wind to purify it, the cold to make it put forth roots, and the heat to develop it, making it reach its proper maturity. Then, It gives the virtue to machines to cut it, to thresh it, to grind it, and so, it is made into the substance of bread; and calling the fire to cook it, It brings it to the mouth of the creature, so that he can eat of it and conserve his life. See, therefore, how many ways my Will has worked in the development of that seed, how many created things It has called upon in order to make that seed reach the point of becoming bread for the mouths of creatures!

Now, who takes the last step on the way of my Will and the fulfillment of the last Act of my Supreme Volition? Whoever takes that bread and eats it as a carrier of the Divine Volition in himself; and, as he eats the bread, he eats my Volition in it to increase the strength of his body and soul, in order to fulfill everything in the Divine Will. The creature, it can be said, is the center of repose in which my Will aspires to reach the creature with all Its ways and in the constant work that It does in all creatures.

— Luisa Piccarreta

❖ ❖ ❖

4

God is the Primary Cause of what is and happens,
we are secondary causes

St. Thomas teaches that the act of every agent, whether God or man, is to bring something into being. In the case of man, whether he is building a house, a career, or a family, man works to make things happen, which is to say, to bring something into being. But, as St. Thomas taught, none of man's actions would be possible without God who gives man his life, his talents, his powers, his opportunities, his very breath and movement. God, we must understand, is the "first agent" of man's acts, all of them (save the sinful), and without God's agency, no action on the part of the creature is possible.

In this regard, St. Thomas wrote: "Being is the proper effect of the primary agent, and all other things produce being because they act through the power of the primary agent. Now, secondary agents, which are like particularizers and determinants of the primary agent's action, produce as their proper effects other perfections which determine being."

It follows, then, that human agents must produce their effect because they are subordinated to the first agent and act through his power. From St. Thomas we learn that man is never the principal cause of good actions, only a cooperating, secondary cause. Moreover, God not only empowers our actions, but he *directs* our actions, when we allow Him to do so, by ordering them to some good end, in accordance with his Divine Will.

St. Thomas: "It is clear, for example, that all the men in an army work to bring about victory, and they do this by virtue of being subordinated to the leader, whose proper product is victory... Besides, in the case of all causes that are ordered, that which is last in this process of generation and first in intention is the proper product of the primary agent [i.e., the end for which the action was initiated]. For instance, the form of a house, which is the proper product of the builder, appears later than the preparation of the cement, stones, and timbers, which are made by the lower workmen who come under the builder. Now, in every action, actual being is primarily intended, but is last in the process of generation. In fact, as soon as it is achieved, the agent's action and the patient's motion come to rest. Therefore, being is the proper product of the primary agent, that is, of God; and all things that give being do so because they act by God's power... [Just as] fire is the proper cause of all things that are afire, ...everything that brings something into actual being does so because it acts through God's power."

—*diarist (St. Thomas,* Summa Contra Gentiles)

❖   ❖   ❖

5

It is God's touch that will animate Adam

In his famed painting of the creation of man, Michelangelo drew Adam as the ultimate expression of human duality. The powerful physique of Adam charged with physical potential to do anything, is countered by the arm that weighs heavily on the knee, the lolling head and the fixed yearning gaze on the apparition of God. It is God's touch that will animate Adam, God's infusion of His own Divine spark, the immortal soul, which will raise man above all other creatures.

— *Vatican Dossier*, "Under the gaze of the Sistine"

❖   ❖   ❖

6

As I instill my Being within yours, you should, in everything, take that which is mine and, in everything, leave behind that which is yours

Having received Holy Communion, I wondered how I could draw myself closer than ever to blessed Jesus; and He said to me:

"In order to draw yourself more closely to Me, so as to arrive at losing your being within Me, as I instill my Being within yours, you should, in everything, take that which is mine and, in everything, leave behind that which is yours. You must do this in such a way that you always think of holy things, as well as only those things that concern what is good — the Honor and Glory of God. Therefore leaving your mind, you take the Divine.

"Consequently, if you speak or do good, and you do so only for love of God, then leave behind your mouth and hands to take my Mouth and Hands. If you walk paths that are holy and just, then you will walk with my own Feet. If your heart loves only Me, then you will leave your heart to take Mine. Hence you will love Me with my very same Love, and so forth with all the rest. Thus, you will remain clothed with all of my things, and I with all of your things. Accordingly I will place with you Myself, and those things which are Mine. Could there be closer union than this?

"If a soul arrives at a point of no longer recognizing itself, but only the Divine Being within itself, it is the fruit of good Communions. Moreover this is the Divine Purpose which I desired to communicate to souls. But how much my Love remains frustrated! Further, how few fruits are gathered by souls from this Sacrament, up to the point where the majority remain at best indifferent, if not nauseated, by the Divine Food."

— Luisa Piccarreta

❖ ❖ ❖
7
"May it be done unto me according to Thy Word"

When the Archangel Gabriel appeared to Mary to request her consent to the Incarnation, Mary's response through him to the Father—her 'Fiat' to the Primary Cause—becomes our model, the model of all secondary causes. As we secondary causes imitate her Fiat in the things that the Father asks of us, we in our measure will find in our acts the fecundating action of God whose Spirit overshadows what comes from us, as it must if what we do is to be good and have worth in God's eyes.

— diarist

❖ ❖ ❖
8
"Be ye perfect!"

The call to perfection that Christ issues in one sense is a call to return to Adam's innocence before the Fall. And what was this innocence? It was moral perfection to be sure, but not only moral. Everything that Adam did, every step he took, word he uttered, had that *right touch* that God imparted to his creation when he "saw that it was good." Everything that Adam did as he moved about Paradise was good (and perfect) because before sin entered the world there was no separation between man and God, between primary and secondary causes, between God's Goodness and man's acts, no division of wills, nor of purpose, nor of method, not even in the performance of the most ordinary acts.

It is not that Adam had the power and perfection of God, for he did not, but he had the perfection proper to a creature without flaw, who allowed himself in all his acts to be moved by the Primary Cause of those acts. And in so doing Adam gave perfect expression to his free will (which we understand to mean the freedom to do, or not do, not anything at all but the right thing, not just anything Adam wished but the just things God wished for Adam's sake).

When that free will was tested, Adam and Eve chose unwisely and by their fateful act of self-will drew down a fatal wedge between creature and Creator to be felt immediately in everything that Adam and Eve were to do thereafter, and continues on ever since in every walk of life. Nothing thereafter in our life in this world would ever be quite right, not even to the taking of a single step.

It is hard for us to imagine that the taking of a single step would be different when done with God than when done without Him. But it is surely so. I believe it was St. Louis Marie de Montfort who said that Mary in stooping over to pick up a straw merited more for the Church in that simple act than did the all the acts of the Apostles because it was done in God.

The Creator of original goodness sent Christ into this flawed world to call us back to Himself and to the felicity of a perfect world. Believing this we must believe perfection is possible in all the ordinary acts that make up life, a perfection begun in time in this world and perfected in eternity in His Kingdom.

Belief in our perfectibility, morally and in every other respect, is part and parcel of the gift which the Father gives us in Christ Jesus, in whom and through whom we are re-created as new beings, free of Adam's sin. A perfect life, then, is the life to which we are called in Christ. But is there not a great, hidden mystery in Christ's call, for he did not call us back to the perfection of Adam before he sinned, to that of the creature before the Fall, but to something infinitely higher: *"Be ye perfect as your Father in heaven is perfect!"*

– diarist

❖   ❖   ❖

9

Adam before he sinned, seasoned all his acts with
the nourishment of our Will

Do you know what the acts of creatures are without the fullness of our Will? They are as foods without seasoning and without nourishment; instead of being tasty, they are disgusting to the human palate; and, likewise, their acts disgust the Divine Palate. They are like unripe fruits which do not contain either the right sweetness or the flavor; they are as flowers without perfume, without color; they are as vases, full, yes, but of things old, fragile and tattered… All that, however, can serve as a strict necessity for man and even as a show of the Glory of God. Now, on the contrary, with what pleasure will one not eat a food well seasoned and nourishing? How it strengthens all the person! The aroma of the seasoning alone whets the appetite and makes one avid to eat it.

And so, Adam before he sinned, seasoned all his acts with the nourishment of our Will, whetting the appetite of our Love; and We took his acts as food most pleasing for Us. In exchange, we gave him our choice food, our Will. But after sin, poor thing, he lost the direct way of communication with his Creator. Pure love no longer reigned in him; love was divided with fear, with timidness; and he no longer had the absolute dominion of the Supreme Will. After sin, the same acts that he had done before no longer had the same value...

But with all that, my Will did not completely leave man. Although no longer able to be the fountain of Life and base that sustains man, because he subtracted himself from It, It offered Itself as medicine so that he would not lose everything. Thus, my Will is medicine, sanctity, conservation, food, Life and Fullness of the highest Sanctity according to what the creature wants of It; It offers Itself to take away the fever of the passions, the weakness, the impatience, the dizziness of pride, the sickness of attachments, and so with all the rest of the evils... If the creature wants It as food, It gives Itself as food so he develops strength and grows more in sanctity. If he wants It as life and fullness of sanctity, oh, then my Will makes merry because It sees man returning to the bosom of his origin from where he came forth; and It offers Itself to give him the likeness of his Creator, unique purpose of his creation. My Will never leaves man. If It did leave him, he would dissolve into nothing. If he does not lend himself to becoming holy by my Will, at the least It uses ways to save him.

—Luisa Piccarreta

❖   ❖   ❖
10
Fiat VoluntasTua, Sicut In Coelo Et In Terra

What is it about Luisa Piccarreta that distinguishes this holy woman from all others? Quickly said and with simple words: she was the first to live in the Divine Will with perfect imitation of the Humanity of our Lord:

"My food is to do the Will of my Father"… and the perfect imitation of the most Holy Virgin: "Let it be done unto Me…"

The Saints and the Church have known until now the conformity with the Will of God, the complete abandonment, even the *Union* with the Will of God, with his Divine Volition. We can see examples of this from such Saints as St. Francis de Sales or St. Vincent de Paul (and, for that matter, hundreds of other Saints) in the expression: "to empty oneself of himself and unite his will totally to God's such that there is only one will with his." We could say that this is the highest point. And how does Luisa's doctrine differ from this union of wills? Let us take the answer from her writings. In the chapter dated Oct. 6, 1922 (Vol. 14), Luisa asks the question how is it that she was the first to *Live in the Divine Will* after so many centuries and so many Saints in the Church. Our Lord responds: "…moreover, it is certain that I have called you first over other souls. Because to no other soul, however much I have loved them, have I shown *How To Live In My Will, The Effects, The Marvels, The Riches That The Creature Receives Who Acts In My Supreme Will.* Search the lives of the Saints as much as you wish or in books of doctrine and you will not find the wonders of *My Will Working In The Creature And The Creature Acting In My Will. The Most You Will Find Is Resignation, Abandonment, The Union Of Wills, But The Divine Will Working In The Creature And The Creature In My Will You Will Not Find This In Anyone.* This signifies that the time had not arrived in which my kindness would call the creature to live in such a sublime state. Moreover, even the way I ask you to pray is not found in any other…"

This is to say that from the union of wills, which has been already experienced, Luisa enters into the unity of *Wills* and into the *Activity* of that *Unity*, to the *Activity And Life* of the creature in the *Divine Will*, along with its effects, etc.

– *José Luis Acuña R.*

❖   ❖   ❖

11

"…that the Kingdom of the Supreme Fiat might come over the earth…"

Who, until now, has ever requested with interest, with insistence, sacrificing his own life so that the Kingdom of the Supreme FIAT might come over the earth and that It triumph and establish Its dominion? No one! It is true that ever since I came to the earth the Church prays the

"Our Father" which asks that my Kingdom come so that my Will be done on earth as It is in Heaven. But who thinks of what they are asking for? It can be said that all the importance of this request remained in my Will and that creatures pray it only to pray it, without really comprehending, nor having real interest in obtaining what they are asking for.

— Luisa Piccarreta

❖   ❖   ❖
12
"…everything that creatures do is by my grace…"

It is true that everything that creatures do is by my grace, but the same grace wants to find the affirmation, disposition and good will of creatures. Therefore, to reestablish the Kingdom of my Will on earth, there must be sufficient acts by creatures to keep my Kingdom from remaining suspended and enable it to descend and take form upon the very acts which creatures have formed in order to obtain such an immense good. This is why I urge you so much to make our rounds in all our works, our Creation and Redemption. I do it to have you contribute your acts, your "I love You," your adoration, your recognition and your "thank You" over all our works. Many times I have made these rounds with you; and, as you finish your journey in our Will, you repeated, to honor Us, your refrain which is so pleasing to Us: "*Supreme Majesty; your little daughter comes before You; and I sit on your paternal knees, to request your FIAT, your Kingdom, that it may be known by all. I ask for the triumph of your Will so that It will establish Its dominion and reign in all. I am not alone in making this request. Together with me are all your works, your own Will. Therefore, on behalf of all, I request, I beg your FIAT.*"

Oh, if you only knew how powerfully your refrain impacts our Supreme Being. We find Ourselves asking for all our works and begging for our own Volition. Heaven and earth kneel to petition the Kingdom of our Eternal Volition. Then, if, in truth, you want this Kingdom, continue with your acts so that when the established number has been completed, you can obtain that for which you sigh with such insistence.

— Luisa Piccarreta

❖   ❖   ❖
13
"Because We never stop, our works are completed and always remain beautiful…"

It doesn't matter how many evil acts creatures do. I never leave my works but conserve them always with my Power and Creative Force for love of those who offend Me. I love them always without ever ceasing. Because we never stop, our works are completed and always remain beautiful, doing good to everyone. And if We would stop, each thing and everything would end in ruin; and no good would be completed. Therefore, I also want you with Me in this, always resolute, without ever leaving my Will doing what you have done until now, to attentively listen to Me, to be the narrator of my Will.

— Luisa Piccarreta

❖   ❖   ❖

14
I will influence the creature in every way to make my Volition reign.

My daughter, whatever is not enjoyed today will be enjoyed tomorrow. What appears darkness now, because of minds that are blind, will change to sunlight for those who will have eyes to see. Oh, what great good they will do! Let us, then, continue what we have done. Let us do what is necessary so that nothing is lacking, neither assistance nor light, nor good, nor surprising truths so that my Volition might be known and reign. I will use all the means of Love, of grace, of chastisements. I will influence the creature in every way to make my Volition reign. And when it seems as though the true good should die, it will rise more beautiful and majestic. Therefore, take courage, my daughter, do not despair; trust in Me… I will think of everything and will defend the rights of my Volition to make It reign.

— Luisa Piccarreta

❖   ❖   ❖

15
"I ask you to give me only what I have given you"

Think very much of this, that I ask you only to give Me what I have given you, to love Me with My love; and realize, therefore, that the reason and purpose of everything you do is to allow Me to act in you. And the more you try to do this, the more you will believe in My love for you—because you will have permitted Me to give it to you more. You must use your freedom for this alone, to allow Me to act in you, to live in you. And the more you permit Me to love you, the more I will show you what you are in yourself, your utter misery without Me—not to reject you, but to draw you more and more closely to My Heart. It is My delight to see you trust Me more and more as you see more and more your own misery. It is my joy to give you this precious grace of boundless trust in My Love for you. That is how I rectify you; that is how you become Me.

— A Servant of God

❖ ❖ ❖

16
We are who we are by an act of God

Whatever bodily or seminal causes may play a part in reproduction, whether by the influence of angels or of men or other animals, or by the intermingling of the two sexes, and whatever longings or emotions of the mother may affect the features or the color while the fetus is still soft and pliable, nevertheless, every nature as such, however affected by circumstances, is created wholly by the Supreme God. It is the hidden and penetrating power of His irresistible presence which gives being to every creature that can be said to be, whatever its genus and species may be. For, without His creative act, a nature would not only not be in this or that genus; it simply could not have being at all.

— St. Augustine

❖ ❖ ❖

17
In him we live and move and have our being

St. Paul wrote that "In him we live and move and have our being," and to this we must add, "and accomplish all that we do" for, in the words of Our Lord (as we must ever remind ourselves), *without him we can do nothing.*

— diarist

❖ ❖ ❖

18
Always work together with Me — as if we were together doing the same thing

My dearest daughter, working for Christ makes the human work disappear, and Christ makes arise the divine work. For this reason, always work together with Me—as if we were together doing the same thing. If you suffer, do it as if you were suffering with Me; if you pray, if you work, make everything run in Me and together with Me. Thus you will lose the human works in everything, only to find them again as Divine. Oh, how immense is the wealth that creatures could acquire working this way, but it does not interest them!

— Luisa Piccarreta

❖   ❖   ❖
19
For God nothing is impossible

In the Gospel of Luke, the angel Gabriel announces to Mary that she will bear the Messiah, and when she asks "how shall this be done?" the angel answers that "with God nothing is impossible."

We must always remember and believe that this is so in anything that God asks us to do, that his infallible Will will accomplish in us the work that he asks of us, be the work big or little, important, or seemingly very ordinary. Our God is the God of both extraordinary things and of very ordinary things. He numbers the very hairs on our head, so when we cut them, we can be sure that He knows and takes interest, hard as that is to believe. He has an interest in everything we do, that it be done well and for our benefit, just as would a loving parent whose son or daughter we are. When the entire world begins to live this way, taking the Lord's interests to heart, knowing He has our interests at heart, the world will be transformed. Meanwhile, will we not see our own lives transformed if we let God into even the smallest of our acts? How could it be otherwise?

— diarist

❖   ❖   ❖
20
Unless the Lord builds the house, those who build it labor in vain

Unless the Lord builds the house,
   those who build it labor in vain.
Unless the Lord watches over the city,
   the watchman stays awake in vain.
It is in vain that you rise up early
   and go late to rest,
eating the bread of anxious toil;
   for he gives to his beloved sleep.

— Psalm 127: 1-2 (RSV)

❖ ❖ ❖

21
"I'll do it my way"

Remember the popular song that Frank Sinatra used to sing, *"My Way,"* with its line "I did it *my* way"? It's the song of a soul seemingly separated in his heart from God, from his Will, from *his* Ways. At no point does a holy soul ever want to sing, "I'll do it my way."

But does this mean that what is unique about a person, about what that person does—inimitably different from any other person—must somehow be effaced? It can hardly be so since our very uniqueness is from God; God has given each of us a unique part to play in his creation, one that belongs to no one else.

The difference between a holy soul and the Sinatra song is that the holy soul is doing all that it does, the unique things that it alone can do, in God's way for that soul, in the way that God ordained when He gave it unique life and a unique mission. There is no division between divine and human creativity here. When the creature acts in his or her unique, God-given way, God is present in this action as the silent, primary creative cause. And this is what constitutes the difference between acts that are merely *original* and acts that are *authentic*. A person's acts are *authentic* in the measure they echo the Creator's creative will for that soul.

— diarist

❖ ❖ ❖

22
"I feel that I am the object of His special action"

Jesus Himself is my Master. He Himself educates and instructs me. I feel that I am the object of His special action. For His inscrutable purposes and unfathomable decrees, He unites me to Himself in a special way and allows me to penetrate His incomprehensible mysteries. There is one mystery which unites me with the Lord, of which no one—not even angels—may know. And even if I wanted to tell of it, I would not know how to express it. And yet, I live by it and will live by it forever. This mystery distinguishes me from every other soul here on earth or in eternity.

— St. Maria Faustina Kowalska

❖   ❖   ❖

23
The Lord has made all things

Because of him his messenger finds the way,
   and by his word all things hold together.
Though we speak much we cannot reach the end,
   and the sum of all our words is: "He is the all."
Where shall we find strength to praise him?
   For he is greater than all his works.
Terrible is the Lord and very great,
   and marvelous is his power.

       . . .

Who has seen him and can describe him?
   Or who can extol him as he is?
Many things greater than these lie hidden,
   For we have seen but a few of his works.
for the Lord has made all things,
   and to the godly he has granted wisdom.

       — Sirach 43:26-29, 31-33 (RSV)

❖   ❖   ❖

24
All through the night they caught nothing

All through the night they caught nothing. Just after daybreak Jesus was standing on the shore, though none of the disciples knew it was Jesus. He said to them, "Children, have you caught anything to eat?" "Not a thing," they answered. "Cast your net off to the starboard side," he suggested, "and you will find something." So they made a cast, and took so many fish they could not haul the net in. Then the disciple Jesus loved cried out to Peter, "It is the Lord!"

       — John 21:3-7 (NAB)

❖   ❖   ❖

25
On secondary causes

The picture we have in the Gospels of the Apostle Andrew is meager but instructive nonetheless. Andrew is the brother of Peter, and is always depicted as Peter's presumably younger, more reticent brother, although, according to John's Gospel, it is Andrew who brings Peter to Jesus, and not the other way around. Certainly the two brothers are very different. Where Peter is bold and outspoken, Andrew comes across as retiring, perhaps even shy. There is only one incident in the Gospel where Andrew stands out, but it is quite interesting. It occurs in the Gospel of John's account of the feeding of the multitude. A very large crowd, eager to hear words from the miracle worker, has followed Jesus into an isolated place in the hills and now it is late and people are getting hungry. Jesus asks his disciples how were they to "buy bread so that these people may eat." Philip answers that two hundred days wages would not be enough to give them even a little, an answer that implied the task was impossible. Then Andrew pipes up with the information that a lad there had five barley loaves and two fish. What prompts Andrew to offer this piece of seemingly irrelevant information if not that somehow he feels it might be relevant after all. But he isn't at all sure about this and so immediately adds the disclaimer, to protect himself from a ludicrous notion as it were, "But what are they among so many?" But that he offers the information at all is significant and, of course, fundamental to the great miracle about to take place.

Another secondary cause involved here should not be overlooked. Why would a lad have carried five loaves and two fish into the hills? Why would he have made Andrew aware of it? We don't know of course any of the answers as to what moved these actors, these secondary causes, to act as they did, only that their having done so made an essential contribution to the way Primary Causality carried out its work.

There is of course a still more compelling example of the role of secondary causes. Mary at the wedding feast of Cana (*John 2:1-11*), like the disciples, brings to the Lord's attention the needs of those assembled: "They have no wine." But unlike Andrew's hesitation, it is Mary who sets things in motion, "Do as he commands" she tells the wine steward. Jesus' retort here that his "hour is not yet come," is also instructive of the part secondary causality plays in God's purposes, for Our Lord's retort suggests that without Mary's intercession this miracle would not have taken place.

Finally, it is instructive to note the other factors in these miracles, the lad and his charity in giving away his food, the steward and waiters and their obedience in fulfilling instructions. These are the actors Our Lord makes use of in accomplishing his work, in ways we as his secondary causes are more than likely unaware of. But here we can see how simple, ordinary acts done in the right spirit may contribute to extraordinary things.

— diarist

❖ ❖ ❖
26
Gamaliel's advice

In the 5ᵗʰ chapter of *Acts* (*v. 34-42*) we see Gamaliel, a learned and respected member of the Sanhedrin, advising his fellow Sanhedrin members on how to treat the Apostles who were now before the council. They had been arrested for preaching about the Name of Jesus. This is the same Gamaliel the Apostle Paul spoke of as his teacher in the Law of Moses.

A Pharisee in the Sanhedrin named Gamaliel, a teacher of the law, respected by all the people, stood up, ordered the Apostles to be put outside for a short time, and said to the Sanhedrin, "Fellow children of Israel, be careful what you are about to do to these men. Some time ago, Theudas appeared, claiming to be someone important, and about four hundred men joined him, but he was killed, and all those who were loyal to him were disbanded and came to nothing. After him came Judas the Galilean at the time of the census. He also drew people after him, but he too perished and all who were loyal to him were scattered. So now I tell you, have nothing to do with these men, and let them go. For if this endeavor or this activity is of human origin, it will destroy itself. But if it comes from God, you will not be able to destroy them; you may even find yourselves fighting against God"

Gamaliel's point is telling: what is not of God in the end comes to naught. Our Lord told us this in many different ways — that only what comes from him bears fruit in what we do. A house built on sand (on purely human devices) will collapse. The fig tree that produces no fruit, season after season, will be cut down. Unless the Lord builds the house, the man who builds it builds it in vain. Our Lord said it plainly: *Without me you can do nothing.* The moment we forget this, profitability departs and what we think we are accomplishing will eventually be cast aside as worthless.

— diarist

❖ ❖ ❖
27
Thou hast wrought for us all our works

O Lord, thou wilt ordain peace for us,
    Thou hast wrought for us all our works.
O Lord our God, other lords besides thee have ruled over us,
    but thy name alone we acknowledge.
They are dead, they will not live;
    they are shadows, they will not arise;
    to that end thou hast visited them with destruction
    and wiped out all remembrance of them.
But thou hast increased the nation, O Lord,
    thou hast increased the nation;
    thou art glorified;
    thou hast enlarged all the borders of the land.

— Isaiah 26:12-15 (RSV)

❖   ❖   ❖

28

It is I who arm you though you know me not

Thus says the Lord to his anointed, Cyrus,
    whose right hand I grasp,
Subduing nations before him,
    and making kings run in his service:…
It is I who arm you, though you know me not,
    so that toward the rising and the setting of the sun
    men may know that there is none beside me.

— Isaiah 45:1, 5-6 (NAB)

Commentary: Note how the Lord accomplished his work through Cyrus though Cyrus does not know God. And yet he was anointed (to accomplish a work of the Lord). The Lord grasps his right hand. It is the Lord who arms him. And because this is so, nations run before him.

Is it any different with us? Is not God, the author of all goodness, the real author of whatever good thing any of us may do? Yet, like Cyrus, we are mostly unaware of our anointing. And we are free and we can refuse this anointing and anoint ourselves, so to speak, pursuing our own worthless ends. But in the measure that what we do is worth anything, faith tells us God has called us to this deed, this work, be it big or small. And like with Jonah, he has his ways of keeping us to the appointed task.

— diarist

❖ ❖ ❖
29
"Was the baptism of John from heaven or from man?"

And they came again to Jerusalem. And as he was walking in the temple, the chief priests and the scribes and the elders came to him, and they said to him, "By what authority are you doing these things, or who gave you this authority to do them?" Jesus said to them, "I will ask you a question: answer me, and I will tell you by what authority I do these things. Was the baptism of John from heaven or from man?"… So they answered Jesus, "We do not know," and Jesus said to them, "Neither will I tell you…" *(Mk 11:27-33 RSV).*

Why did Jesus not tell them? They did not know because they did not want to know, and telling them would not have made them know. We see that to know truth we must want to know the truth, otherwise our life will remain in darkness, for, as we see from this Gospel passage, truth will not be revealed to a soul indisposed.

This lesson has a bearing in what *we* do as well. For us to know God's will and to do as He wishes, we must be open and attentive to that will in everything we do. *"The eyes of the handmaid are on the hands of the master."* If we turn our eyes from God, how can we pretend to be doing his bidding? How can we say we didn't know when the truth is we didn't want to know?

– diarist

❖ ❖ ❖
30
Any truth spoken by anyone is spoken
by the Holy Spirit (Ambrosiaster)

Now concerning spiritual gifts, brethren, I do not want you to be uninformed…. No one can say, "Jesus Christ is Lord" except by the Holy Spirit. Now there are varieties of gifts, but the same Spirit; and there are varieties of service, but the same Lord; and there are varieties of working, but it is the same God who inspires them all in everyone. To each is given the manifestation of the Spirit for the common good *(I Cor 12:1-7 RSV).*

Commenting, Chrystostom writes, "Paul calls the gifts spiritual because they are the work of the Spirit alone, owing nothing to human initiative."

❖   ❖   ❖

31

He himself is the Lord of both the work and the worker

I have come to understand today that even if I did not accomplish any of the things the Lord is demanding of me, I know that I shall be rewarded as if I had fulfilled everything, because He sees the intention with which I begin, and even if He called me to himself today, the work would not suffer at all by that, because He himself is the Lord of both the work and the worker. My part is to love Him to folly; all works are nothing more than a tiny drop before Him. It is love that has meaning and power and merit. He has opened up great horizons in my soul—love compensates for the chasms.

— *St. Maria Faustina Kowalska*

❖   ❖   ❖

32

Neither he who plants nor he who waters is anything, but only God who gives the growth

What then is Apollos? What is Paul? Servants through whom you believed, as the Lord assigned to each. I planted, Apollos watered, but God gave the growth. So neither he who plants nor he who waters is anything, but only God who gives the growth. He who plants and he who waters are equal, and each shall receive his wages according to his labor (*I Cor 3:5-8 RSV*).

Commenting on this, Theodoret of Cyr writes, "Our labor is in vain without the help of God." *And Augustine:* "Since the Apostles would not have accomplished anything if God had not given the increase, how much more true is this of you or me, or anyone else of our time…"

❖   ❖   ❖

33

I have formed my Life in you, and my Will is acting in you and in your acts

My daughter, rise up, rise up more, more—so much that you arrive at the Bosom of Divinity. Your life will be amidst the Divine Persons. Behold, to make you achieve this I have formed my Life in you, and I have enclosed my Eternal Volition in whatever you do so that it flows in everything in a wonderful and surprising manner. *My* Will is acting in you in some continual and actual act. Because I have formed my Life in you, and my

Will is acting in you and in your acts, then your volition has been impregnated by Mine and transfused into Mine. Thus my Will has life on earth.

— Luisa Piccarreta

❖ ❖ ❖

34

*Can any one of you, however much you worry, add one single cubit
to your span of life? (Mt 6:27)*

Jesus tells us nothing happens without God, that He is behind everything that takes place in this world, everything except disorder. All processes that are ordered and therefore good are of his making, including those we do, when they are good, for God is the author of all goodness and all goodness is in God, ours included.

The man who remembers this as he goes about his day will keep to the order of God in his life. The person who does not is bound to breed disorder, be it little or much, in everything that person does. The saint of course orders things closer to perfection than the one who is not a saint, much as a virtuoso at the piano performs better than those who are not. Most of us are still learning to play, some better than others. But those who apply themselves rightly soon begin to make music, no matter how imperfectly, and everyone in their hearing knows it and begins to delight in the sound.

— diarist

❖ ❖ ❖

35

*It was your right hand, your arm,
and the light of your face…*

We heard with our own ears, O God,
our fathers have told us the story
of the things you did in their days,
you yourself, in days long ago.

To plant them you uprooted the nations:
to let them spread you laid peoples low.
No sword of their own won the land;
no arm of their own brought them victory.
It was your right hand, your arm
and the light of your face: for you loved them.

It is you, my king, my God,
who granted victories to Jacob.
Through you we beat down our foes;
in your name we trampled our aggressors.

For it was not in my bow that I trusted
nor yet was I saved by my sword:
it was you who saved us from our foes,
it was you who put our foes to shame.
All day long our boast was in God
and we praised your name without ceasing.

— Psalm 43 (44):1-9 (Grail)

❖   ❖   ❖

36
Let your life on earth be entirely merged in Mine

My Will in you must be as the main gear of the watch: if this turns, all the other gears turn. The watch marks the hours and the minutes, so that the accord is in the motion of the main gear; and if the main gear does not move, everything remains stopped. Thus, the main gear in you must be my Will, which must give movement to your thoughts, to your heart, to your desires, and to all…

Let your life on earth be entirely merged in Mine. Do not do a single act that does not go through Me; and every time you merge yourself in Me, I will pour into you new grace and new light… When the soul, merging herself in Me, makes her immediate acts with Me, I then feel Myself so greatly attracted to her that I do together with her that which she does, and I change her action into Divine…

Who will be the souls in whom I reflect the reverberations of my sufferings and my life? Those who have my Fiat for life will absorb in themselves my reflections, and I will be generous in allowing them to participate in whatever my Will works in Me. So, I await souls in my Will, ready to give them true control and complete glory over every act and pain that they suffer.

Outside my Will, I do not acknowledge deeds or sufferings. I might say, "I have nothing to give you. Whose will animated you in doing or suffering that? Seek your reward therefrom."

— Luisa Piccarreta

❖   ❖   ❖
37
In all possible ways we should combat the spirit of arbitrary self-will

In all possible ways we should combat the spirit of arbitrary self-will and the impulse to shake off all restraint. lt is a spirit that whispers to us: This is beyond my strength, for that I have no time, it is too soon yet for me to undertake this, I should wait, my monastic duties prevent me—and plenty of other excuses of like kind. He who listens to this spirit will never acquire the habit of prayer.

Closely connected with this spirit is the spirit of self-justification: when we have been carried away into wrong-doing by the spirit of willful arbitrariness and are therefore worried by our conscience, this second spirit approaches us and sets to work on us. In such a case the spirit of self-justification uses all kinds of wiles to deceive the conscience and to present our wrong as being right. May God protect you against these evil spirits.

— *Schema Monk Agapii, Staretz of Valamo*

❖   ❖   ❖
38
Entrusting the source and fountainhead
of all human activities to God

In order to purify and heal a man, divine grace begins first of all by entrusting the source and fountain-head of all human activities to God. In other words, grace turns man's consciousness and power of free will towards Him, so that, using this as its starting point, it may in due course effect healing of all man's powers by means of their own activity: the source has been healed and sanctified, and so all the faculties dependent on that source are gradually purified from this same fountain-head.

— *Theophan The Recluse*

❖   ❖   ❖
39
I am your life

Sister Mary, a Swiss native and convert to Catholicism, was inexplicably drawn to faith by the mysterious action of grace. Until that point in her adult life she did not even know that Jesus was the Son of God. Following her conversion, she became a nun and Jesus began to speak to her and asked her to write down the things he told her. Some were meant for her personally, but most for all of us:

I am the Source: come and draw from it! I will give you what you need at every moment: strength, joy, courage, meekness, patience, charity, wisdom… At every moment. But come…I am your life.

— Sister Mary of the Holy Trinity

❖ ❖ ❖

40

I will be with your mouth and teach you what you shall speak

The Lord said to Moses: "Come, I will send you to Pharaoh that you might bring forth my people, the sons of Israel, out of Egypt." But Moses said to God, "Who am I that I should go to Pharaoh, and bring the sons of Israel out of Egypt… I am not eloquent…but I am slow of speech and tongue." Then the Lord said to him, "Who has made man's mouth? Who makes him dumb, or deaf, or seeing, or blind? Is it not I, the Lord? Now therefore go, and I will be with your mouth and teach you what you shall speak."

— Ex 3:10-11; 4:10-12 (RSV)

Jesus said to his disciples: "Beware of men; for they will deliver you up to councils, and flog you in their synagogues, and you will be dragged before governors and kings for my sake, to bear testimony before them and the Gentiles. When they deliver you up, do not be anxious how you are to speak or what you are to say; for what you are to say will be given to you in that hour; for it is not you who speak, but the Spirit of your Father speaking through you."

— Matt 10: 17-20 (RSV)

❖ ❖ ❖

41

The most important work is not that which you do,
it is that which you allow Me
to do among you

The most devout nun in the convent is not she who accomplishes the most visible work; it is she who does the most invisible work, who knows best how to efface herself, to inconvenience no one, to be cheerful with others, and to have a soul that is transparent, so that I may be discovered through her. The most important work is not that which you do, it is that which you allow Me to do among you.

— *Jesus, to Sister Mary of the Holy Trinity*

❖   ❖   ❖
42
I do not force your will in any thing.

I do not force your will in anything. I move your will without forcing it. Can you understand that? I provide exterior things for you to consider and contemplate, I provide the exterior things that you need in order to grow in grace and understanding, each thing that happens to you, in just the way it happens, when it happens and all the circumstances in which it happens—and every little detail is fashioned with loving care by My Providence. Not only that, but My Love operates within the very depths of your soul to enlighten your mind so that you will be able to understand the things that happen to you just as I wanted you to understand them—and I even move your will to love and to choose as I love and as I would have you choose. But for all that I do not force your will. I respect the freedom in you which I created.

Yes, under the very influx of My grace, powerful as it is—really just because it is so powerful—your will remains your own. It is your will that moves your understanding to rest on what your will would enjoy. If your will seeks to enjoy My Goodness, it moves your understanding to contemplate My suffering on the Cross, and when, by a more intense act of love your will seeks to delight more in My Goodness, it moves your understanding to penetrate My Love for you on the Cross still more.

That is your freedom. But all the time this is happening; it is I, Jesus, your God, operating deep within you, so deep that I am totally hidden from you, yet doing everything, it is I Who am moving your will to this act of love, all the while I am enlightening your intelligence to understand what your will would enjoy.

And therefore you must not wait to be moved by My grace—as though I would do something to you first, and then, as a result, you would begin to love Me. No! Just as in the natural order, it is I who move you to your every act, yet you move yourself to pursue the good you desire, so in your supernatural life, as soon as you are directing your mind to Me in order to be more united with Me in love, it is I Who am moving you to do this—you are receiving my grace.

— Our Lord to a Servant of God

❖ ❖ ❖
43
Remember the Lord as you work

Whatever your occupation, great or small, reflect that it is the omnipresent Lord Himself who orders you to perform it and who watches to see how you are carrying it out. If you keep this thought constantly in mind you will fulfill attentively all the duties assigned to you and at the same time you will remember the Lord.

— Theophan The Recluse

❖ ❖ ❖
44
The Lord enters into our daily lives and has things for us to do

The great exemplar of this reality that God is the primary cause and we are but secondary causes is the Blessed Virgin, who when carrying Jesus in her womb knew that her part in what was happening to her was her consent. This is a paradigm for us. The Lord enters into our daily lives and has things for us to do, things the purpose of which He alone knows. If we assent, our cooperation will allow divine work to be accomplished, whether it be big or small, perhaps as small as the baking of a cake, or the making of a phone call, or a bright smile to some lonely face. But it will be He who accomplishes this work in us and through us for the ends He has in mind. Humble work on our part by which, if done for God, we too like Mary magnify the Lord.

— diarist

❖ ❖ ❖
45
If you ask anything in my name, I will do it

Jesus said to Thomas, "I am the Way; I am Truth and Life. No one can come to the Father except through me. If you know me, you will know my Father too. From this moment you know him and have seen him." Philip said, "Lord, show us the Father and then we shall be satisfied." Jesus said to him, "Have I been with you all this time, Phillip, and you still do not know me? Anyone who has seen me has seen the Father, so how can you say, 'Show us the Father'? Do you not believe that I am in the Father and the Father is in me? What I say to you I do not speak of my own accord: It is the Father, living in me, who is doing his works.

"You must believe me when I say that I am in the Father and the Father is in me; or at least believe it on the evidence of these works. In all truth I tell you, whoever believes in me will perform the same works as I do myself, and will perform even greater works, because I am going to the Father. Whatever you ask in my name I will do, so that the Father may be glorified in the Son. If you ask me anything in my name, I will do it."
— John 14:6-14 (The New Jerusalem Bible)

❖   ❖   ❖
46
Jesus sees two fishermen casting their nets into the sea.
He calls out to them,
"Come after me and I will make you
fishers of men" (Mark 1:17)

He calls out to us who are busy doing whatever it is we do in this life, and tells us that if we come after him, he will give this work new purpose, new ends that exceed anything we had in mind, ends that he has in mind. When the primary cause of all goodness enters into our world of secondary causes, and these secondary causes—we, in what we do—follow His lead, good things of an unforeseen nature are bound to follow.

Thus it happened that a small band of fishermen and a tax collector and the like were able to change the entire world. Who can say what will happen when any secondary cause allows the primary cause of all things to enter in and lead it? This is how the Kingdom will be built, through secondary causes, through his coming and leading, first on the shores of Galilee, and then on the clouds of heaven.

But it will be through us that He establishes his kingdom, through his saints and chosen ones who follow him through thick and thin. When we work, when we do anything at all, let us follow him, his lead, let us come after him and allow him to accomplish his purposes in us, whatever they may be. We can be sure that they will exceed our poor notions.

—diarist

❖   ❖   ❖
47
Whoever lives in my Will becomes my substitute for everyone,
defends Me from everyone, and protects my motion,
that is, my very Life

My beloved daughter, I so love those acts that have been done in my Will that, as soon as the soul enters into It to act, my light surrounds it; and I run to ensure that my Act and the soul's act are one. Since I am the first Act of all creation, without Me as the First Mover all created things would remain paralyzed, impotent, and incapable of the slightest motion. Life consists in motion; without it everything is dead. I am, therefore, the First Mover who makes all other motion possible. So, it is my first Act that sets the creature into motion. It's like a machine; after the first gear starts to move, all the other gears move. You see, therefore, how it is almost natural that whoever acts in my Will also acts in my own first Act and therefore, in the actions of all creatures…

So, I say that whoever lives in my Will becomes my substitute for everyone, defends Me from everyone, and protects my motion, that is, my very Life.

— *Luisa Piccarreta*

Commentary: From what Our Lord says here, we can see how the motive of self-will, "to do it my way," adversely affects the mechanism set in motion by God to accomplish his purposes. The cultural ideal of "doing one's own thing" thus is destructive of the common good, a fact that hardly anyone seems to grasp anymore.

Put this in the context of some simple acts like preparing a meal, or hammering a nail, or adding a column of figures: how one goes about these simple acts has profound consequences — hard to see, difficult to describe — but it makes all the difference in the world in what spirit that meal was cooked, that nail was hammered, those numbers were added.

As Jesus said in *Mathew 25:40, Truly I say to you, as you did it to one of the least of these my brethren, you did it to me.* Is it so foreign to our understanding that a nail driven in the wrong spirit may attach the board, but a nail driven in the right spirit will help re-attach creation to its Maker?

— *diarist*

❖   ❖   ❖

48

Why is it that things are not going well with you just now?

I think [your difficulty] is because you wish to remember the Lord, forgetting worldly affairs. But worldly affairs intrude into your consciousness and push out the remembrance of the Lord. What you should do is just the reverse: you should busy yourself with worldly affairs, but think of them as a commission from the Lord, as something done in His presence. As things are now, you fail both on the spiritual and on the material level. But if you act as I have explained, things will go well in both spheres.

– Theophan The Recluse

❖   ❖   ❖

49

Whom shall I send?

In the year King Uzziah died, I saw the Lord seated on a high and lofty throne, with the train of his garment filling the temple. Seraphim were stationed above....

"Holy, holy, holy is the Lord of hosts!" they cried out one to the other, "All the earth is filled with his glory!" At the sound of that cry, the frame of the door shook and the house was filled with smoke.

Then I said, "Woe is me, I am doomed! For I am a man of unclean lips, living among a people of unclean lips; yet my eyes have seen the King, the Lord of hosts!"

Then one of the seraphim flew to me, holding an ember which he had taken with tongs from the altar. He touched my mouth with it. "See," he said, "now that this has touched your lips, your wickedness is removed, your sin purged."

Then I heard the voice of the Lord saying, "Whom shall I send? Who will go for us?" "Here I am," I said; "send me!"

– Isaiah 6:1-2a, 3-8 (NAB)

❖   ❖   ❖

50

It's immediately apparent whether the creature is acting and suffering in the divine way: whether love alone is behind its actions and sufferings

My daughter, it is praiseworthy and good to accept mortification and suffering as penance and as a punishment; but it has no connection with the divine way of acting. I did much and suffered much, but my sole purpose in all of that was Love of my Father and of men. So, it's immediately apparent whether the creature is acting and suffering in the divine way: whether love alone is behind its actions and sufferings. If it has other ends, even if they are good ones, then it is acting only on the level of a creature. The merit that he receives, then, will be only what a creature can acquire, not the merit that is divine, since these two ways of acting are not the same. If he adopts my way of acting, however, the fire of Love will destroy every disparity and inequality, and will make as one the creature's work and my own.

— Luisa Piccarreta

❖   ❖   ❖
51
Petering out

[Regarding Peter] why did almighty God permit the one He had placed over the whole Church to be frightened by the voice of a maidservant and even to deny Christ himself? This we know was a great dispensation of the divine mercy, so that he who was to be the shepherd of the Church might learn through his own fall to have compassion on others.

— Pope Gregory the Great

Commentary: Yes, and compassion on ourselves as well. We must not be hard on ourselves when we see ourselves failing in some way. Yes, let us weep as Peter did, but not lose heart as Judas did. Let us remember that these things were foreseen in Peter by Our Lord before they happened. Our Lord foresees our failures too, and does not reject us. Let us remember what became of Peter, how Our Lord took this weakness and made it into a strength by his grace.

Let us believe this for ourselves, *that our weakness and failings and yes, our betrayals, are building blocks in the hands of a master craftsman, who wants to make saints of us all, and is doing so in just this way.* "Come unto me all you who are weary and burdened, and I will give you rest." What burdens us more than our sins and failures? And what greater rest than grace?

— Anonymous

❖ ❖ ❖

52

*The greater the work that I want to accomplish, the more ordinary
I made the chosen soul appear*

My precious daughter, my Supreme Will always brings about the greatest of works in souls that are virginal and unknown—and not merely those who are virgins by nature, but those who are virginal in their affections, in their heart, in their thoughts. True virginity is the divine shadow, and only by means of my shadow can I fecundate my greatest works.

I elected a Virgin who was unknown to all but well-known to Me. If true virginity is my shadow, the fact that I elected an unknown virgin is because of divine jealousy. I wanted Her all for Myself, so I made Her unknown to everyone else. Because this Heavenly Virgin was unknown, I was able to make Myself better known and to clear the way for everyone to learn about the Redemption. The greater the work that I want to accomplish, the more ordinary I made the chosen soul appear.

— Luisa Piccarreta

❖ ❖ ❖

53

Your life and Ours must be as one

Know that whoever lives in my Will must rise to such heights that they live in the bosom of the Sacrosanct Trinity. Your life and Ours must be as one. It is necessary; it is proper that you know where you stand and in whose company, and that you conform to everything that We do. Thus you will live in our Bosom with full awareness, willingly, without compulsion, and with love.

— Luisa Piccarreta

❖ ❖ ❖

54

See, I place my words in your mouth

The word of the Lord came to me thus: "Before I formed you in the womb I knew you, before you were born I dedicated you, a prophet to the nations I appointed you."

"Ah, Lord God!" I said, "I know not how to speak; I am too young."

But the Lord answered me, "Say not, 'I am too young.' To whomever I send you, you shall go; whatever I command you, you shall speak. Have no fear before them, because I am with you to deliver you, says the Lord."

Then the Lord extended his hand and touched my mouth, saying, "See, I place my words in your mouth! This day, I set you over nations and over kingdoms. To root up and to tear down, to destroy and to demolish, to build and to plant."

— Jeremiah 1:4-10 (NAB)

❖ ❖ ❖

55
The soul who perfectly hopes in me ...must necessarily put
no hope in herself or in the world
or in her own weakness

I, the true and just doctor, give you whatever I see your weakness needs to make you perfectly healthy and to keep you healthy. My Providence will never fail those who want to receive it. Whoever wants to experience my goodness in my Providence has only to look at those who hope in me, who knock and call out not just with words but with love enlightened by most holy faith... So I tell you, my providence will not fail those who truly hope in me, but it will fail those who hope not in me but in themselves... But the soul who perfectly hopes in me and serves me with her whole heart and will must necessarily put no hope in herself or in the world or in her own weakness. This true and perfect hope is more or less perfect in proportion to the soul's love for me, and thus she experiences my Providence more or less perfectly.

— The Dialogue of St. Catherine of Siena

❖ ❖ ❖

56
I raise you up to Myself

Know, my daughter, that between Me and you there is a bottomless abyss, an abyss which separates the Creator from the creature. But this abyss is filled with My mercy. I raise you up to Myself, not that I have need of you, but it is solely out of mercy that I grant you the grace of union with Myself.

— St. Maria Faustina Kowalska

❖ ❖ ❖

57

*When We will have finished making of you the first copy of a soul
who lives in our Will, other copies will follow*

You have much to receive from Us in order to learn our ways and form
the first copy of a soul who lives in our Will. It is the greatest work we
have to do… Our will desires to transform you entirely into Ourselves. It
wishes to leave in you our Will as divine actor to duplicate what We do.
Thus our images will emanate from Us; and our Will, working in you,
will consume as many others.

Oh, how the purpose of Creation will be fulfilled. The echo of our Will
shall be the echo of our same Will possessed by you. There will be
reciprocal correspondence, reciprocal love. We will be in complete
harmony, and the creature will be fused with its Creator. Nothing will be
lacking in our joy and in our happiness over those whom we issued forth
into Creation. The *"Let Us make man in our own image and likeness"* will
have full meaning and effectiveness. Our Will, being the only actor in the
creature, will bring fulfillment to all; and Creation will bring Us its divine
culmination; and We will receive it in our bosom as our work, just as we
made it issue forth.

— Luisa Piccarreta

❖ ❖ ❖

58

"That which is born of the Spirit is spirit"

The dwelling, animation, operation of the Holy Spirit in the soul of the
apostle is the great secret of all spiritual fecundity…. Meditate on this
marvel. All acts accomplished under the movement…of the Holy Spirit
have the power thereby to give birth to Christ, to increase Christ and
extend the rays of the Father's complacency over his creation.

— Our Lord to an anonymous French nun

❖ ❖ ❖

59

Psalm 106 (107):10-16 (Grail)

Some lay in darkness and in gloom,
prisoners in misery and chains, having defied the words of God

and spurned the counsels of the Most High.
He crushed their spirit with toil;
they stumbled; there was no one to help.

Then they cried to the Lord in their need
and he rescued them from their distress.
He led them forth from darkness and gloom
and broke their chains to pieces.

Let them thank the Lord for his goodness,
for the wonders he does for men:
for he bursts the gates of bronze
and shatters the iron bars.

The Psalmist tells us that our God is not an abstraction, an ideational plug in the metaphysical bathtub to keep life's meaning from draining out. No, He is the dynamic cause and source of every good thing we have.

Let us not think there is any difficulty that the Lord cannot handle, whether it is the parting of the Red Sea or the bursting of bronze doors. Or the simple matter of finding that, lo and behold, that matter that seemed so hopeless has somehow now been taken care of, even though we may have failed to ask him for that favor.

A mother does not feed her child because it asks for food. It is what a mother does. And will our heavenly Father not also, when we allow ourselves to be his child?

— diarist

❖ ❖ ❖

60

The Power of God is with us until the end of time

In St. Paul we read: "Christ is the power and the wisdom of God." *And in the Gospel, Jesus said*: "Lo, I will be with you always, even until the end of time." Does this not mean that God's power and wisdom will be with us, enabling us to do the Father's will, even as Christ did? He did nothing, said nothing, except as he saw the Father doing it, speaking it (*John's* gospel). This is our model but not only our model, for he will be with us to accomplish these things in us, as he promised, until the end of each of our times on earth.

— diarist

❖   ❖   ❖
61
Nobility will prevail in you if… you will try to enter into your nothingness;
that is to say, if you will attain perfect knowledge of yourself

Not your will but my Will alone should remain in you to dominate like a
King in his royal palace. My spouse, this absolutely must prevail between
you and Me. Otherwise, we will have to bear with the discord of an
imperfect love from which dark shadows will rise over you and cast
disharmony and disagreement of operation, inappropriate to the mutual
nobility which absolutely must reign between Me and you, my spouse.

This nobility will prevail in you if, from time to time, you will try to enter
into your nothingness; that is to say, if you will attain perfect knowledge
of yourself. You must not stop there, because after you have established
your nothingness, I want you to disappear into Me. You must do all you
can to enter into the infinite power of my Will. From It, you will derive
all the graces you need to raise you up into Me, to do everything with Me
without reference to yourself.

— *Luisa Piccarreta*

❖   ❖   ❖
62
The lives of the faithful, their praise, sufferings, prayer, and work,
are united with those of Christ and with his total offering,
and so acquire new value (CCC 1368)

In Blessed Dina Bélanger's writings, Jesus helps us to see the divine "new
value" which our acts can ultimately attain when they are done in us by
the reigning Divine Will. Through [these] writings, Jesus invites us to
unite our acts to his always and everywhere with a new and deeper
understanding of what we are doing. In this way, the unity for which He
prayed at the Last Supper can be fulfilled in us.

The doctrine that human acts achieve their true and highest dignity only
when they are performed in us by Jesus—or, we might say, by the Divine
Will of the Father, the Son, and the Holy Spirit—is not new… What is
new in the recent private revelations is the understanding that it is
possible for souls of good will *to participate fully in the divine-human acts of
Jesus and Mary* and to allow the Divine Will to reign in all of their
thoughts, words, and actions *during their lives on earth.*

— *Hugh Owen*

❖　❖　❖
63
The Story of Babel

The whole world spoke the same language, using the same words. While men were migrating in the east, they came upon a valley in the land of Shinar and settled there. They said to one another, "Come, let us mold bricks and harden them with fire." They used bricks for stone, and bitumen for mortar. Then they said, "Come, let us build ourselves a city and a tower with its top in the sky, and so make a name for ourselves; otherwise we shall be scattered all over the earth."

The Lord came down to see the city and the tower that the men had built. Then the Lord said: "If now, while they are one people, all speaking the same language, they have started to do this, nothing will later stop them from doing whatever they presume to do. Let us then go down and there confuse their language, so that one will not understand what another says."

Thus the Lord scattered them from there all over the earth, and they stopped building the city. That is why it was called Babel, because there the Lord confused the speech of all the world. It was from that place that he scattered them all over the earth.

— Gen 11:1-9 (NAB)

The 18th century German mystic, Blessed Anne Catherine Emmerich, had this to say about the story of Babel: "The building of the Tower of Babel was the work of pride. The builders aimed at constructing something according to their own ideas, and thus resisted the guidance of God.... They thought not of God, they sought only their own glory. Had it been otherwise, as I was distinctly told, God would have allowed their undertaking to succeed."

— Blessed Anne Catherine Emmerich

❖　❖　❖
64
Whoever leaves what is upright leaves the correct path. He leaves the holy, the beautiful, the useful and the boundaries in which God has placed him

My daughter, all the Divine Science is contained in upright works. This is because uprightness contains all the beauty and good that one can find — one finds order, usefulness, beauty and skill. A work is only good for as much as it is ordered to good; but, if the threads appear crooked, and conducted in a crooked manner, one won't understand anything of that work. Moreover they won't see anything other than something disordered, which will be neither useful nor good.

Accordingly, what I have done, from the greatest to the least, is seen as orderly; and it all serves a useful purpose... Now the creature, for as much as he is good, will contain that much corresponding to Divine Science within himself. Hence, for as much as the creature is just, that many good works will come forth from him. However, a twisted thread in the creature's works is enough to disorder the creature and the works that go forth from him, darkening the Divine Science that his works contain.

Whoever leaves what is upright leaves the correct path. He leaves the holy, the beautiful, the useful and the boundaries in which God has placed him. Moreover, leaving what is upright, he becomes like a plant that doesn't have much earth beneath it. Thus, under the rays of a burning sun or in times of ice and winds, such a plant will dry up the influences of the Divine Science. It is the same with crooked works. Where there is lacking in the creature much substance of the Divine Science, the creature won't do anything other than dry up amid his disorder.

— Luisa Piccarreta

❖ ❖ ❖

65
My daughter, disperse yourself in Me

My daughter, disperse yourself in Me. Disperse your prayer in Mine in a way that yours and Mine are one single prayer, and it cannot be known which is yours and which is Mine. Your pains, your work, your volition, your love—dispense them all in my pains, my work, etc., in a way that the one blends in the other so as to form one single thing, so much so that you could say, "What is Jesus' is mine"; and I, "What is yours is Mine."

Suppose that you pour a glass of water into a larger container of water. Would you know how to discern, afterwards, which is the water from the glass and which is from the container? Certainly not. Therefore, to your greatest gain and for my greatest contentment, often repeat to Me in what you do: "Jesus, I pour this in You to be able to do not my will but yours." Then I immediately pour my acts in you.

— Luisa Piccarreta

❖ ❖ ❖
66
Let me act

Jesus, speaking to this sister: Yes, you see the beautiful things that I make with the tiniest seeds… because they are surrendered to my action. What would I not make with acts of confidence, of faith, of hope, of charity, surrendered to my Omnipotence?

Yes, be My little seed… Let me act. But let your obedience be perfect; like the seed surrendered to My action. You know that the grain of wheat must die so that it may yield fruit.

— Sister Mary of the Holy Trinity

❖ ❖ ❖
67
They caught a great number of fish and their nets were tearing

While the crowd was pressing in on Jesus and listening to the word of God, he was standing by the Lake of Gennesaret. He saw two boats there alongside the lake; the fishermen had disembarked and were washing their nets. Getting into one of the boats, the one belonging to Simon, he asked him to put out a short distance from the shore. Then he sat down and taught the crowds from the boat. After he finished speaking, he said to Simon, "Put out into deep water and lower your nets for a catch." Simon said in reply, "Master, we have worked hard all night and have caught nothing, but at your command I will lower the nets." When they had done this, they caught a great number of fish and their nets were tearing. They signaled to the other boat to help and before long both boats began to sink under the load of fish. When Simon Peter saw this, he fell at the knees of Jesus and said, "Depart from me, Lord, for I am a sinful man." For astonishment at the catch of fish they had made seized him and all those with him… Jesus said to Simon, "Do not be afraid; from now on you will be catching men." When they brought their boats to the shore, they left everything and followed him (*Luke 5:1-11*).

We see that Simon Peter and his friends had been working all night to no avail. Their boat was empty, a necessary condition for the miracle that is to follow, for first we must know that our own efforts have achieved us nothing. Then Jesus gets into Peter's boat and everything changes. Peter listens to the Lord and obeys him, and because he does, they catch a quantity of fish beyond anything they had ever experienced, enough to astound them. So much so that thereafter they understand their true work will be to work with this Master. They leave their work and follow him to do his work in them.

— diarist

❖   ❖   ❖

68

I want you to remain near Me — like an infant — to always ask for my
help and assistance, acknowledging your nothingness and
expecting everything from Me

So that I can pour my graces into your heart, it is necessary for you to convince yourself that by yourself you are nothing and are capable of nothing. I look with much approval and bestow gifts and graces upon souls that are wary of attributing to themselves the good effects that result from their own works made in correspondence to my graces. The souls that consider my gifts and graces — given to them by my Love — to have been acquired by themselves, are committing many thefts. You ought always to tell them, "The fruits that are produced in my garden are not to be attributed to me, a miserable wretch, but are the result of the gift of Divine Love, bestowed in profusion by his Heart."

Remember that I am generous and pour torrents of graces on souls that know themselves — souls that do not usurp anything for themselves and understand that everything is accomplished by means of my grace…

I cannot enter into hearts that stink with pride — souls so puffed up with themselves that there is no place in their hearts for Me… You must be like an infant in swaddling bands who, unable to move by himself, even to walk or move a hand, must rely on its mother for everything. In that way, I want you to remain near Me — like an infant — to always ask for my help and assistance, acknowledging your nothingness and expecting everything from Me.

— Luisa Piccarreta

❖   ❖   ❖

69

Is it not I who have done everything in your life?

Sister Mary complains to Our Lord, "I have wasted all my time. I have squandered my life; so far I have done no good."

Our Lord replies, "If you obey My voice, that is a great good; I will do the rest. Is it not I who have done everything in your life? I will continue to work in you in death and after your death."

— Sister Mary of the Holy Trinity

❖ ❖ ❖

70

Turn away from evil, learn to do God's will; the Lord will strengthen you
if you obey him… Wait for the Lord, then follow in his way

First principle: if we wish to work synergistically with God, we must be sure that what we are doing is what He wants us to do. God never follows our will unless we are first following His. So the first thing is, we must be sure we ARE doing God's will in our work. How can we know that? Well, we can be sure if what is done is done under obedience.

Now, submitting a matter to the respected judgment of another doesn't mean abandoning one's own intentions in the matter at hand. St. Augustine advised us to *Love God and do what you please,* so if we love God we can indeed do as we please, this because in loving God we will be wanting only what pleases Him. The disposition of love is to want what the beloved wants, and, as Augustine implies, it works both ways in this love affair between God and the soul. The function of a spiritual director is to protect the soul against mistaken notions and to increase objectivity. And objectivity increases in the measure that the soul submits a matter to a judgment not his own.

But there's more to be seen here. If God wants something for us, there will be signs, will there not? Won't things begin to fall into place, desire grow stronger, doors open, people turn supportive, and in the end so too the spiritual director? The suavity of God! All are signs to us that God is behind this work, is blessing it, and is doing the things that are not ours to do but His. We for our part do our best in what he gives us to do, leaving the results to him who initiates this work in the first place.

— diarist [Psalm antiphon, *Office of Reading*]

❖ ❖ ❖

71

It is God who…gives you the intention and the powers to act

So, my dear friends, you have always been obedient; your obedience must not be limited to times when I am present. Now that I am absent it must be more in evidence, so work out your salvation in fear and trembling. It is God who, for his own generous purpose, gives you the intention and the powers to act. Let your behavior be free of murmuring and complaining so that you remain faultless and pure, unspoilt children of God surrounded by a deceitful and underhand brood, shining out among them like bright stars in the world, proffering to it the Word of life.

—Philippians 2:12-16a (The New Jerusalem Bible)

❖   ❖   ❖
72
When you work, you are inclined to think too much that the fruit
depends on the branches; it is the roots that require care

See with what materials I founded My Church:
- a few souls of goodwill,
- grace flowing through the Sacraments (so soberly instituted),
- the redemptive work of the Cross,
- the Omnipotence of the Holy Spirit, My Spirit.

That is all!

Was it a well-coordinated organization? Not even that.
Nevertheless My Church was founded, surrendered to the impetuous breath of life, to the initiative of those who are Mine.
It was founded because its roots were established.

When you work, you are inclined to think too much that the fruit depends on the branches; it is the roots that require care...

Souls of goodwill are needed, and without great exterior show,
- souls entirely surrendered to the action of grace through the Sacraments,
- entirely surrendered to the redemptive action of the Cross,
- entirely surrendered to the invisible and powerful action of the Holy Spirit,
- "victim" souls, united to the Victim of Calvary and of the Altar, not passively, but like Him, following Him...

That is sufficient. My little daughter, do you understand?

– Sister Mary of the Holy Trinity

❖   ❖   ❖
73

If one could see a soul truly united to God, one would not be able to distinguish between them.

— Johann Tauler

❖   ❖   ❖
74

Surrender to God and he will do everything for you

— Antiphon, Office of Readings

❖   ❖   ❖
75

This was the sole purpose for the Creation

My Will permeates all of creation. There is nothing on which my Volition has not put its seal. When it pronounced the FIAT to create all things my Will took possession and became the life and sustenance of all things. Now this Volition of Mine wishes all things to be encompassed in Itself so that It will receive correspondence for Its noble and divine acts. It wants to see the air, the breeze, the perfume and the light of Its Will flow through all human acts, so that flowing together, the acts of creatures and those of my Will may be fused into one.

This was the sole purpose for the Creation, that the emanations of all wills be as one continuous will. This is what I want, that is what I propose, and that is what I expect. This is the reason I am so eager for my Will to be known. I want to make known Its worth and Its effects so that those souls who live in my Will, by doing acts in my Will, can diffuse throughout all things the continuous emanations of their wills into Mine as so much perfumed air.

I want these souls to multiply themselves in all their human acts, investing these acts in my Will and conferring these acts with my Will so that at last I may achieve the purpose of all Creation. My Will can then repose in these souls to form the new generation, and then all created things will have a double seal: the seal of the FIAT at the moment of Creation and the seal of the echo to my FIAT coming from all creation.

— Luisa Piccarreta

❖ ❖ ❖
76
In Whom we live and move and have our being

Paul speaks of Our Lord "*in whom we live and move and have our being.*" We are here because, as *Genesis* tells us, God willed us to be. But each one of us is here because of parents who brought us forth. So there are two causes for the fact of our existence. The primary cause is God's will. But when God created man, he told him to "increase and multiply," and that of course is what secondary causes have been doing ever since. But it is wise to remember it was a particular thought of God, the author of life, that ordained each of us to a particular womb and then stirred us to the miracle of life. *In Whom we live and move and have our being.*

– diarist

❖ ❖ ❖
77
You are my eyes, my ears, my mouth, my hands, my feet

My daughter, those who use their senses to offend Me distort my image within them. Sin makes the soul dead: not that she actually dies, but she becomes dead to all that is Divine. If, instead, the soul makes use of her senses to give Me glory, then I can say, "You are my eyes, my ears, my mouth, my hands, my feet." I thereby conserve within this soul my Creative work. If, in addition to giving Me glory, the soul includes suffering, satisfaction, and reparation for others, then she conserves within herself my Redemptive work.

By bringing these works of Mine to ever greater perfection in herself, the soul gives rise to my Sanctifying Work, sanctifying everything and conserving it within herself. So all that I have accomplished in Creation, in Redemption and in Sanctification, I infuse a participation of this within the soul: it is all there, if the soul corresponds to my work.

– Luisa Piccarreta

❖ ❖ ❖
78
God's works must be done by Him and not wrought chiefly by man

Know that what man deems perfection in himself is in God's sight faulty. For all the things a man does, which he sees or feels or means or wills or remembers to have a perfect appearance, are wholly fouled and sullied unless he acknowledges them to be from God. If a work is to be perfect it must be wrought in us not chiefly by us, for God's works must be done by Him and not wrought chiefly by man.

— St. Catherine of Genoa

❖   ❖   ❖

79

Let Me do everything! You will see that I will do everything, and do it well

Commenting on the great teaching Our Lord imparted to Sister Consolata: Our Lord's watchword to all souls whom He calls to high perfection in the path of love is simply this: *Allow Me to do it!*

Yes, let Jesus do it! And why not? Has anyone else the sanctification of the soul more at heart than He? Is anyone else able to sanctify her? Who can perceive her real needs as well as He? To Him alone are known the designs which God has for the soul. Being omnipotent, He can do everything; being faithfulness itself, He will keep all His promises.

Why then should one not entrust oneself to Him and give Him a free hand so that He can work in the soul as absolute and uncontested Master? Why not submit to Him one's own opinions, one's thoughts, aspirations, desires, preoccupations? Why not adapt oneself trustingly at each moment to His actions which alone are always sanctifying? That is what Jesus desired from Sister Consolata.

— Lorenzo Sales, IMC

Sept. 22nd,1935: You see, Consolata, sanctity means self-forgetfulness in everything, in thoughts, desires, words… Allow Me to do it all! I will do everything; but you should, at every moment, give Me what I ask for with much love!

Sept.24th, 1935: Consolata, I have every claim upon you, but you have only one duty: to obey Me. I require a docile will which permits Me to act, which lends itself to everything, which trusts in Me and serves Me always in peace and joy, no matter what the situation is.

Nov. 18th, 1935: Let Me do everything! You will see that I will do everything, and do it well, and that My little victim will become fruitful in love and in souls.

Aug. 22nd, 1934: Think no longer about yourself, about your perfection, on how to attain to sanctity, or about your defects, your present and future troubles. No, I will see to your sanctification, to your sanctity. You must henceforth think only of Me and of souls; of Me to love Me, and of souls to save them!

Oct. 15th, 1935: Let Me do everything! Act as though only I existed. Of yourself there should remain only the continual act of love and an extreme docility to do simply and always whatever I desire directly or indirectly through your superior or your Sisters.

— Sister Maria Consolata

❖   ❖   ❖
80
It is not that we do nothing

All true discipline is nothing other than docility to God's Will — it is not that we do nothing — rather, we do everything in our power to allow God to act in us, as perfectly as we give up our thoughts and ideas.

— A Servant of God

❖   ❖   ❖
81
All of creation is to Me what the body is to the soul of a creature

All of creation is to Me what the body is to the soul of a creature, as the skin is to the fruit. I am in continuous, current action with man; but created things conceal Me, just as the body conceals the soul. Yet without a soul the body would have no life. In the same way I approach man through all created things, I touch him and give him life. I am hidden in the fire, and I approach man with its heat. If I were not in the fire, it would give no heat. It would be like a painted fire, it would give no heat. As I approach man in the fire he does not recognize me, nor does he greet Me. I am in the water, and I approach him by quenching his thirst. If I were not in the water it would not quench man's thirst; it would be dead water. Yet as I visit man he passes before Me without so much as a nod. I am hidden in man's food; and I visit him by giving him substance, strength and flavor. If I were not present in his food then man, though he ate, would be in a continual fast. Yet despite all this, while deriving his nourishment from Me, man turns his back on Me. I am hidden in the sun and I visit man with my Light almost at every moment.

But ungrateful man responds to this with continuous offences. I visit man in everything, in the air which he breathes, in the flowers that perfume him, in the gentle, refreshing breeze, in the rolling thunder, in everything. My visits are innumerable. Do you see how much I love man? And you, being in my Will, participate with Me when I visit man to give him life.

— Luisa Piccarreta

❖   ❖   ❖

82

The Word of God has but to give a gesture of command and everything falls into place; each creature performs its own proper function

"In the beginning was the Word, and the Word was with God, and the Word was God. All things were made through him, and without him nothing was made." In these words John the theologian teaches that nothing exists or remains in being except in and through the Word… While remaining unchanged with his Father, he moves all creation by his unchanging nature, according to the Father's will. To everything he gives existence and life in accordance with its nature, and so creates a wonderful and truly divine harmony.

To illustrate this profound mystery, let us take the example of a choir of many singers. A choir is composed of a variety of men, women and children, of both old and young. Under the direction of one conductor, each sings in the way that is natural for him; men with men's voices, boys with boys' voices, old people with old voices, young people with young voices. Yet all of them produce a single harmony. Or consider the example of our soul. It moves our senses according to their several functions so that in the presence of a single object they all act simultaneously: the eye sees, the ear hears, the hand touches, the nose smells, the tongue tastes, and often the other parts of the body act as well as, for example, the feet may walk.

Although this is only a poor comparison, it gives some idea of how the whole universe is governed. The Word of God has but to give a gesture of command and everything falls into place; each creature performs its own proper function, and all together constitute one single harmonious order.

— St. Athanasius

❖   ❖   ❖

83

They went out and proclaimed the good news everywhere, while the Lord worked with them and confirmed the message by the signs that accompanied it

In Mark's Gospel (16:17-20), as Our Lord is about to ascend to the Father, his final instruction to the apostles is that they are to go out into all the world and proclaim the Gospel to the whole of creation, to do in effect what He had done and shown them how to do.

And then Jesus said that signs would accompany this declaration, signs of great wonder, of healings, casting out demons, speaking in new tongues, grave dangers overcome. And after the Lord had thus spoken to them, he *"was taken up into heaven and sat down at the right hand of God. And they went out and proclaimed the good news everywhere, while the Lord worked with them and confirmed the message by the signs that accompanied it."*

In a non-canonical manuscript of *Mark*, we read, *"And all that had been commanded them they told briefly to those around Peter. And afterward Jesus himself sent out through them, from east to west, the sacred and imperishable proclamation of eternal salvation."* Are we not to believe that Jesus is still working today through those who wish to serve Him, who stand around Peter, who wish to proclaim eternal salvation in his Name? And should we not look to Him to perform new prodigies for his Name's sake?

—diarist

❖   ❖   ❖

84

When you have filled yourself with Me — go outside and operate together with Me — as if you and I were one thing alone

I want to teach you the way you must be with Me. First, you must enter inside of Me, transform yourself in Me, and take for yourself what you find in Me.

Second, when you have filled yourself with Me — go outside and operate together with Me — as if you and I were one thing alone. Do this in such a way that if I move, you move; if I think, you think my same thought. In other words, that which I do, you will do.

Third, for a moment, remove yourself from Me — with this work that we have done together — and go into the center of the creature. Give to all and to each everything that we have done in unison; that is, give to each one my Divine Life. Then immediately return to Me, to give Me, in the name of everyone, all the glory that they should have given Me. Pray, implore forgiveness, repair, and love,…yes, love Me for everyone! Satiate Me with love!

— Luisa Piccarreta

❖ ❖ ❖
85

Before I formed you in the womb I knew you, before you were born I dedicated you, a prophet to the nations (Jeremiah 1:4-5, 17-19)

Each of us has been conceived by God to express something of Him in this world, something which we alone can give voice to. Each of us speaks for God then and is a prophet in that sense. *"But do you gird up your loins; stand up and tell them all that I command you" (v. 17a)*. In other words, do in life what I have endowed you to do, use the gifts I have given you to accomplish my work in you.

"Be not crushed on their account, as though I would leave you crushed before them; for it is I this day who have made you a fortified city, a pillar of iron, a wall of brass, against the whole land: against Judah's kings and princes, against its priests and people. They will fight against you but not prevail over you, for I am with you to deliver you, says the Lord" (v.17b-19).

When we give ourselves to some good work that the Lord wishes to accomplish in us, the Lord, as primary cause of that good, will not allow anything to stop us. We become as it were pillars of iron, a wall of brass. But this only in so far as we, as secondary causes, acknowledge that this is all that we are, secondary. *In him alone we move and have our being.*

— diarist

❖ ❖ ❖
86
My thoughts are not your thoughts

Man must always bear in mind that God is the Creator, and that in his divine presence he must be aware that he is weak and inadequate, as befits a creature made of clay, and that he is not to make demands or give orders, but is to accept the will of God at each moment, which ordinarily does not coincide with the will of men: "For my thoughts are not your thoughts, nor are your ways my ways, says the Lord. As high as the heavens are above the earth, so high are my ways above your ways and my thoughts above your thoughts" *(Isaiah 55:8-9).*

Knowing then that the ways of the Lord are more perfect than the ways of men, foolish is every mortal "who talks back to God. Will perchance the clay say to the potter: Why have you created me so? Or does not the potter have a right over the clay?" *(Rom 9:20-21).*

– Our Lady to Consuelo

❖   ❖   ❖

87

In receiving this divine light, my daughter, I wish to see thee
very attentive, and very quick and diligent in following it up in deed

Mary speaks: Happy is the soul to whom the Most High manifests his holy and perfect will; but more happy and blessed is he who puts into execution what he has learned. In many ways God shows to mortals the highways and pathways of eternal life: by the Gospels and the holy Scriptures, by the Sacraments and the laws of the holy Church, by the writings and examples of the saints, and especially, by the obedience due to the guidance of its ministers, of whom his Majesty said: "Whoever hears you, hears Me;" for obeying them is the same as obeying the Lord himself. Whenever by any of these means thou hast come to the knowledge of the will of God, I desire thee to assume the wings of humility and obedience, and, as if in ethereal flight or like the quickest sunbeam, hasten to execute it and thereby fulfill the divine pleasure.

Besides these means of instruction, the Most High has still others in order to direct the soul; namely, He intimates his perfect will to them in a supernatural manner, and reveals to them many sacraments. This kind of instruction is of many and different degrees; not all of them are common or ordinary to all souls; for the Lord dispenses his light in measure and weight *(Wisdom 11:21).* Sometimes He speaks to the heart and the interior feelings in commands; at others, in correction, advising or instructing; sometimes He moves the heart to ask Him; at other times He proposes clearly what He desires, in order that the soul may be moved to fulfill it; again He manifests, as in a clear mirror, great mysteries, in order that they may be seen and recognized by the intellect and loved by the will. But this great and infinite Good is always sweet in commanding, powerful in giving the necessary help for obedience, just in his commands, quick in disposing circumstances so that He can be obeyed, notwithstanding all the impediments which hinder the fulfillment of his most holy will.

In receiving this divine light, my daughter, I wish to see thee very attentive, and very quick and diligent in following it up in deed. In order to hear this most delicate and spiritual voice of the Lord, it is necessary that the faculties of the soul be purged from earthly grossness and that the creature live entirely according to the spirit; for the animal man does not perceive the elevated things of the Divinity (*I Cor 2:14*). Be attentive then to his secrets (*Is 34:16*) and forget all that is of the outside; listen, my daughter, and incline thy ear; free thyself from all visible things (*Ps 44:11*).

And in order that thou mayest be diligent, cultivate love; for love is a fire, which does not have its effect until the material is prepared; therefore let thy heart always be disposed and prepared. Whenever the Most High bids thee or communicates to thee anything for the welfare of souls, or especially for their eternal salvation, devote thyself to it entirely; for they are bought at the inestimable price of the blood of the Lamb and of divine love. Do not allow yourself to be hindered in this matter by thy own lowliness and bashfulness; but overcome the fear which restrains thee, for if thou thyself art of small value and usefulness, the Most High is rich (*I Pet 1:18*), powerful, great, and by Himself performs all things (*Rom 10:12*). Thy promptness and affection will not go without its reward, although I wish thee rather to be moved entirely by the pleasure of thy Lord.

— Our Lady to Venerable Mary of Agreda

❖ ❖ ❖

88

I desire thee to assume the wings of humility and obedience
(Mary to Venerable Mary of Agreda)

The Incarnation, the Word's assumption of flesh and the human condition, must also be seen as the descent of that which is primary in the order of power and causality into that which is secondary. Is not this why Jesus is always withdrawing to pray? For having voluntarily limited himself in this way, he must like us depend upon prayer for his own effectiveness, even though, as the Father's Word, "*all things were made through him and without him was not anything made that was made*" (*John 1:3*). Mary's child renewed creation through humility and obedience. Can such a mother desire anything less for all her children?

— diarist

❖   ❖   ❖
89
The will of God is the cause of all things (St. Thomas)

Since both intellect and nature act for an end…the natural agent [you and I] must have the end and the necessary means predetermined for it by some higher intellect; as the end and definite movement is predetermined for the arrow by the archer.

– St. Thomas Aquinas

❖   ❖   ❖
90
For unto us a child is given

In the following we see barren women who by the mercy of God bear sons, and glimpse something about the mysterious interplay of primary and secondary causalities. We see how the very helplessness of these women is used by the Lord to accomplish extraordinary things. The accounts remind us that the hopelessness of the human situation is God's opportunity. He reveals himself through our weaknesses and desperations. What is lovely about these stories is that barrenness is transformed into fruitfulness, not only to fulfill these women, but for the good of many. This must give us hope that barrenness and failure at the level of secondary causality all happen within the providence of God's primacy and are never the last word.

Judges 13:2-7, 24-25a (NAB)
There was a certain man from Zorah, of the clan of the Danites, whose name was Manoah. His wife was barren and had borne no children. An angel of the Lord appeared to the woman and said to her, "Though you are barren and have had no children, yet you will conceive and bear a son.… No razor shall touch his head, for the boy is to be consecrated to God from the womb. It is he who will begin the deliverance of Israel from the power of the Philistines."

Luke 1:5-15, 18, 76- 80 (RSV)
In the days of Herod, King of Judea, there was a priest named Zechariah, of the division of Abijah; and he had a wife of the daughters of Aaron, and her name was Elizabeth. And they were both righteous before God, walking in all the commandments and ordinances of the Lord blameless. But they had no child, because Elizabeth was barren, and both were advanced in years.

Now while he was serving as priest before God when his division was on duty...[there appeared to him] an angel of the Lord....And Zechariah was troubled when he saw him, and fear fell upon him. But the angel said to him, "Do not be afraid, Zechariah, for your prayer is heard, and your wife Elizabeth will bear you a son, and you shall call his name John.... He will be filled with the Holy Spirit even from his mother's womb. And he will turn many of the sons of Israel to the Lord their God."

And Zechariah said to the angel, "How shall I know this? For I am an old man, and my wife is advanced in years."

We know that Zechariah was struck dumb because of his skepticism, and remained so until his wife delivered their son. But when he regained his voice, he announced a glorious prophesy: "And you, child, will be called the prophet of the Most High; for you will go before the Lord to prepare his ways, to give knowledge of salvation to his people in the forgiveness of their sins, through the tender mercy of our God, when the day shall dawn upon us from on high to give light to those who sit in darkness and in the shadow of death, to guide our feet into the way of peace." And the child grew and became strong in spirit, and he was in the wilderness 'til the day of his manifestation to Israel .

I Samuel 1:1-2, 11 (RSV)
There was a certain man of Ramathaim-Zophim of the hill country of Ephraim, whose name was Elkanah the son of Jeroham, son of Elihu, son of Tohu, son of Zuph, an Ephraimite. He had two wives; the name of the one was Hannah, and the name of the other was Peninnah. And Peninnah had children, but Hannah had no children....

Greatly afflicted by her barrenness, Hannah cried to the Lord: "O Lord of hosts, if thou wilt indeed look on the affliction of thy maidservant, and remember me, and not forget thy maidservant, but wilt give to thy maidservant a son, then I will give him to the Lord all the days of his life, and no razor shall touch his head."

The Lord heard this woman and used her barrenness for high purpose, giving the world the prophet Samuel. And then there is the most seminal story of all in Sarah, Abraham's aged, barren wife, through whom God would bring forth a Chosen People, people likewise barren in their own old age but out of whom would come the Savior, this time of a young Virgin. "For unto us a child is given."

— diarist

❖   ❖   ❖
91
The person who acts in righteousness is righteous (I John 3:7-10)

"No one who is born of God commits sins; for God's nature abides in him and he cannot sin because he is born of God" (I John 3.7). Yet, John tells us elsewhere, *"If we say we have no sin, we deceive ourselves, and the truth is not in us"* (*I John 1:8*). How shall we understand this? In God's chosen souls, we may believe that by his grace only sins of weakness remain, left there providentially by God to remind us of who we are without him, and to impel us to go to him again and again.

The parable of the wheat and the tares is telling: if the weaknesses were removed (that weakness which is not yet rectified in us), there is the risk that the good in us will suffer, since a man who has no failings may very well cease to look to God for strength. Thus can Paul say (*II Cor 12:9*), in complaining about the "thorn" in his flesh from which he suffered greatly,*"Three times I besought the Lord about this, that it should leave me; but he said unto me, 'My grace is sufficient unto you, for my power is made perfect in weakness.' I will all the more gladly boast of my weaknesses, that the power of Christ may rest upon me. For the sake of Christ, then, I am content with weaknesses, insults, hardships, persecutions, and calamities; for when I am weak I am strong."*

We do not know what Paul's "thorn" amounted to. Some think it may have been a moral weakness of some sort, others that it was some kind of sickness or physical affliction. Whatever the case, the same truth applies. No matter what our weakness might be, insofar as this weakness moves us to seek the mercy of God, again and again, his power is being made perfect in us. Paul understood this for us as well.

In St. Catherine's *The Dialogue,* the Father refers to this condition in Paul: "Sometimes my providence leaves my great servants a pricking, as I did to my gentle apostle Paul, my chosen vessel. After he had received my Truth's teaching in the depths of me the eternal Father, I still left him the pricking and resistance of his flesh.

"Could I and can I not make it otherwise for Paul and the others in whom I leave this or that sort of pricking? Yes. Then why does my providence do this? To give them opportunity for merit, to keep them in the self-knowledge whence they drew true humility, to make them compassionate instead of cruel toward their neighbors so that they will sympathize with them in their labors."

—diarist

❖   ❖   ❖
92
What have you that you have not received?

St. Paul says, *"What have you that you have not received!"* What we have received is our human nature, our intelligence, our family, our education, our teachers and so on. Whatever we have that is good we have received. Then the only thing that is ours of ourselves is our nothingness and our sins. Our good actions have God as their first cause, and our ability to perform them is also from God. Again, St. Paul says that God is in us both to will and to achieve. It seems to us that we are the first cause of our good actions, but really we are the second cause, and we are a cause of them only because God is moving us, though we experience and have to act as if we were moving ourselves, which we are—but when we do, we have to realize that God is moving us as second cause. This is the Dominican and Thomist resolution of the apparent conflict between freedom of the will and the omnipotence of God.

God however is not responsible for the disorder of our sins, though we could not accomplish them without His concurrence. But the first cause is our own choice of them. Therefore all we have OF OURSELVES (that is independent of God) is our sins and our nothingness. And our sins have been forgiven—the guilt is gone, though the memory of them remains.

But by His gracious gift, as St. Paul put it, we are what we are. And that is the image of God. The likeness to Him, lost by sin, is restored by grace—through the redemption and consequent sanctification.

So you must acknowledge the goodness of God in you in order to be grateful and to make acts of gratitude for the gift of your nature, of your marriage, of your friends, of all that is good, but especially of your friendship with God in Jesus.

— Fr. Raphael Simon, O.C.S.O.

❖   ❖   ❖
93
On predestination and the dignity of human causality

St. Paul says: *We know that in everything God works for good with those who love him, who are called according to his purpose. For those whom he foreknew he also predestined to be conformed to the image of his Son, in order that he might be the first-born among many brethren. And those whom he predestined he also called; and those whom he called he also justified; and those whom he justified he also glorified. What then shall we say to this?* (Rom. 8:28-31a RSV).

St. Thomas says: "*It is fitting that God should predestine men. For all things are subject to His providence.*" But St Thomas goes on to say that predestination here does not leave out human causality, such as, for example, the effectiveness of the prayer of the saints. Some might argue, he notes, that if we are predestined, then it must mean that our spiritual destiny "*cannot be furthered,*" not even "*by the prayers of the saints.*" The reasoning here is, "*if a thing can be helped it can also be hindered. But predestination cannot be hindered by anything. Therefore it cannot be furthered by anything.*"

St. Thomas argues quite otherwise. It is true, he says "*in no possible way can predestination be furthered by the prayers of the saints. For it is not due to their prayers that anyone is predestined by God.*" But predestination, he says, can be "*helped by the prayers of the saints, and by other good works; because providence, of which predestination is a part, does not do away with secondary causes but so provides effects, that the order of secondary causes falls also under providence. So, as natural effects are provided by God in such a way that natural causes are directed to bring about those natural effects, without which those effects would not happen; so the salvation of a person is predestined by God in such a way, that whatever helps that person towards salvation falls under the order of predestination; whether it be one's own prayers, or those of another; or other good works, and suchlike, without which one would not attain to salvation. Whence the predestined must strive after good works and prayer; because through these means predestination is most certainly fulfilled. For this reason it is said: 'Labor the more; that by good works you may make sure your calling and selection' (2 Peter 1:10).*"

St. Thomas concludes his argument by stating, "*Nor is this [reliance on secondary causes] on account of any defect in the power of God, but because He employs intermediary causes, in order that the beauty of order may be preserved in the universe; and also that He may communicate to creatures the dignity of causality.*"

—diarist

❖   ❖   ❖
94
A Great Mystery

The providence of God produces effects through the operation of secondary causes... Wherefore, that which flows from free-will is also of predestination.

— *St. Thomas Aquinas*

❖   ❖   ❖
95
Everything I have created depends upon Me totally

Everything that I have created depends on Me totally, as much for its slightest movement and operation as for its very substance and existence. I, Who have given the creature its natural powers of operation, do not fail in moving it to the perfection of that operation which is its end and purpose. For all things reach their end by a perfection of operation, a perfection of activity according to the measure of My Wisdom, by which they participate in the Infinite Activity of God. And therefore We provide each thing, not only with its nature and powers, the principles of its operation by which it is able to operate, but We move it to its perfect operation, delighting to see the actuality of both its being and its activity depending on Ourselves, having its very existence in Us, the imitation of Our Perfect Being Which is Pure Activity.

And in this We are glorified, that every particle of being and perfection in the creature, its matter, its form, its substance, its powers, and consummating everything else, its operations, its activity, proceed from Us, totally. In your ignorance, and in your pride, you think that you do things of yourself and because you think that you are the ultimate source of what you do, you are constantly anxious and preoccupied with the success of your undertakings. And therefore when you succeed, you take glory to yourself, and when you fail you are depressed because you are separated from the ultimate goodness which you would find in yourself, and in which you would delight. Can you see, then, why in the Gospel I exhorted My followers again and again to contemplate and consider creatures I had made without reason, the birds of the air, the flowers of the field? Being without reason, it was evident that they depended totally on My Providence to reach their end — and it is manifest to your very senses how very perfectly they reach it. But men, because they have the use of reason and can foresee, and because their fallen nature disposes them to see things outside of Me, rely on their own providence instead of on Mine. They really think that they are taking care of themselves—which they could, as instruments of My Providence. For they should use the reason I have given them to provide for the things which that reason teaches them that they need.

But the providence of men is only part of My Providence. Just as it is I Who have given them their reason, it is I Who direct that reason and move it totally to its end—so that the providence of men is contained in My Providence as a ship is in the sea wherein it moves. That was why Paul said: "I use the things of this world as though I use them not." Because even as he, Paul, was directing things by his own reason and will in using them, so he was himself being directed by Me: as things were his instrument so he is the instrument of Christ. And as I am the Principle of his life, so I am the Principle of his operation, and of your life and your activity, of everything you do. *"Without Me you can do nothing."*

– A Servant of God

❖ ❖ ❖
96

It is you who have accomplished all we have done.

—Isaiah 26:12b
(NAB)

❖ ❖ ❖
97

God will condemn what we have done, but he will save
what he himself has done in us

Happy are we if we do the deeds of which we have heard and sung. Our hearing means having them planted in us, while our doing them shows that the seed has borne fruit. By saying this, I wish to caution you, dearly beloved, not to enter the Church fruitlessly, satisfied with mere hearing of such mighty blessings and failing to do good works. *For we have been saved by his grace,* says the Apostle, *and not by our works, lest anyone may boast; for it is by his grace that we have been saved.* It is not as if a good life of some sort came first, and that thereupon God showed his love and esteem for it from on high, saying: "Let us come to the aid of these men and assist them quickly because they are living a good life." No, our life was displeasing to him; whatever we did by ourselves was displeasing to him;

but what he did in us was not displeasing to him. He will, therefore, condemn what we have done, but he will save what he himself has done in us.

– St. Augustine

❖   ❖   ❖
98
Primary Cause empties himself and becomes like one of us, in all things save sin

St. Paul puts it starkly: The divine Son of God did not deem his divinity something to be clung to but *"emptied himself taking the form of a servant"* (*Phil 2:7*). The great ontological chasm between Primary Cause and the multitude of secondary causes is mysteriously bridged and even in some still more mysterious way dissolved. Even as Jesus "emptied himself" to become Son of Man, we are called to empty ourselves so that we can become adopted sons of God. The mystery of salvation is hidden in this mutual, self-emptying action. Jesus said: *"He who loses his life for my sake will find it (Matt 10:39).*

We are kidding ourselves if we think we can fathom very much of what this means. Jesus, who is the Word of God of whom it is revealed, *"all things were made through him and without him was not anything made that was made (John 1:3),"* empties himself of his status as Creator and enters his creation as a creature, one among many. As God's Word, he is (to use St. Thomas' term) the expression of the Primary Cause of everything that exists in the created order. We creatures, objects of his creation, are never more than "secondary causes," working in the created order as he, the Primary Cause, allows. So in emptying himself, the Word of God, the Primary Cause, lowers himself to our status as secondary causes. He who is the cause of every created thing has now confined himself in what he has created, and to all its limitations.

As John Paul II has written in *Redemptor Hominis*, quoting from Vatican II's *Gaudium et Spes* "He worked with human hands, he thought with a human mind. He acted with a human will, and with a human heart he loved. Born of the Virgin Mary, he has truly been made one of us, like to us in all things except sin, he, the Redeemer of man."

The full reasons Jesus took on our nature are hidden in the deepest mysteries of God's Providence of Love, but one purpose is perfectly clear:

He entered creation to restart it after the devastation wrought by Adam, by becoming the New Adam and doing everything right this time, all in accordance with the Father's will, and in so doing, to fulfill the Father's original plan for Adam when He created the first man in His image.

It is, after all, the proper function of a secondary cause to serve the purposes of a Primary Cause. This is easy to see. A commercial company will get nowhere if the employees do not heed the will of their employer. The same goes for the foot soldiers of an army with respect to its general. Good order quickly turns to disorder when that which is secondary is no longer subject to that which is primary. An employee who habitually comes late and takes overlong lunch hours will eventually lose out because he has disturbed the order proper to the business environment. If all the employees took advantage of the company in this way, the company itself would suffer before long. And so with God's creation. The original order and perfection of creation was lost through sin. Sin broke the harmonious connection between God as Primary Cause and us as his secondary causes. It is restored in the measure we live in the One whom the Father sent to restore his order, which is to say in the measure that we allow Christ to live and act in us. It is to this perfection that Christ called us when he said, *"Be ye perfect as your heavenly Father is perfect."* Be the perfect image and likeness of the Father you were meant to be.

Quoting *Gaudium et Spes*, John Paul II writes "He [Jesus] who is the 'image of the invisible God' (*Col 1:15*) is himself the perfect man who has restored in the children of Adam that likeness to God which had been disfigured ever since the first sin. Human nature, by the very fact that it was assumed, not absorbed, in him, has been raised in us also to a dignity beyond compare. For, by his Incarnation, he, the Son of God, in a certain way united himself with each man."

This is an awesome realty. In his becoming part of us, part of the created order, he reveals to us that our proper destiny is to become part of him, part of the divine order. In taking on our human nature, we are extended an invitation to take on his divine nature. This is the destiny the Father wills for us, and reveals to us in the New Adam. In becoming man, the Council document says, "Christ the Lord, the new Adam, in the very revelation of the mystery of the Father and his love, fully reveals man to himself and brings to light his most high calling."

The New Adam, then, by his thirty-three years of life on earth, answers the question of who we are, and shows us how we are to live and for what. How did Jesus live? He lived by doing the Father's will, in all things. For what did He live? To accomplish the Father's will. *"Not my will but thy will be done."* Who are we in light of Him? Children of God: *"Beloved, we are God's children now; it does not yet appear what we shall be, but we know that when he appears, we shall be like him" (I John 3:2).* By his Incarnation, death and Resurrection, Jesus restores the proper order between the primacy of God's causality and ours. But there is more. In a profound and mysterious way Our Lord's Incarnation—the Son of God taking on flesh—combines what is fully divine with what is merely human and in so doing truly makes into one what is primary and what is secondary in the order of causality. Is this not his meaning when he said, "The Father who dwells in me is doing his works" *(Jn14:10)*? Does this not also apply to all who become Our Lord's brothers and sisters?

— diarist

❖ ❖ ❖

99

The Gift is not for us alone and so to receive it we must make it known

And I coming on earth, had to do as a God; I had to complete in everything the work of man; I had to raise him to the first point of his origin, by giving him the possession of my Will. And, although many make use of my Coming as remedy for their salvation, and therefore take my Will as medicine, as strength, as antidote in order not to go to Hell, I still wait so that souls rise up who will take It as Life; and in making It known, they take possession of It. In this way I will complete the work of my Coming upon the earth and will have the fruit of the Divine Graft formed anew with the creature…

Therefore, the forerunner of the Gift that I want to give to the creature of my Will is the knowledge of It. The knowledge prepares the way… For however much knowledge enters into the soul, so much more is it stimulated to desire the Gift… And so in these times, the sign that I want to give the Gift of my Volition is the knowledge of It. Therefore, be attentive and do not flee from anything that I have manifested to you about my Will, if you want Me to place my last signature on the Gift that I long to give to creatures.

— Luisa Piccarreta

❖   ❖   ❖

100

Behold I am the God who is isolated from creatures

Behold I am the God who is isolated from creatures. I live in their midst; I am the life of each one of their acts; yet they consider Me to be irrelevant… Yet, being among men, I am the light of their every thought, the sound of their every word, the movement of their every act, the footstep of their every walk, the palpitation of every heart. Nevertheless, ungrateful man leaves Me in isolation, never giving Me a "thank you," not an "I love you." I am abandoned in man's intelligence because man uses for his own ends the light I give him, perhaps even to offend Me. I am abandoned in man's words, whose sounds often blaspheme Me. I am abandoned in his acts, which man uses to bring Me death. I am abandoned in his steps; and I am abandoned in his heart—a heart devoted to disobedience and to loving what does not pertain to Me.

Oh, how this solitude weighs upon Me! But so great are my Love and my magnanimity that, although being much more than a sun, I continue on my course—always searching to find someone willing to accompany Me in the midst of such solitude! When I find such a soul, I continually accompany it and fill it to overflowing with my graces.

— Luisa Piccarreta

❖   ❖   ❖

101

The void of human action in the Divine, when filled, will transform the world with blessings and wonders

My daughter, in my Will there is the void of human action in the Divine, and this empty space must be filled up by whoever lives in my Will. The more you take care to live in my Will and make It known to others, the sooner this void will be filled. Then my Will, seeing the human will stirring within It, as if returning to the beginning from whence it came, will feel satisfied in seeing Its longings for the human race fulfilled.

There may be few of these human wills, but even if It found just one alone, with no others, my Will, with Its Power, could recover everything. But it is always a human will that must come into my Will and fill up all that the others do not do. This will be so acceptable to Me that the heavens will be torn asunder to allow my Will to descend and to reveal the blessings and wonders that It contains. Each new entry that you make into my Will gives me the incentive to give you additional knowledge and to tell you about other wonders, because I want you to know the good that you do so that you value It and desire to possess It. When I see that you love and value It, I will give you possession of It.

Knowledge is the eye of the soul; the soul without knowledge is blind concerning those goods and truths. In my Will, there are no blind souls; rather, each new acquisition of knowledge leads them to a broader perspective.

— Luisa Piccarreta

❖ ❖ ❖
102
The Celestial Creator, when He sees the soul in his Will, takes it in his arms and,
placing it on his lap, lets it operate with his own hands

My daughter, it is true that to live in my Volition is a gift and the possession of the greatest gift. But the gift that contains infinite value, which is money that rises at every instant, light that never dims, sun that never sets, putting the soul in its place as established by God in the Divine Order and, therefore, taking its place of honor and of sovereignty in Creation, is not given except to one who is disposed and should not waste It, and to one who will esteem and love It so much, even more than its own life, who is ready to sacrifice its own life in order to let this Gift of my Volition have supremacy over all, esteeming It more than life itself. Indeed, one's own life is nothing in comparison to It. Therefore, first I want to see that the soul truly wants to do my Will and never its own, that it is ready to sacrifice anything to do Mine, and that in all it does, it asks Me always, even on loan, the Gift of my Volition.

When I see that it does everything with the loan of my Volition, I gift It to the soul as a gift because, by asking for It again and again, it has formed the empty space in its soul in which to put the Celestial Gift. Living habitually on the loan of this Divine Food, it has lost the taste for its own volition; its palate is ennobled and is not adapted to the vile foods of its own ego. Therefore, seeing itself in possession of the gift that it longed for, yearned for and loved so much, the soul will live by the Life of that Gift, will love It and will give It the esteem that It deserves.

The Celestial Creator, when He sees the soul in his Will, takes it in his arms and, placing it on his lap, lets it operate with his own hands and, with the power of the "Fiat" with which He made all things, lets all his reflections descend upon the creature in order to give it the likeness of his operation. This is why the operation of the creature becomes light, is united to the single act of its Creator and is constituted in the Eternal Glory and continuous praise of its Creator. Therefore, be attentive, and make sure that the most important thing for you is to live in my Volition, so you will never descend from your origin, that is, from the bosom of your Creator.

– Luisa Piccarreta

❖   ❖   ❖

103
See my Will at work in the creature

Continuing in my usual state, I heard my adorable Jesus praying within me, saying: "My Father, I beseech You that our Will be one with the will of this little daughter of our Will. Her will is a legitimate birth from our Will. Oh, for the honor and dignity of our Eternal Will, permit that nothing comes from her that is not born of our Will and that she knows nothing other than our Will alone. To obtain this, I offer You all the acts of my Humanity which were done in our adorable Will…

"Come! Come everyone, angels, saints, wayfarers, all generations; come and see the greatest wonder and miracle ever seen: my Will at work in the creature! …

"My Will must be like the air we breathe: though it is not seen, it is felt; it gives life; it penetrates everywhere, even to the deepest tissues, so as to give life to every heartbeat. Wherever it enters, whether in darkness, great depths, or the most secret places, it constitutes the life of everything. So, my Will shall be more than air in you. Coming out of you, It will make Itself the life of everything. Be more attentive, therefore, and follow the Will of your Jesus, because watchfulness will show you where you are and what you are doing. Knowledge will make you appreciate and esteem more highly the divine palace of my Will.

"Suppose someone finds himself in the palace of a king and he doesn't know that the building belongs to the king. It will make no impression on him; he will be distracted and go about speaking and laughing. He will not be disposed to receive the gifts of the king. But if he knew that it was the king's palace, he would look carefully at everything and value them. He would walk on his tiptoes, whisper, and watch wide-eyed to see from which room the king would enter. He would be in expectation of receiving great gifts from the king. You see, vigilance is the path of knowledge. Knowledge changes the person and things, disposing him to receive great gifts. So, since you know that you are in the palace of my Will, you will receive always, and you will receive much so as to be able to give to all your brothers."

— Luisa Piccarreta

❖ ❖ ❖
104
It is Christ, in you

It was God's purpose to reveal to them how rich is the glory of this mystery among the gentiles; it is Christ among you, your hope of glory: this is the Christ we are proclaiming, admonishing and instructing everyone in all wisdom, to make everyone perfect in Christ. And it is for this reason that I labor, striving with his energy which works in me mightily.

— Colossians 1:27 – 29 (The New Jerusalem Bible)

❖ ❖ ❖
105
Prayer

O Mary Immaculate, Queen of apostles, deign to bless these simple pages. Grant that all who read them may really *understand* that, if it please God to use their activity as an ordinary instrument of His Providence, in pouring out His heavenly riches upon the souls of men, this activity, if it is to produce any results, will have to *participate, somehow, in the nature of the Divine Act* as Thou didst behold it in the bosom of God when He, to Whom we owe the power of calling thee our Mother, became incarnate in thy virginal womb.

— Dom Jean-Baptiste Chautard, O.C.S.O.

❖

144

- IV -

Work, What We Do

❖ ❖ ❖
1
Be grafted onto Him and the fruits will be copious

Ask God humbly for light and you will be able to understand and assimilate all that I am teaching you. He will help you because God gives Himself to men without limit or measure, and He providentially looks after all creation for we are the work of His hands. The Lord does not leave unassisted by his graces those whom He has chosen....

The works of the man who possesses God are generosity, dedication, and love; these are the perfumes which are pleasing to the Lord. In the garden of the Beloved, the flowering is increasingly luxuriant. Be grafted onto Him and the fruits will be copious. Moistened with the water of his grace, they will not lose their charm. He forms in the soul his divine beauty, and it is eternal, as God is eternal.

— Our Lady to Consuelo

❖ ❖ ❖
2
Without me you can do nothing

These are the bookends for the conduct of our life in the world, on the one end when the Father tells us, as He did on Mt. Tabor, *"This is my beloved Son, listen to him."* And on the other end, when Jesus says, *"Without me you can do nothing."* Thus, to re-phrase an old popular song, we must "listen while we work" if we want to do any good in this life.

— diarist

❖ ❖ ❖
3
Laborare est orare

The old piety, "Pray as if everything depended upon God, work as if everything depended upon you," does not really get it right. Work done properly will itself be a prayer.

—diarist

❖   ❖   ❖

4
Mary at needlework in Egypt

In view of their great poverty, and of the great difficulty of sufficient employment [for Joseph] as a carpenter, the great Lady resolved to assist him by the work of her hands to earn a livelihood. She immediately executed her resolve by seeking to obtain needlework... As all that She attended to or busied herself with was so perfect, the reputation of her skill soon spread abroad, so that She never was in want of employment...

In order to obtain the indispensable victuals and clothing, furnish the house ever so moderately, and pay the necessary expenses, it seemed to our Queen that She must employ all day in work and consume the night in attending to her spiritual exercises. This She resolved upon, not for any motives of gain, or because She did not continue in her contemplations during the day; for this was her incessant occupation in the presence of the infant God... But some of the hours, which She was wont to spend in special exercises, She wished to transfer to the night-time in order to be able to extend the hours of manual labor, not being minded to ask or expect God's miraculous assistance for anything which She could attain by greater diligence and additional labor on her own part. In all such cases we ask for miraculous help more for our own convenience than on account of necessity. The most prudent Queen asked the eternal Father to provide sustenance for her divine Son; but at the same time She continued to labor. Like one who does not trust in herself, or in her own efforts, She united prayer with her labors, in order to obtain the necessities of life like other men.

— Venerable Mary of Agreda

❖   ❖   ❖

5
Fiat: the perfect response of the creature to the Creator

Mary's response to the archangel Gabriel, *"May it be done unto me according to thy word,"* is the perfection of response of the creature to the Creator, the secondary cause to the Primary Cause. Mary is the model for all our actions in this life, seeing them as responses to the fecundating action of God who must overshadow what is to come from us if it is to have worth in his eyes and accomplish his purposes.

— diarist

❖ ❖ ❖

6
Doing what we do in the presence of God

You will find an important remark on this subject [by Brother Lawrence on the practice of the presence of God] in his conversations, where he said that this presence of God must be maintained more by the heart and by love than by the understanding or by discourse. "In the ways of God," he said, "thoughts amount to little whereas love counts for everything. And it is not necessary," he continued, "to have important things to do." I am describing a lay brother in the kitchen to you, so let me use his own expressions:

"I flip my little omelet in the frying pan for the love of God, and when it's done, if I have nothing else to do, I prostrate myself on the floor and adore my God who gave me the grace to do it, after which I get up happier than a king. When I can do nothing else, it is enough for me to pick up a straw from the ground for the love of God."

—*Joseph de Beaufort*, The Ways of Brother Lawrence

❖ ❖ ❖

7
Little acts are great acts when willed by God

One should not look at how much or how little one does, but rather if it is something willed by God. This is because God looks more at the little act, if it is done according to his Will, than the great act done without It.

— *Luisa Piccarreta*

❖ ❖ ❖

8
The Lord does the building

"Should you build me a house to dwell in?... In all my wanderings among the Israelites, did I ever utter a word...to ask: why have you not built me a house of cedar?" *(II Sam 7:5,7).*

David has had success against all his enemies and now is at rest, living in a house of cedar. He reflects on the fact that the ark of God dwells in a tent, and tells the prophet Nathan that he wants to do something about it, to build something appropriate for the Lord. But the Lord reveals to Nathan that this is not to be. He tells Nathan to tell David that the Lord does the building, not David, and reminds David everything that David has and has accomplished comes from the Lord's hands.

Yet, we read in *Haggai* (*1:1-8 NAB*) that when the Jews were brought back from Babylonian exile for the express purpose of rebuilding the destroyed temple and they instead pursued personal interests, the Lord admonishes them, "Is it time for you to dwell in your own paneled houses, while this house lies in ruins?" He tells them "Consider your ways! You have sown much, but have brought in little; you have eaten, but not been satisfied; you have drunk, but not been exhilarated; have clothed yourselves, but not been warmed; And whoever earned wages earned them for a bag with holes in it." So the Lord tells them, "Go up into the hill country; bring timber, and build the house. That I may take pleasure in it and receive my glory."

What are we to make of this? David, full of righteous zeal, wants to build for God and is told to lay off; the returning Jews, thinking only of themselves, neglect to build and are told to get cracking. In David's case, he wants to do something God does not want, in the case of the returning Jews, they neglect what He wants. In both cases, secondary agents pre-empt God's primacy and pursue their own agendas, pious or otherwise.

St. Thomas tells us that the creature satisfies the Creator's justice by receiving, for it is the very nature of the Creator to give and of the creature to receive what is given. Is it not so then that when Our Lord asks a work of us, He has already placed the work in our hearts, and put the means for doing it in our hands. Working independently of His Will does not please Him, however good the motive and, truthfully, in the end, where does it get us? "Consider your ways. You have sown much, but have brought in little; you have eaten but not been satisfied…" As the Psalmist (*127:1*) reminds us ,"*Unless the Lord builds the house, they labor in vain who build it.*".

– diarist

❖   ❖   ❖
9

Amen, Amen I say to you, whoever believes in me
will do the works that I do (John 14:12)

It is quite evident that the faithful absolutely need the help of the Divine Redeemer, since He himself said, "*Without Me you can do nothing.*" … Still, it is necessary to state, astonishing as this may seem, our Lord needs the help of his members....This is not due to any poverty or weakness on his part, but rather because He himself has disposed it thus for the greater honor of his spotless Spouse. As He was dying on the Cross, He left to his Church, without any contribution on her part, the limitless treasure of Redemption but when it came to the distribution of this treasure, He not only shares with his Church the work of sanctification of souls, but He wills it in some way to be due to their action. A tremendous mystery indeed, about which we can never meditate enough: the salvation of great numbers of souls depends upon prayers and voluntary mortifications, suffered for this purpose by the members of the Mystical Body of Christ and on the collaborative work that the pastors and the faithful, in particular the fathers and mothers of families, must bring to Our Lord.

– Pope Pius XII, Encyclical Mystici Corporis Christi

❖ ❖ ❖

10

If you are inside the Church, the gates of hell
will not prevail against you

St. Ambrose in his *Exposition of the Gospel of Luke*, commenting on Peter's profession of faith at Caesarea Philippi, recalls that "Christ is the stone," and that "Christ did not refuse this beautiful name to his disciple so that he, too, would be Peter, and have in the stone the strength of perseverance, the indestructibleness of faith." Then Ambrose adds, for our benefit, "You also can make the effort to be a stone. Your stone is your actions. Your stone is your thoughts. Your house is built on this stone, so that it will not be lacerated by any tempest of the evil spirits. If you are a stone, you will be inside the Church because the Church is on the stone. If you are inside the Church, the gates of hell will not prevail against you."

– Pope John Paul II

❖ ❖ ❖

11

Oh, Jesus, give me your holy hand and the light of your intelligence
and write together with me

Luisa Piccarreta was an uneducated person, not even having attended high school, yet she has given us some of the most profound spiritual writings ever penned.

What she wrote was written in obedience, listening to what Our Lord was telling her, and recording it because this is what He wanted her to do. For her, writing was a sacrifice, always against the grain of what by nature she would have chosen to do. She relied upon Him to accomplish in her the work He desired.

I write out of obedience. I offer everything to my sweet Jesus, in union with the sacrifice of his obedience, so as to obtain the grace and the strength to do as He wants. And now, O my Jesus, give me your holy hand and the light of your intelligence, and write together with me.

— Luisa Piccarreta

❖   ❖   ❖

12
*Always work together with Me — as if we were
doing the same thing together*

My dearest daughter, working for Christ makes the human work disappear, and Christ makes arise the divine work. For this reason, always work together with Me—as if we were together doing the same thing. If you suffer, do it as if you were suffering with Me; if you pray, if you work, make everything run in Me and together with Me. Thus you will lose the human works in everything, only to find them again as Divine. Oh, how immense is the wealth that creatures could acquire working this way, but it does not interest them!

— Luisa Piccarreta

❖   ❖   ❖

13
I begged Him to help me

Occasionally He assigned work for me to do in a given hour, and I tired myself to please Him. When unsuccessful, I begged Him to help me. Many times He obliged by doing the work with me so that I would be free—not for entertainment—but almost always to have more time for prayer. It happened, therefore, that either by myself or with Him, the work that was to occupy me all day was finished in a short time. He kept drawing me toward prayer and held me completely absorbed in contemplation of the many lights and graces bestowed by Him on creatures.

— Luisa Piccarreta

❖ ❖ ❖
14

If you get to work, all your difficulties will disappear and fall away like the scales of a fish.

— Our Lord to Luisa Piccarreta

❖ ❖ ❖
15

St. Thomas quotes a gloss on Psalm 118:82 by Lombard, defending the Dominican view of study:

"People who do nothing but study the word of God are not being idle, nor is the person who works outwardly of more value than the person whose study is devoted to knowing God. Wisdom is the greatest of all works, and Mary, who listened, is put before Martha, who served."

— Peter Lombard

❖ ❖ ❖
16

Act with an upright intention of pleasing God alone

Peace puts all the passions in their place. But what triumphs over everything, what establishes the entire good of the soul and what sanctifies everything, is doing everything for God — to act with an upright intention of pleasing God alone. Acting uprightly is what directs, rules, and corrects the virtues themselves, even obedience. In other words, it is like a maestro who directs the spiritual music of the soul.

— Our Lord to Luisa Piccarreta

❖ ❖ ❖
17

When you think, act, or speak, let it be for the glory of God and not the self

Work only becomes fruitful when it is praying, when it is offering to the divine intentions. And by this same token, prayer only becomes fruitful when it is work or suffering, which means sacrifice to the divine intentions, a host of praise, gratitude, reparation.

— Our Lord an anonymous French nun

❖ ❖ ❖
18

He who has completed his mission on earth can say that his mission is finished, but for whoever has not completed it must do so from heaven

Luisa Piccarreta was bed-ridden for 60 some years, a victim soul who kept a diary of Our Lord's dealings with her over those years. Her spiritual director was St. Annibale di Francia (recently canonized by John Paul II) to whom she had entrusted her diaries recording Our Lord's communications to her concerning His call to mankind to live life in the Divine Will. This holy priest was to see to the publication of her writings, even during her lifetime. She, as authoress, was not to be mentioned in the work. But the priest had taken ill before the project could be completed and was near death and Luisa was concerned that the work would be abandoned and the Lord's purposes frustrated. While in this state of inquietude, Our Lord came to Luisa and made her understand the following:

My daughter, whoever has been given a mission and has barely had an opportunity to begin, or has not been able to complete the entirety of his missions because at the best moment I call him to heaven, he will continue his mission from there, so that it may bring into the depths of the soul its deposit of good relating to the knowledge which the soul acquired in this life. In heaven he will understand with greater clarity and understanding the great good of the knowledge of the Supreme Fiat. He will plead with the Fiat, indeed he will ask all of heaven to pray, that the knowledge be known throughout the earth; he will impetrate that clearer light be given to whoever must work in making it known. This is true especially because every knowledge concerning my Will will bring the blessed greater glory, greater happiness, and as they are known throughout the earth their glory and happiness will be doubled, because this will be the fulfillment of the soul's mission which had been placed in his will to do.

He…who has completed his mission on earth can say that his mission is finished; but for whoever has not completed it must do so from heaven.

As for you, your mission is very long, and neither will you be able to complete it on earth. Until all the knowledges are known upon the earth and the Kingdom of the Divine Will is known, your mission cannot be said to be completed. In heaven you will have much to do; my Will, which held you so occupied upon earth on behalf of its Kingdom, will not leave you—you will still work with it in heaven. It will keep you always in its company so that you will do nothing other than descend and ascend from heaven to earth to help establish my kingdom with decorum, honor, and glory. This will be your great contentment, happiness, and highest glory in seeing your smallness which, united to my Volition, has transported heaven upon earth and the earth into heaven. You could not have any greater gratification than this—seeing the glory of your Creator completed by his creatures, the natural order re-established, all of creation with its full splendor, and seeing man, our dear jewel, in his place of honor. How great will be Our, and your utmost satisfaction, glory, and unending happiness to see the purpose of creation realized

Then Luisa had a vision of St. Annibale di Francia after his death. He appeared to her and explained the value of having known about the wonders of living in the Divine Will. Referring to the publications of her writings, he said:
But that which surprised me the most are those few publications which I was able to put out regarding the Divine Will. Each saying, being turned into a sun, and with its rays investing all other lights, forms such a surprise of beauty that the soul remains rapt in enchantment. You cannot know how surprised I was in finding myself in the midst of this light and these suns. It was a great contentment for me and I thanked our Greatest Good Jesus that He had given me the occasion and the grace to do it...

— Luisa Piccarreta

❖   ❖   ❖

19

A man carrying a jug of water

Go into the city, and a man carrying a jug of water will meet you; follow him, and wherever he enters, say to the householder, "The Teacher says, 'Where is my guest room, where I am to eat the Passover with my disciples?'" (Mark 14:13).

A man carrying a jug of water. Was he an angel? Was he just a simple servant on his daily rounds, whom God moved to be where he was and do as he did? The man, whoever he was, was simply doing his duty carrying water to this house perhaps in preparation for the Passover feast our Lord was to celebrate. Perhaps this water here was the very water Our Lord used to wash the disciples' feet. We might see the water as a distant echo of the first feast at Cana where that extraordinary transformation took place involving water.

But now, the man carrying the water would identify the place where, not water, but wine would be transformed, to become Sacred Blood to forever change our lives. And might not there be some such hidden significance in any one of our little acts, when fitted into God's purposes? As we are told, "all things work together for the good, for those who serve the Lord." We likely never know in this life, in some gesture of ours, some chance meeting, some word spoken, what is being accomplished in God's

Providence. As we see, this includes a humble person carrying a jug of water and in this humble way fulfilling one essential, tiny, barely noticed step in a sequence that would redeem the world.

– diarist

❖   ❖   ❖
20
Regarding the characteristics of the temporal kingdom during the millennium

And they shall build houses and inhabit them; and they shall plant vineyards, and eat the fruits of them, and drink the wine…and the works of their hands shall be multiplied. My elect shall not labor in vain.

– Justin Martyr

❖   ❖   ❖
21
The glorious liberty of the children of God

My son, you must diligently see to it that wherever you are and in whatever you do—I refer to your external actions—you are interiorly free and act as your own master, that is, everything should be subject to you and you should be subject to nothing.

You are to be lord and master of your actions and not their slave nor hired servant. You are to be a true Israelite, redeemed from captivity and enjoying the glorious liberty of the children of God.

You must keep your head above the contingencies of the present and contemplate the eternal. Look on ephemeral things with one eye and with the other gaze upon celestial things.

Don't allow temporal things to so attract you that you find yourself clinging to them, but use them for your spiritual advantage as God, the Supreme Maker, who has left nothing disordered in His creation, has designed and ordained them.

– Imitation of Christ

❖   ❖   ❖
22
The work of our hands

Let us love God, my friends, let us love God, but let it be through the work of our hands, let it be by the sweat of our brow.

– St. Vincent de Paul

❖   ❖   ❖
23
God will not give you anything, unless you work with all your strength

Complete serenity of mind is a gift of God; but this serenity is not given without our own intense effort. You will achieve nothing by your own efforts alone; yet God will not give you anything, unless you work with all your strength. This is an unbreakable law.

— Theophan The Recluse

❖   ❖   ❖
24
The chief enemy of life in God is a profusion of worldly cares

The chief enemy of life in God is a profusion of worldly cares. This profusion of cares impels a man into an endless round of secular activities. Every day, from morning till night, it drives him from one job to another, not giving him a moment's rest, leaving him no time to turn to God and to remain for a while uplifted in prayer to Him.

— Theophan The Recluse

Commentary: Theophan adds that a man enters a monastery precisely to get away from the "multitude of cares which gnaw at the minds of laymen." "It is this freedom from anxiety," he says, "resulting from the ordered sequence of the monastic life that enables the monk to remain constantly with God and in God." But one must recall that Joseph was not a monk and yet lived this way. A lay person can understand the monastery as a monastery of the heart, and the "ordered sequence of the monastic life" as a life lived in the quiet, recollected pursuit of the work that God has given us, whether it is going to our place of work, taking our children to their activities, waging battle, or whatever. One can do these things with the interior quietness and steadfastness of a monk or with the frenzy that so sadly characterizes our secular age.

For anyone who learns to cultivate the interior life, one's day need not be frenzied. Such a person, no less than the monk, can "remain constantly with God and in God." There are many examples that, with grace, such a life is possible. Like the Mexican woman, Conchita Armida, recently declared venerable by the Vatican. She was a devoted wife, ran a large household of many children, wrote some 60 volumes of remarkable spiritual reflection, founded an order of priests and an order of contemplative nuns. Her many children never thought of her as a saint, only as a great mom, but "great moms" can be saints too.

— diarist

❖   ❖   ❖
25
On listening to Schubert's Piano Trio in B flat, D. 898, Andante movement

It was as if the music sought to touch something beautiful, ever so deftly so as not to disturb its order. Each note saying, "here, see," with the notes that follow whispering "and here too." Music that did not presume to be that beauty itself. What would it be like if everything were touched this way?

— diarist

❖   ❖   ❖
26
The man in whose presence you felt loved

We visited the old priest in the hospice where he stayed because of advanced Parkinson's disease, and within minutes he began to tell us of his new vocation. He says he has found a new vocation, a new work, and that he does not think of himself as a patient there awaiting death but as a worker. And so he is, shuffling through the halls behind his wheel chair for support, visiting the dying.

He had grave difficulty talking, but somehow it didn't seem to prevent him from communicating to us or the stream of visitors who come to see him, even if only with a few words. But it was not what he said that was telling, he let us know. Often he could utter little more than a word or two, but the effect seemed to have great power because now it is not him speaking but the Spirit through him.

This is the man of whom a highly successful Jewish entrepreneur said once to me, when asked if he remembered meeting this priest, "Ah, yes, the man in whose presence you felt loved."

— diarist

❖   ❖   ❖
27
Serve Me in the moment

I was reflecting on how a man might serve the Lord by just walking through the halls of a hospice barely able to speak. I prayed this prayer:

"Lord, I want to serve you, but I don't know what I should do."
And I seemed to hear Our Lord answer:

"Serve me in the moment."

"How Lord?"

"By believing in my mercy for you and for those present to you, now, in this very moment, no matter what you, or they, may have been doing or not doing in the preceding moment. Remember Dismas. If you do as I say, you will experience joy and your joy will be my witness."

— diarist

❖   ❖   ❖

28

Souls who live in the sacrament of the present moment

Obedient to God's command and the special fulfillment of his will, and resigned to their human condition, they [souls to whom God's good pleasure has become their own] exist oblivious to both its joys and sorrows in the fullness of God's enduring mercy. He finds these souls sunk in apathy and takes possession of their heart. Living in God in this way the heart is dead to all else and all else is dead to it. For it is God alone who gives life to all things, who quickens the soul in the creature and the creature in the soul. God's word is that life. With it the heart and the creature are one. Without it they are strangers. Without the virtue of the divine will, all creation is reduced to nothing, with it, it is brought into the realm of his kingdom where every moment is complete contentment in God alone, and a total surrender of all creatures to his order. It is the sacrament of the present moment.

— Jean-Pierre de Caussade

❖   ❖   ❖

29

Surrender and Assent

The practice of this excellent theology is so simple, so easy, and so accessible that it need only be wished for it to be had. This indifference, this love so perfect, so universal, is both active and passive, insofar as what we do through grace, and what grace accomplishes in us, requires nothing more than surrender and assent. In fact it is everything that God himself ordains and mystical theology expounds in a multitude of subtle concepts which it is often better for us not to know, since all that is required is oblivion and surrender.

It is enough, then, for us to know what we must do, and this is the easiest thing in the world. It is to love God as the mighty all in all, to rejoice in him and to fulfill our duty conscientiously and wisely. Simple souls who follow this path, so straight, so clear and so safe, have only to walk with guarded step in confidence, and all the admirable propositions of mystical theology, which involve tribulation and inward grace, are carried out, unnoticed by them, through God's will. While they think only of loving and obeying him, his will operates in a way that the more committed souls are, the more withdrawn and detached from everything in themselves, the more perfectly the work is accomplished; whereas their own opinions, searching, and cleverness can only be opposed to the way God acts in which lies all their good. He sanctifies, purifies, guides, enlightens and makes them useful to others. He makes them his apostles by ways and means that seem to point to the contrary.

— Jean-Pierre de Caussade

❖   ❖   ❖

30

Keep your eyes on what you have been given to do,
leaving God to do what He will

Everything in the present moment tends to draw us away from the path of love and passive obedience. It requires heroic courage and self-surrender to hold firmly to a simple faith and to keep singing the same tune confidently while grace itself seems to be singing a different one in another key, giving us the impression that we have been misled and are lost. But if only we have the courage to let the thunder, lightening and storm rage, and to walk unfaltering in the path of love and obedience to the duty and demands of the present moment, we are emulating Jesus himself. For we are sharing that passion during which our Savior walked with equal firmness and courage in the love of his father and in obedience to his will, submitting to treatment which seemed utterly opposed to the dignity of so holy a saint.

Jesus and Mary, on that dark night, let the storm break over them, a deluge which, in apparent opposition to God's will, harms them. They march undaunted in the path of love and obedience, keeping their eyes on what they have to do, and leaving God to do what he will. They groan under the weight of that divine action, but do not falter or stop for a single moment, believing that all will be well provided they keep on their course and leave the rest to God.

— Jean-Pierre de Caussade

❖   ❖   ❖
31

You can tell a saint
By the way he sits
And the way he stands
By the way he picks up things
And holds them in his hands.

— old saying

❖   ❖   ❖
32

And whatsoever you do, in word or in deed, do everything in the name of the Lord Jesus, giving thanks to God the Father through him.

— Col 3:17 (RSV)

❖   ❖   ❖
33

Why do we not season all our actions with the spirit of faith and charity?

Had we the power to work visible miracles, or at least to accomplish great things with ease, how zealously we should use this power, and what an honorable duty we should consider it to turn this capital to profitable advantage! With how much zeal do great artists and poets practice their art and continually produce new and more beautiful works!

If we only considered what power every good work possesses for the increase of grace and the gain of eternal happiness, we should let no moment pass without loving God, adoring Him, and praying to Him, and we should be ashamed to draw one breath without sighing to God; we should even rejoice with the Apostles to suffer something for God's sake (Cf. *Acts 5:41*). If we knew how greatly we may enhance our dignity by a single act of virtue, we should purchase the opportunity at any price. We could not bear to lose one chance out of a hundred offered to us.

No man would be so cruel as not willingly to cure a sick person, or to enrich a poor one, if he could do so by one small act of charity, or by a short prayer. But are we not much more cruel to ourselves if we refuse to augment the heavenly beauty, glory and treasures of our soul at an equally insignificant cost? Why do we not season all our actions with the spirit of faith and of charity? For we should then acquire a higher degree of grace, which is nobler than all the things of nature and greater than miracles.

– Fr. Matthias J. Scheeben

❖   ❖   ❖

34
There will be no "I shall do," and "You shall do."
These shall disappear and be replaced by "we" will do

Not your will but my Will alone should remain in you to dominate like a King in his royal palace. My spouse, this must absolutely prevail between you and Me. Otherwise, we will have to fear with the discord of an imperfect love from which dark shadows will rise over you and cause disharmony and disagreement of operation, inappropriate to the mutual nobility which absolutely must reign between Me and you, my spouse. This nobility will prevail in you if, from time to time, you will try to enter into your nothingness, that is to say, if you will attain perfect knowledge of yourself. You must not stop there, because after you have established your nothingness, I want you to disappear into Me. You must do all you can to enter into the infinite power of my Will. From It, you will derive all the graces you will need to raise you up into Me, to do everything with Me without reference to yourself.

I want that there be no "you" and "I." There will be no "I shall do," and "You shall do." These shall disappear and be replaced by "we" will do. Everything will be "ours." You, as any faithful spouse would do, will take common action with Me and guide the destiny of the world.

– Luisa Piccarreta

❖   ❖   ❖

35
I am aware of the smallest act, even when they are so small
as to be considered "nothings"

If a soul has done much, yet has not acted within my Will, then one could say that she has done nothing. I take account of everything that ends in my Will. Since it is as if my own Life were involved in the acts performed by souls in my Will, it is only to be expected that I be aware of even the smallest things. I am aware of them even when they are so small as to be considered 'nothings' because I feel the smallest act the creature does in my Will, is being done by first taking it from my Will and then acting.

— Luisa Piccarreta

❖   ❖   ❖

36

Just when I need it, a new light shines on my problems

I know that the Kingdom of God is within us. Jesus has no need of books or doctors of the Church to guide souls. He, the Doctor of doctors, can teach without words. I have never heard Him speak, but I know that He is within me. He guides and inspires me every moment of the day. Just when I need it, a new light shines on my problems. This happens not so much during my hours of prayer as when I'm busy with my daily work.

— Ste. Thérèse of Lisieux

❖   ❖   ❖

37

Set me as a seal upon your heart, and
as a seal upon your arm *(Song of Solomon 8:6)*

The heart gives life and strength to the arm by means of the blood which it sends forth; otherwise, that member would wither up. And in the same way, the contemplative life, a life of union with God, thanks to the light and the constant assistance the soul receives from this closeness to Him, gives life to our external occupations and it alone is able to impart to them at the same time a supernatural character and a real usefulness. But without contemplation, everything is sick and barren and full of imperfection.

— Jean-Bapriste Chautard O.C.S.O.

❖   ❖   ❖

38

The Blind Beggar

Bartimaeus, the blind beggar, in *Mark*, on hearing that Jesus is passing by the roadside where he is sitting, cries out to Jesus for mercy, which leads to a two-fold miracle. He sat on the side of the road, hoping for something good to happen to him, if only to receive a piece of bread. On hearing that Jesus is near, he cries out to Him for help over the remonstrances of those around him who tell him to be quiet. And despite his infirmity, he gets up to call attention to himself and when called comes directly to Jesus and tells Jesus plainly what he wants. And two great mercies are given to this beggar—his sight, and the grace to follow "the way," for his eyes were opened not only to the sensible world about him but to the Truth standing before him. How many of Bartimaeus' prayers, tears, cooperating judgments and timely actions laid the groundwork for these miracles. Would these miracles have occurred without them?

— diarist

❖ ❖ ❖

39

Each man's work will become manifest

For no other foundation can any one lay than that which is laid, which is Jesus Christ. Now if anyone builds on the foundation with gold, silver, precious stones, wood, hay, stubble—each man's work will become manifest; for the Day will disclose it, because it will be revealed with fire, and the fire will test what sort of work each one has done. If the work which any man has built on the foundation survives, he will receive a reward. If any man's work is burned up, he will suffer loss, though he himself will be saved, but only as through fire.

— I Cor 3:11-15 (RSV)

❖ ❖ ❖

40

For a work to be perfect it must be wrought not chiefly by us

Know that what man deems perfection in himself is in God's sight faulty. For all the things a man does, which he sees or feels or means or wills or remembers to have a perfect appearance, are wholly fouled and sullied unless he acknowledges them to be from God. If a work is to be perfect it must be wrought in us not chiefly by us, for God's works must be done by Him and not wrought chiefly by man.

— St. Catherine of Genoa

❖ ❖ ❖

41

The lives of the faithful, their praise, sufferings, prayer, and work, are united with those of Christ and with his total offering, and so acquire new value (CCC 1368)

In Blessed Dina's writings, Jesus helps us to see the divine "new value" which our acts can ultimately attain when they are done in us by the reigning Divine Will. Through [these] writings, Jesus invites us to unite our acts to his always and everywhere with a new and deeper understanding of what we are doing. In this way, the unity for which He prayed at the Last Supper can be fulfilled in us.

– Hugh Owen

❖   ❖   ❖

42
What is new in the recent private revelations

The doctrine that human acts achieve their true and highest dignity only when they are performed in us by Jesus—or, we might say, by the Divine Will of the Father, the Son, and the Holy Spirit—is not new… What is new in the recent private revelations is the understanding that it is possible for souls of good will to participate fully in the divine-human acts of Jesus and Mary and to allow the Divine Will to reign in all of their thoughts, words, and actions during their lives on earth.

– Hugh Owen

❖   ❖   ❖

43
It is a mark of great wisdom neither to be hasty in our actions nor stubbornly maintain our private opinions

It is a mark of great wisdom neither to be hasty in our actions nor stubbornly maintain our private opinions. It is also wisdom neither to believe everything we hear, nor to pour it immediately into another's ear. Seek counsel from one who is wise and honest and ask instruction from one you esteem; do not follow your own devices. A good life makes us wise in the eyes of God and makes us knowledgeable in many things. The humbler you are in heart and the more you submit yourself to God, the wiser will you be in everything, and greater peace will be yours.

– Imitation of Christ

❖   ❖   ❖

44
Holiness in the ordinary

When Chagall was growing up as a child in Byelorussia, this was a region where the *Hasidim* flourished, a mystical Jewish movement in which the disciple, it was said, did not visit his master to learn some mysterious new doctrine but just to see how his master tied his shoelaces. It was understood that the greatest mysteries of life could be discovered not through talk but through the simplest and most banal of daily actions.

St. Louis de Montfort said that Mary taught more by the way she stooped to pick up a straw than all the writings of the Apostles. Romano Guardini said that you should be able to recognize a Christian by the way he climbed a tree. Is Guardini referring here simply to the way a person moves, or to the way he takes up his cross? Is there a difference?

— diarist

❖   ❖   ❖
45
He must increase. I must decrease

This is true not only of us ontologically, at the level of our being, but in our operations as well. Our operations as secondary causes must lose themselves in the primary cause that moves us in the first place. Even here we must disappear as it were. That is the perfection of our movement, to be moved purely by the One who moves all things in perfect ways. Not without our freely given cooperation, to be sure, but with his inspiration intact.

— diarist

❖   ❖   ❖
46
Getting our marching orders

Paul, in speaking of Christ's appearances after the Resurrection, describes how Jesus first appeared to Cephus (Peter), and then to the twelve, and then to "the five hundred," (not mentioned elsewhere in the Gospels) and to James and the apostles, and "last of all," Paul says, "as one untimely born, he appeared also to me."

This is cause of great wonderment, as Paul goes on to say, "for I am the least of the apostles, unfit to be called an apostle, because I persecuted the Church of God."

Paul remembers the time when, as Saul, those who stoned Stephen to death laid their cloaks at his feet, their ringleader, and how he traveled about the region inciting bloody opposition to the early Church. All this he did in the belief that he was serving the God of Israel, and he would have kept doing it were it not for the fact that, one day, on the way to

Damascus to persecute the beginnings of the Church there, a voice came to him and asked, *"Saul, Saul, why do you persecute me?"*

So Paul enters into a dialogue with the Lord and, given little room to do otherwise being blind, he does what he is told. Forgiven for past crimes against Christ and his Church, Paul enters a new life and a new work, so that now he could say, "I am what I am," an apostle, "by the grace of God," and then he goes on to say, "and his grace towards me was not in vain. On the contrary, I worked harder than any of them, though it was not I, but the grace of God which is with me" *(I Cor 15:10 RSV).*

If Christ has a work for any one of us to do, must we too not believe that He will let us know, in a fitting time and manner?

Paul was on his way to do something he thought was right to do, and God said, *No, don't do that,* and then caused things to happen which changed Paul, and through him all of us, for without his epistles like those to the *Romans,* the *Corinthians,* and indeed to us all, the faith today would not be the same. Paul is a paragon of great wrongs made right. But as Paul would be the first to say, *"It was not I."* To quote the words of George Bernanos in *The Diary of a Country Priest,* echoing St. Paul, *"Everything is grace."*

— diarist

❖   ❖   ❖
47
Labor in the Lord is not in vain

Therefore, my beloved brethren, be steadfast, immovable, always abounding in the work of the Lord, knowing that in the Lord your labor is not in vain .

— I Cor 15:58 (RSV)

❖   ❖   ❖
48
Where fun gives way to folly

When a task you've once begun
Never let yourself have fun,
Be the labor great or small,
Do it yourself or not at all.

— Anonymous

❖ ❖ ❖
49
It is Jesus who works in me

I believe quite simply that it is Jesus Himself, hidden deep in my poor little heart, who works within me in a mysterious manner and inspires all my daily actions.

— *Ste. Thérèse of Lisieux*

❖ ❖ ❖
50
I can say that I am no longer attached to my own ideas or feeling

Now I can say that I am no more attached to my own ideas or feelings than I am to material possessions. If I think of something and speak about it and the other sisters like the idea, I find it quite natural that they grab it as if it belonged to them, for such a thought is the Holy Ghost's, not mine. St. Paul insists that "without the Spirit of love we cannot call God our Father." So this Spirit is at liberty to make use of me to transmit a worthwhile thought to someone else, and I have no right to consider that such a thought belongs exclusively to me.

— *Ste. Thérèse of Lisieux*

❖ ❖ ❖
51
Rising in the morning

Rising in the morning, stand as firmly as possible before God in your heart, as you offer your morning prayers; and then go to the work apportioned to you by God, without withdrawing from Him in your feelings and consciousness. In this way you will do your work with the powers of your soul and body, but in your mind and heart you will remain with God.

— *Theophan The Recluse*

❖ ❖ ❖
52
Those who work with my help will not sin (Sirach 24:22)

We may understand sin here as any act which is contrary to God's will. The act need not be ostensibly moral in nature. Adam's sin was not moral in the customary sense of the word. He did not break one of the Ten Commandments, not literally. He simply did not do what God asked.

Sin at heart is doing anything that is contrary to what God asks of us. And this can pertain, can it not, to the simplest of things. Jesus said, *"Without me you can do nothing."* This statement is not only factual but hortatory: *Without me you should not try to do anything, for what is done entirely on your own is worthless in the eyes of God who alone is the author of right action. It is worthless because without God no act has the perfection that would be proper to it if God did it with us.* Our Lord tells us, *"Be ye perfect as your heavenly Father is perfect."* Without Christ's perfection at work in us, can we do anything pleasing to the eyes of the Father? *Those who work with my help will not sin.*

— diarist

❖ ❖ ❖
53
Putting God's Work into Practice

Providence is a reality; and we must not merely conceive this reality theoretically: we must act upon it in our lives… It is not easy to express what I mean. A piece of news arrives: something has happened. The web of things and events and claims closes in around us. It—the situation—but no, it is not an "it" at all! At the deepest level of our minds we know it is a *He!*
You must not force yourself to believe this, but must merely face the facts. Listen carefully, be on the alert, and one day you will realize that He is looking at you, speaking to you, challenging you. And then you will enter into unity with Him and act out of this encounter, from this situation of being spoken to and challenged—and that is Providence! You will not be merely thinking, but acting. You will be open to God, and Providence will be present.

What does this mean? It means that Providence is not a ready-made machine but is created from the newness of the freedom of God and also from our small human freedom. Not just anywhere, but here. Not just at any time, but now. It is a mystery of the living God, and you will experience it to the extent that you surrender yourself to it, not letting it merely pass over you, but cooperating with it. You are being called. God is calling you into the weft of his providential creation. You must realize in your conscience what is at stake. You must set to work with your hands. You must use your freedom. As a living person, you must stand within the living activity of God.

— Romano Guardini

❖   ❖   ❖
54
Father and Son

I have come to understand that there are things that a son must learn about himself that can only be learned through a father, or someone functioning as a father. One of those things is the special thrill of cooperative work, experienced when a young son is invited to work alongside his father on some project and then at some point is allowed to grab hold and do some operation by himself. The boy fumbles a bit and his father reaches to steady his hand or correct an angle, and for a moment it looks like it might end in disaster. But then suddenly the work falls into place and the boy hears his father utter those magic words, "Nice going, son." The pleasure such praise arouses in a boy cannot be overstated. But more important than that, a boy's introduction into cooperative work with his father, and the experience of being trusted with a piece of that work and of being able to accomplish it, all to the music of his father's praise, takes the boy out of himself and of that world his mother had nurtured him in since his birth. A new appetite is being aroused, moving the boy to leave that world and trail after his father, hungry for more of this male affirmation. And to the extent that the father stops to satisfy this need in his son, the child quite naturally becomes his.

A mature and healthy father is thus able to guide his son into experiences of the objective world, and open him up to the satisfactions of addressing that world, of confronting its problems and solving them, however minute the scale initially. And he corrects his son too, in a way that enables the son to accept it, teaching him the need to conform to a reality outside himself, to find the right angle, apply just the right pressure, use the correct tool, face a mistake like a man and re-do the operation until it is right, and so on. In the process, the son absorbs his father's values and way of seeing things, of walking and talking, and more importantly the boy absorbs his father's self-confidence, his patience and objectivity, and learns through all this the ego-pleasure of standing on his own two feet and coping. In short he discovers the pleasures and discipline of being a man. It is not something a mother can accomplish for her son, or a wife for her husband. Thus from the hands of a father, or an older man functioning as a father, the son experiences desires and satisfactions of a kind he otherwise would not suspect existed. Without a functioning father, unaware of the manly satisfactions that await his struggle with an objective order, the boy will seek gratification elsewhere, in imagination and in extensions of that easy, intimate, accepting world where the mother's love was originally felt and cherished. In the process, the son withdraws from his father, assuaging the guilt with bitter reflections about the old man's indifference. The boy grows up a rebel, secret or overt, and the father of such a rebel becomes at worst a roadblock to be knocked aside, and at best an irrelevance, like an out-of-season window piece that no one pays attention to.

This is the story of many today. Young boys have a natural longing for a relationship with their fathers. By nature they look to him but increasingly, for whatever reason, he is not there for them, not in a way that really matters. It is not an issue of blame; many fathers today were essentially fatherless themselves. But whatever the case, the fatherless boy now looks to his mother and comes to believe that whatever it was he needed would come only from women's hands. But no woman, however loving and supportive, can ever quite make up for that father and the ineffable thrill a father confers when he tells the boy at his side, "Good work, son."

One can hear St. Joseph saying the same words to Jesus as the boy stood at his side in the family workshop and lent his small hands to some task. And is not this the same affirmation the mature Jesus received from his heavenly father that time at the river Jordan? *This is my beloved Son in whom I am well pleased.* What sort of life does a man have when this affirmation was missing in his formative years? What restless lifelong hunger does its absence give rise to?

— diarist

❖ ❖ ❖
55
Being in the Lord produces good works

I heard a voice from heaven say to me: *"Write this down: Happy now are the dead who die in the Lord!"* The Spirit added, *"Yes, they shall find rest from their labors, for their good works accompany them."*

— Rev. 14:13 (NAB)

❖   ❖   ❖
56
A well-known writer and man of the world visits his monk

In what follows, a well-known satirist writes of his visit with an aged Benedictine monk on the Isle of Wight, a monk responsible, the author says, for the salvation of his soul. In this visit the two are discussing the author's recent work as a TV writer and his frustrations and misgivings regarding his chosen and highly successful career as a satirist. In the writer's own words:

We were rounding back up to the monastery, having taken a shortcut through the garden. He was leaning heavily on my arm by now.

"Work is so important, isn't it, dear? Work works in unknown ways. If work is done well, conscientiously, joyfully, I think it has an effect far beyond what's actually made or grown or sold."

"*Laborare est orare.*" [to work is to pray]

"Very good. You do remember."

"I thought that applied only to monk work."

"I don't see why. *Laborare est orare* doesn't mean we actually mumble prayers while we work, does it? You'd drive the other chaps barmy. The work itself is prayer. Work done as well as possible. Work done for others first and yourself second. Work you are thankful for. Work you enjoy, that uplifts you. Work that celebrates existence, whether it's growing grain in the fields or using God-given skills — like yours. All this is prayer that binds us together and therefore to God. "

"My work is prayer?"

"Why is the work you have chosen less valuable than mucking out the cows?"

He nodded towards a monk who was hosing out the cattle pens.

"I guess I muck out sacred cows."

Finally, I got a real laugh!

I thought about work as prayer. Driving a truck? Logging a forest? Slinging hash? Selling cars? Teaching school? Working as a GS12, or in the IRS or the DMV, or a fire department? All this done joyfully, thankfully, unselfishly, conscientiously becomes…prayer?

Why not? Not in the pious sense of nice, polite requests floating up to a capricious Godhead; rather a force, vital and alive, part of the quotidian fabric, producing — at a depth unknown to pollsters, spin doctors, demographers, and other calibrators of human emotion — widespread outcomes throughout society? Innumerable small acts of generosity and goodwill, binding us closer, motivating us, giving us little boosts of hope and faith in each other. Changing the world, even.

Why not indeed? For a man who didn't see the everyday world as separate from the sacred. Who saw God everywhere, shining out from the down-to-earth and battered and untidy and defeated. Who was a commonsense saint, a saint of what could be done, not should be done, a practical saint, a saint of imperfection....

"How about atheists? If they work in the spirit you're describing, would that be prayer?"

"Of course. God loves atheists as much as he does believers. P-p-probably more."

"Comforting for us atheists."

"What you must ask yourself, Tony dear, is this: do you do the work you've chosen with joy and gratitude? Do you do it conscientiously? Do you do it for others first and yourself second?"

– Tony Hendra

❖   ❖   ❖

57

Martha, Martha, thou art anxious and troubled about many things (Luke 10:41)

> My son, do not busy yourself with many matters;
>   if you multiply activities you will not go unpunished,
> and if you pursue you will not overtake,
>   and by fleeing you will not escape.
>
> There is a man who works, and toils, and presses on,
>   but is so much the more in want.
> There is another who is slow and needs help,
>   who lacks strength and abounds in poverty;
> but the eyes of the Lord look upon him for his good;
>   he lifts him out of his low estate
> and raises up his head,
>   so that many are amazed at him.
>
> Good things and bad, life and death, poverty and wealth,
>   come from the Lord.
> The gift of the Lord endures for those who are godly,
>   and what he approves will have lasting success.
> There is a man who is rich through his diligence and self-denial,

and this is the reward allotted to him:
when he says, "I have found rest, and now I shall enjoy my
   goods!" he does not know how much time will pass
   until he leaves them to others and dies.
Stand by your covenant and attend to it,
   and grow old in your work.

Do not wonder at the works of a sinner,
   but trust in the Lord and keep at your toil;
for it is easy in the sight of the Lord
   to enrich a poor man quickly and suddenly.
The blessing of the Lord is the reward of the godly,
   and quickly God causes his blessings to flourish.

— Sirach 11:10-22 (RSV)

❖   ❖   ❖

58

For when I am weak, then I am strong

I know a man in Christ who fourteen years ago was caught up to the
third heaven—whether in the body or out of the body I do not know, God
knows…. He heard things that cannot be told, which man may not utter.
On behalf of this man I will boast, but on my own behalf I will not boast,
except of my weaknesses…. And to keep me from being too elated by the
abundance of revelations, a thorn was given me in the flesh, a messenger
of Satan to harass me, to keep me from being too elated. Three times I
besought the Lord about this, that it should leave me; but he said to me,
"My grace is sufficient for you, for my power is made perfect in
weakness." I will all the more gladly boast of my weaknesses, that the
power of Christ may rest upon me. For the sake of Christ, then, I am
content with weaknesses, insults, hardships, persecutions, and calamities;
for when I am weak, then I am strong.

— 2 Corinthians 12:2-10 (RSV)

❖   ❖   ❖

59

It is so manifestly his work that often I hardly know what I am writing

While I was convalescing, I began to write poetry. I held my crucifix in
my right hand so that my good Master could guide my pencil. What a
surprise! My brain was teeming with ideas; I did not have to search for

rhymes, they came spontaneously to end the lines. I was very touched by this. The ease with which I write dates from that time. Since then, but when I am alone so that it is not obvious, I never write without the One who inspires me in my hand; that is my secret, it is Jesus who is the author. And as confirmation, I can say that when in the presence of my sisters I try to put some lines together "without him," I succeed only with difficulty or not at all. At such times I need dictionaries which are hardly of any use.

Our Lord was beginning to fulfill his prediction: *You will do good by your writings.*

He takes pleasure in making me write in the seclusion of the infirmary; it is there that he favors me to a greater extent with his inspirations. It is so manifestly his work that often I hardly know what I am writing. I am impelled by a gentle and superior force and, on reading over what I have written, I have often been surprised to find I have expressed ideas that have not passed through my mind.

Subsequently, Jesus gave me to understand that he not only wanted me to be united to him in my life, but that his action in me and through me was to be deep-rooted.

— Blessed Dina Bélanger

❖　❖　❖

60

Whatever the blessed man does prospers

Happy the man who follows not the
　counsel of the wicked
Nor walks in the way of sinners,
　nor sits in the company of the insolent,
But delights in the law of the Lord
　and meditates on his law day and night.

He is like a tree
　planted near running water,
That yields its fruit in due season,
　and whose leaves never fade.
Whatever he does, prospers.

— Psalm 1 (NAB-emphasis added)

❖ ❖ ❖
61
On submitting the question of what we are to do to God

If love of obedience to God grows in me, I will first ask him, by the simple means of prayer, which is at everyone's disposal, whether it is his will that I make that journey, do that job, pay that visit, buy that object, and then I will act or not. But whatever the decision, it will be an act of obedience to God and no longer a free initiative of mine. It is clear that normally I shall hear no voice in my short prayer and I shall not be told explicitly what to do. But this is not necessary to make my action an act of obedience. In so doing, I have submitted the question to God. I have emptied myself of my own will. I have renounced deciding for myself and I have given God the chance to intervene in my life, if he so wishes. Whatever I now decide to do, based on the ordinary criteria of discernment, will be obedience to God… The will of God thus penetrates one's existence more and more, making it more precious and rendering it a "living sacrifice, holy and acceptable to God" (*Rom 12:1*).

– *Father Raniero Cantalamessa, O.F.M.*

❖ ❖ ❖
62
Who am I that I should go to Pharaoh and lead the children of Israel out of Egypt?

Moses was tending the flock of his father-in-law Jethro, the priest of Midian. Leading the flock across the desert, he came to Horeb, the mountain of God. There an angel of the Lord appeared to him in fire flaming out of a bush. As he looked on, he was surprised to see that the bush, though on fire, was not consumed. So Moses decided, "I must go over to look at this remarkable sight, and see why the bush is not burned."

When the Lord saw him coming…God called out to him from the bush, *"Moses! Moses!…Come no nearer! Remove the sandals from your feet, for the place where you stand is holy ground. I am the God of your father,"* he continued, *"the God of Abraham, the God of Isaac, the God of Jacob."…*

"The cry of the Israelites has reached me, and I have truly noted that the Egyptians are oppressing them. Come, now! I will send you to Pharaoh to lead my people, the Israelites, out of Egypt." But Moses said to God, "Who am I that I should go

to Pharaoh and lead the Israelites out of Egypt?" He answered, *"I will be with you; and this shall be your proof that it is I who have sent you: when you bring my people out of Egypt, you will worship God on this very mountain."*

— Exodus 3: 1-6, 9-12 (NAB)

❖ ❖ ❖

63

Show forth your work to your servants;
    let your glory shine on their children.
Let the favor of the Lord be upon us:
    give success to the work of our hands,
    (give success to the work of our hands).

— Psalm 89 (90):16-17 (Grail)

❖ ❖ ❖

64

Works without charity are dead

He [Jesus] then said, "Charity is the virtue that gives splendor to other virtues, and works without charity are dead."

"My eye pays no attention to works not done in the spirit of charity — they are not accessible to my Heart. Therefore, be attentive and do your works — even the smallest ones — with a spirit of charity and sacrifice that is done in Me, with Me, and for Me. I will not recognize, as mine, works that do not have the stamp of both your mortification and mine on them. As money must have the king's image imprinted on it to be accepted as genuine by the king's subjects, so too must your works have the mark of my Cross in order to be accepted by Me."

— Luisa Piccarreta

❖ ❖ ❖

65

Working in the presence of the one for whom we do the work

How can we focus on our work and at the same time on the Lord? Is there a dichotomy here, either I think about my work or I think about God? But does a wife who prepared dinner for her family not do so with her family very much on her heart? Do not the choice of ingredients and the extent of seasonings reflect her desire to please her family even as she focuses on the task at hand with all her mind? While she works, we know where her heart is.

In the *Way of the Pilgrim* we read this tale: a king calls a shoemaker into his presence and asks him to repair his boot. The shoemaker does so in the presence of the king, certainly concentrating on the work with all his powers, but never forgetting in whose presence he is, for whom this work is being done.

God sees the intention of the heart. For whose honor and glory do we do a thing? Jesus said that he who speaks on his own authority seeks his own glory, but he who seeks the glory of him who sent him is true, and in him there is no falsehood *(Jn 7:18)*. The same can be said for what a man or woman says and does, can it not; for the wife who prepares a good meal for her family, for the shoemaker who labors to please his king? Jesus tells us he does nothing on his own accord, nothing for himself, *"but only what he sees the Father doing, for whatever he does that the Son does likewise (Jn 5:19)."*

If we do what we do for God, then can it not be said to be his work, not our own, the work he has given us to do, work that he is doing in and through us, work that he will certainly prosper as he sees fit?

– diarist

❖   ❖   ❖
66

Unless a man is assisted by inner work according to the will of God, he labors in vain at what is external.

– Sts. Barsanouphios and John

❖   ❖   ❖
67

*Act and speak always with the awareness that the Lord is near
and directs everything according to His pleasure*

You tell me that you are subject to distraction. This is the first attack of the enemy which is harmful to our inner order. When you enter into communication with other people or busy yourself with secular affairs, do so in such a way that you still remember the Lord at the same time. Act and speak always with the awareness that the Lord is near and directs everything according to His pleasure. Therefore, if there is something that requires your attention, prepare yourself beforehand so that you will not be withdrawn from the Lord in the course of attending to it, but will remain in His presence all the while. You should pray to be granted this. It is certainly possible to acquire this habit; simply make it a rule from now on always to act in this way.

— *Theophan The Recluse*

❖   ❖   ❖

68

The Lord has made excellent he who is faithful to him (Psalm 4:4)

What, then, is this duty which for each one of us is the very essence of our perfection? It is twofold: a general obligation which God imposes on all mankind; and specific obligations which he prescribes for each individual. God involves each one in different circumstances in which to carry out his purpose. He binds us to his love and influences our purpose so that it may become the object of his grace, showing his mercy by asking from each one no more than he is able to give.

O you who reach after perfection and are tempted to be discouraged by what you read about the lives of the saints and what works of piety they prescribe! Who are daunted by exalted notions of perfection! It is for your consolation that God wishes me to write this. Know what you seem to be unaware of: that God in his mercy has made free everything which is necessary for human existence, such as air, water and earth. Nothing is more essential than breathing, sleeping and eating, yet nothing is more available. In accordance with God's commandment, love and faith are no less essential and common to our spiritual needs, and so the difficulties cannot be so great as we imagine.

Even in things of little consequence, God is easily satisfied by the part souls are to play in the achievement of their perfection. He himself is too explicit for us to doubt it, *"Fear God, and keep his commandments; for this is the whole duty of man" (Ecclesiastes12:13)*. Which is to say, that is all men must do for their part; it is their living faith. Let them do it, God will do the rest. Grace alone will perform the miracles passing the understanding of men, for the ear has not heard, nor the eye seen nor the heart felt what God conceives in his mind, resolves in his will and by his power performs in souls *(I Cor 2:9)*. We present this simple background, this picture so clear, these colors so evenly applied, this composition so admirable, so skillfully perfected. The hand of divine wisdom alone knows how to cover this canvas of love and obedience which souls unconsciously hold up, unquestioning and without bothering to find out what God is adding to it because, trusting and surrendering themselves to him, they are only concerned with doing their duty and think neither about themselves nor what their needs are nor how to obtain them. The more they work at their humble task, however lowly and obscure it may be outwardly, the more God adorns, embellishes and enriches it with the colors he adds. *"The Lord has made excellent he who is faithful to him" (Psalm 4:4 Vulgate).*

— *Jean-Pierre de Caussade*

❖ ❖ ❖

69
The power of God being made manifest in weakness

You remember how you were taught to write when you were small. Your mother put a pencil in your hand, took your hand in hers and began to move it. Since you did not know at all what she meant to do, you left your hand completely free in hers. This is what is meant by the power of God being manifest in weakness.

You could think of that also in terms of a sail. A sail can catch the wind and be used to maneuver a boat only because it is so frail. If instead of a sail you put a solid board, it would not work; it is the weakness of the sail that makes it sensitive to the wind. The same is true of the gauntlet and the surgical glove. How strong is the gauntlet, how frail is the glove, yet in intelligent hands it can work miracles because it is so frail. So one of the things which God continues to try to teach us is to replace the imaginary and minute amount of disturbing strength we have by this frailty of surrender, of abandonment in the hands of God.

— *Orthodox Archbishop Anthony Bloom*

❖ ❖ ❖

70
The union of works with mine is a guarantee of salvation

My daughter, the union of human works with mine is a guarantee of salvation. This is because if two people work in the same field, by working together, they will harvest. Consequently, uniting their works to mine is the same as if they had worked in my field, and as such they will reap in my Kingdom.

— *Luisa Piccarreta*

❖ ❖ ❖

71
Jesus, bless this pen so that everything…may be for the glory of God

As I took the pen in hand, I addressed a short prayer to the Holy Spirit and said: "Jesus, bless this pen so that everything You order me to write may be for the glory of God." Then I heard a voice: "Yes, I bless [it], because this writing bears the seal of obedience to your superior and confessor, and by that very fact I am already given glory, and many souls will be drawing profit from it. My daughter, I demand that you devote all your free moments to writing about My goodness and mercy. It is your office and your assignment throughout your life to continue to make known to souls that great mercy I have for them and to exhort them to trust in My bottomless mercy."

– St. Maria Faustina Kowalska

❖ ❖ ❖
72
*Always have Me present to work with you and it will be
completed with perfection*

If you had been more humble and closer to me you would not have done that work so poorly. But because you thought you could begin, continue and end the work without Me, you succeeded—despite your regret—but not according to my wish. Therefore ask my assistance at the start of everything you undertake. Always have Me present to work with you and it will be completed with perfection. Know that if you always do this, you will acquire the greatest humility. If you do the opposite, pride will reenter you and choke the seed of the beautiful virtue of humility that has been sown in you.

– Luisa Piccarreta

❖ ❖ ❖
73
He is the source of all my activity

Luis Maria Martinez became Archbishop of Mexico City on Feb. 14, 1937. In accepting this position, he wrote:

"When I accepted the archbishopric, I placed upon Our Lord a condition that he would have to do everything and that I would be his megaphone and instrument. He has complied very well; and sometimes when I see myself hurried, I recall the pact."

The task of running such a huge archdiocese was indeed burdensome... The Archbishop continually visited his parishes and administered the sacrament of confirmation, to several thousand each week on average. He was known never to refuse an invitation to preach. He was intimately involved in his seminaries, was himself a director of souls, and wrote many books, some of which remain classics (e.g., his beautiful book on the Holy Spirit, The Sanctifier, *his book on the spiritual life,* The Secrets of the Interior Life, *and the book that was his own personal favorite,* Only Jesus).

Indeed, his was a life of "world wind activity" and yet when someone suggested his office entailed hardships too great for him, particularly at a time when, in addition to everything else, the Mexican government was taking hostile measures against the Catholic Church, he demurred. 'He does not know the peace in which I live!' For I know that Jesus arranges it all, he does all for me... I feel that he is the source of all my activity: he speaks, he works in me, he preaches; he directs, he governs, he decides everything. He arranges for me even the most difficult things... This idea has dominated me: that Jesus does my work, and that I do the work of Jesus!"

— Archbp. Luis Maria Martinez

❖　❖　❖
74
What I desire is not merely your work but yourself

On New Year's Day , 1941, Mary of the Holy Trinity wrote down a list of resolutions. Among them: "[To] do one thing at a time, giving myself to it entirely — doing it as perfectly as I can."

Again, in this list of resolutions, she wrote a second time, "To do one thing at a time, with all my heart and soul."

Shortly afterwards, Our Lord told her: "Yes, work is a joy and a great dignity for man; but what I desire is not merely your work, but *yourself.* You dishonor Me when you leave Me to think only of your work."

— Sister Mary of the Holy Trinity

❖　❖　❖
75
Acquiring the interior life

I would be depriving myself of one of the most effective means of acquiring this interior life if I failed to strive after a *precise* and *certain* faith

in the active presence of Jesus within me, and if I did not try to make this presence within me not merely a living, but an *extremely vital* reality, and one which penetrated more and more into all the life of my faculties. . .
In *proportion* to the intensity of my love for God, my supernatural life may increase at *every* moment by a *new* infusion of the grace of the active presence of Jesus in me; an infusion produced...by each meritorious act (virtue, work, suffering...) [and] by the Sacraments, especially the Eucharist. It is certain that, by *every* event, person or thing, Thou, Jesus, *Thou Thyself*, dost present Thyself, objectively, to me, at *every* instant of the day. Thou dost hide Thy love beneath these appearances and dost *request my cooperation to increase Thy life in myself.*

— *Dom Jean-Baptiste Chautard O.C.S.O*

❖ ❖ ❖
76

The Holy Father, John Paul II, in a message for The World Day of Prayer for Vocations, speaks of Jesus as the Father's servant and says we are called likewise to serve the Father. The Pope concluded his message with this prayer to Mary:

Mary, humble servant of God Most High,
    the Son to whom you gave birth has made you the servant of
    humanity.
Your life was a humble and generous service.
You were servant of the Word when the angel
    announced to you the divine plan of salvation.
You were servant of the Son, giving him life
    and remaining open to his mystery.
You were servant of Redemption, standing courageously at the
    foot of the Cross, close to the Suffering Servant and the Lamb,
    who was sacrificing himself for love of us.
You were servant of the Church on the day of Pentecost
    and with your intercession you continue to generate her in every
    believer, even in these our difficult and troubled times.
Let the young people of the third millennium look
    at you, young daughter of Israel,
    who have known the agitation of a young heart
    when faced with the plan of the Eternal God.
Make them able to accept the invitation of your Son
    to give their lives wholly for the glory of God.

Make them understand that to serve God satisfies the heart,
    and that only in the service of God and of his kingdom
    do we realize ourselves in accordance with the divine plan,
    and life becomes a hymn of glory to the Most Holy Trinity.
Amen.

— Papal Message for World Day of Prayer for Vocations, 2003

❖ ❖ ❖
77
Works void of life

Mary is speaking to Luisa: You must know that what does not begin with Jesus, who is within the heart, even though they be the most beautiful external works, can never please Me, because they are void of the Life of my dear Son.

— Luisa Piccarreta

❖ ❖ ❖
78
The consequences of acting without Me

Look, there are statesmen who want to decide the fortunes of nations; but they act without Me; and where I am not, there can be no light. They have only the smoke of their passions, which greatly blind them. Therefore, no good will come from them. They will only succeed in exasperating each other, thereby producing even graver consequences. Poor nations, led by blind men who are full of self-interest! These men will go down in history as laughing stocks—only able to cause ruin and disorder. But let us withdraw. Let us leave them to their own devices, so that they will learn the consequences of acting without Me.

— Luisa Piccarreta

❖ ❖ ❖
79
I am in you to oversee your work

Jesus to Luisa: "Tell Me what you need now."
Luisa's response: "Lord, I need everything, for I have nothing."
Jesus then continued: "Very well, do not fear, for little by little we will do everything. I know how weak you are. It is from Me that you will draw strength, perseverance, and good will to execute what I have told you. I

want your work to be honest. You must keep one eye on Me, and the other on what you are doing. I want creatures to disappear from your consciousness so that, when they tell you to do something, you will do it as if the request came from Me. With your eyes fixed on Me, do not judge anyone. Do not look to see if the task is painful or disgusting, easy or difficult. You shall close your eyes to all that, and you shall open them to Me, knowing that I am in you to oversee your work."

– Luisa Piccarreta

❖   ❖   ❖
80
*Sinning is nothing else than a deviation from that rectitude which
an act ought to have*

Sinning is nothing else than a deviation from that rectitude which an act ought to have; whether we speak of sin in nature, art, or morals. That act alone, the rule of which is the very virtue of the agent, can never fall short of rectitude. Were the craftsman's hand the rule itself engraving, he could not engrave the wood otherwise than rightly; but if the rightness of engraving be judged by another rule, then the engraving may be right or faulty. Now the Divine will is the sole rule of God's act, because it is not referred to any higher end. But every created will has rectitude of act so far only as it is regulated according to the Divine will, to which the last end is to be referred as every desire of a subordinate ought to be regulated by the will of his superior; for instance, the soldier's will, according to the will of his commanding officer. Thus only in the Divine will can there be no sin; whereas there can be sin in the will of every creature; considering the condition of its nature… Such sin always comes of ignorance or error; otherwise what is evil would never be chosen as good.

– St. Thomas Aquinas

❖   ❖   ❖
81
Mary desired to subject herself to the natural order

Venerable Mary of Agreda is writing of Mary and Joseph's flight to Egypt, after the birth of Jesus, and of their labors as they journeyed, accompanied by angels yet having to struggle for everything they needed, while at the same time performing wondrous deeds of charity for others whom they met along the way:

The most prudent Virgin would not rely on miraculous assistance whenever She could provide for the daily needs by her own diligence and labor; for in these matters She desired to subject Herself to the natural order and depend upon her own efforts.

— Venerable Mary of Agreda

❖   ❖   ❖

82

Brother Lawrence: Practices Necessary to Attain the Spiritual Life

The holiest, most ordinary, and most necessary practice of the spiritual life is that of the presence of God. It is to take delight in and become accustomed to his divine company, speaking humbly and conversing lovingly with him all the time, at every moment, without rule or measure, especially in times of temptation, suffering, aridity, weariness, even infidelity and sin.

We must continually apply ourselves so that all our actions, without exception, become a kind of brief conversation with God, not in a contrived manner but coming from the purity and simplicity of our hearts. We must perform all our actions carefully and deliberately, not impulsively or hurriedly, for such would characterize a distracted mind. We must work gently and lovingly with God, asking him to accept our work, and by this continual attention to God we will crush the head of the devil and force the weapons from his hands.

During our work and other activities, even during our reading and writing, no matter how spiritual—and, I emphasize, even during our religious exercises and vocal prayers—we must stop for a moment, as often as possible, to adore God in the depths of our hearts, to savor him, even though in passing and stealthily. Since you are aware that God is present to you during your actions, that he is in the depth and center of your heart, stop your activities and even your vocal prayers, at least from time to time, to adore him within, to praise him, to ask his help, to offer him your heart, and to thank him.

 Nothing is more pleasing to God than to turn away from all creatures many times throughout the day to withdraw and adore him present within.

— Brother Lawrence

❖ ❖ ❖
83
Doing everything tranquilly

Many are the open doors, but the one of righteousness is in Christ. Blessed are they who enter therein and direct their path in holiness and righteousness, doing everything tranquilly.

— Clement of Rome

❖ ❖ ❖
84
Einstein, commenting on his achievements in science

The state of mind which enables a man to do work of this kind is akin to that of the religious worshipper or the lover; the daily effort does not originate from a deliberate intention or program, but straight from the heart.

— Albert Einstein

❖ ❖ ❖
85
If I do all that is in my power, the rest is not my business

O my Jesus, You do not give a reward for the successful performance of a work, but for the good will and the labor undertaken. Therefore, I am completely at peace, even if all my undertakings and efforts should be thwarted or should come to naught. If I do all that is in my power, the rest is not my business. And therefore the greatest storms do not disturb the depths of my peace; the will of God dwells in my conscience.

— St. Maria Faustina Kowalska

❖ ❖ ❖
86
God will not give you anything unless you work with all your strength

Complete serenity of mind is a gift of God, but this serenity is not given without our own intense effort. You will achieve nothing by your own efforts alone; yet God will not give you anything, unless you work with all your strength. This is an unbreakable law.

— Theophan The Recluse

❖   ❖   ❖

87

The Father to St. Catherine: Those who receive more should give more in return

It is only reasonable that those who receive more should give more in return, and the greater the gift, the greater the bond of indebtedness. How greatly were they indebted to me, then, since I had given them their very existence, creating them in my image and likeness! They owed me glory, but they stole it from me and took it to themselves instead. They violated the obedience I had laid on them and so became my enemies. But with humility I destroyed their pride: I stooped to take on their humanity, rescued them from their slavery to the devil, and made them free. And more than this — can you see? — through this union of the divine nature with the human, God was made human and humanity was made God....

Because they owe me so much love, if they refuse it their sin is all the greater, and my divine justice punishes them so much more severely in eternal damnation. False Christians fare much worse there than do pagans. The fire of divine justice torments them the more, burning without consuming; and in their torment they feel themselves being eaten by the worm of conscience, which eats away without eating up — for the damned for all their torment cannot cease to exist. Indeed they beg for death, but cannot have it. They cannot cease to exist. By their sin they can lose the life of grace, but not their very being.

But I have one remedy to calm my wrath: my servants who care enough to press me with their tears and bind me with the chain of their desire. You see, you have bound me with that chain [speaking to St. Catherine] — and I myself gave you that chain because I wanted to be merciful to the world. I put into my servants a hunger and longing for my honor and salvation of souls so that I might be forced by their tears to soften the fury of my divine justice.

Bring then your tears and your sweat, you and my other servants. Draw them from the fountain of my divine love and use them to wash the face of my bride. I promise you that thus her beauty will be restored. Not by the sword or by war or by violence will she regain her beauty, but through peace and through the constant and humble prayers and sweat and tears poured out by my servants with eager desire.

And so I will fulfill your desire by giving you much to suffer, and your patience will spread light into the darkness in all the world's evil. Do not be afraid: Though the world may persecute you, I am at your side and never will my providence fail you.

— The Dialogue of St.Catherine of Siena

❖   ❖   ❖

88
On working with Jesus

A spiritual director of great renown was talking with a spiritual son about recollection, about turning to Jesus while you work. At one point this individual said, "Well, I turn to Jesus in the morning, but then I go to work and I get absorbed and may not think of him again until lunch time." Whereupon the spiritual director answered, "If you have been working for three hours and haven't thought of Jesus, you've accomplished nothing."

— diarist

❖   ❖   ❖

89
One should not look at how much or how little one does,
but rather if it is something willed by God

The more a soul is united and fused with the Will of God, the more it can be said to be holy—and the more it is loved by God. Further, being loved more, so much more is it favored by Him. This is because the life of the soul is nothing other than the product of the Will of God. Moreover, if it is one single thing with Him, could he not love it? Hence one should not look at how much or how little one does, but rather if it is something willed by God. This is because God looks more at the little act, if it is done according to his Will, than the great act done without it.

— Luisa Piccarreta

❖   ❖   ❖

90
Anyone who boasts of worldly achievement is highly worldly himself

God chose what is low and despised in the world, even things that are not, to bring to nothing things that are, so that no human being might boast in the presence of God. He is the source of your life in Christ Jesus, whom God made our wisdom, our righteousness and sanctification and redemption; therefore, as it is written, "Let him who boasts, boast of the Lord."

— I Cor 1:28-31 (RSV)

Commenting on this passage, Theodore of Mopsuestia writes: "Boasting, even if it is of good works, harms the soul of the boaster. Anyone who boasts of worldly achievements is highly worldly himself."

— Pauline Commentary from the Greek Church.

❖   ❖   ❖

91

Grace is already present within us, but it will only act after man has himself acted, filling his powerlessness with its own power

The Lord sees your need and your efforts, and will give you a helping hand. He will support and establish you as a soldier, fully armed and ready to go into battle. No support can be better than His. The greatest danger lies in the soul thinking that it can find this help within itself; then it will lose everything. Evil will dominate it again, eclipsing the light that as yet flickers but weakly in the soul, and it will extinguish the small flame which is still scarcely burning. The soul should realize how powerless it is alone; therefore, expecting nothing of itself, let it fall down in humility before God, and in its own heart recognize itself to be nothing. Then grace — which is all-powerful — will, out of this nothing, create in it everything. He who in total humility puts himself in the hand of the merciful God, attracts the Lord to himself, and becomes strong in His strength.

Although expecting everything from God and nothing from ourselves, we must nevertheless force ourselves to action, exerting all our strength, so as to create something to which the divine help may come, and which the divine power may encompass. Grace is already present within us, but it will only act after man has himself acted, filling his powerlessness with its own power. Establish yourself, therefore, firmly in the humble sacrifice of your will to God, and then take action without any irresolution or half-heartedness.

— Theophan The Recluse

❖   ❖   ❖

92

Whenever thou must perform any ... work, consider beforehand ...

Since this is the most powerful means for the perfection of thy works, I wish that you write this advice into thy heart. Whenever thou must perform any interior or exterior work, consider beforehand whether what thou art going to say or do corresponds with the doings of the Lord, and whether thou hast the intention thereby to honor thy Lord and benefit thy neighbor. As soon as thou art sure that this is thy motive, execute thy understanding in union with Him and in imitation of Him; but if thou findest not this motive let the undertaking rest…

In this imitation consists the fruit of his holy teaching, in which He urges us to do what is most pleasing and acceptable to the eternal God. Moreover from this day on be mindful not to undertake any work, not to speak or even think of anything, without first asking my permission and consulting with me as thy Mother and Teacher. And as soon as I answer thee give thanks to the Lord; if I do not answer after continued inquiry, I promise and assure thee on the part of the Lord that He will, nevertheless, give thee light as to what will be according to his most perfect will. In all things, however, subject thyself to the guidance of thy spiritual director, and never forget this practice!

— Our Lady to Venerable Mary of Agreda

❖   ❖   ❖

93
Playing by the grace of God

Arthur Rubinstein's page-turner once commented that when Rubinstein's fingers touched the keys, it seemed to this man that there was an infinitesimal hesitation in the finger before it struck the key. He did not quite know what to make of this observation. But I have always understood it to mean Rubinstein hesitated in order to allow a purer impulse to arise and play the note. Such performers, it is said, play as they do by the grace of God.

— diarist

❖   ❖   ❖

94
To bear monotony, the tediousness of the same work . . . is to honor Me

To bear monotony, the tediousness of the same work coming round regularly, the absence of novelty, while keeping a joyful heart, is to honor Me — that is to conform oneself to My hidden life. To be joyous simply because I am with you, when you have no other reason for being so, that is to prove to Me that you love Me.

— Sister Mary of the Holy Trinity

❖   ❖   ❖

95

Seek not what is too difficult for you

My son, perform your work in meekness;
    then you will be loved by those whom God accepts.
The greater you are, the more you must humble yourself;
    so you will find favor in the sight of the Lord.
For great is the might of the Lord;
    he is glorified by the humble.
Seek not what is too difficult for you,
    nor investigate what is beyond your power.
Reflect upon what has been assigned to you,
    for you do not need what is hidden.
Do not meddle in what is beyond your tasks,
    for matters too great for human understanding
    have been shown you.
For their hasty judgments have led many astray,
    and wrong opinion has caused their thoughts to slip.

— *Sirach 3: 17-24 (RSV)*

❖   ❖   ❖

96

A given work must not mean more to us than the Lord who gives it

Sister Mary's superior had the sisters all working on a special present for certain benefactors of the convent. The work began to mean too much to Mary and Our Lord remonstrates with her: My little daughter, who would believe that you would pay more attention to a piece of common embroidery than to your Lord! ... You think too much about your lace and you neglect Me... Be quick in finishing that lace that fascinates you too much: is it not My Voice alone that must captivate you?

— *Sister Mary of the Hoy Trinity*

❖   ❖   ❖

97

I have made My manner of working imitable

My love does not spare you the Cross; but your love of the Cross will always increase.

Who can love Me without seeking to imitate Me? I have made Myself imitable in My human life—I have perpetuated My work in My Eucharistic life, and I have made My manner of working imitable…

To pray, to listen to Me, to bear all sufferings patiently, to keep silent so as to give place to charity… My little daughter, it is so easy to live according to My Spirit!

— Sister Mary of the Holy Trinity

❖ ❖ ❖
98
*Your works please Me in the measure in which they teach you to
know yourself and to conquer yourself*

Your works please Me in the measure in which they express your love. If you do them for the pleasure of using your talents, of turning out something good, for your own satisfaction, it is not wrong, but what do they give to your God? Your works please Me in the measure in which they teach you to know yourself and to conquer yourself. Because what have you come to the cloister to do, if it is not that interior work on yourself which makes you master of your soul, so that you may give it to Me?

— Sister Mary of the Holy Trinity

❖ ❖ ❖
99
*The pure and whole work done for God in a pure heart
merits a whole kingdom for its owner*

God is more pleased by one work, however small, done secretly, without desire that it be known, than a thousand done with the desire that people know of them. Those who work for God with purest love not only care nothing about whether others see their works, but do not even seek that God himself know of them. Such persons would not cease to render God the same services, with the same joy and purity of love, even if God were never to know of these. The pure and whole work done for God in a pure heart merits a whole kingdom for its owner.

—St. John of the Cross

❖ ❖ ❖
100
Protect yourself against distraction and…against captivation of the heart

The second snare of the enemy that prevents us from dwelling within, is the cleaving of the heart to some particular thing, and its captivation by this object. This is worse than distraction...

If your heart [has] cleaved to something, you would have had a long drawn-out struggle to shake yourself free. In that case it would have been necessary first to tear the heart away from the thing it was cleaving to, and secondly to engender a revulsion against it. Keep this in mind and protect yourself against distraction and, still more, against captivation of the heart. The remedy is one and the same—not to let the attention withdraw from the Lord and from consciousness of His presence.

— *Theophan The Recluse*

❖　❖　❖

101
This says it all

Wait for the Lord to lead, then follow in his way.

— *Psalm antiphon*

❖　❖　❖

102
I know that there is nothing better for [man] than to rejoice
and to do good in one's lifetime

What advantage has the worker from his toil? I have considered the task which God has appointed for men to be busied about. He has made everything appropriate to its time, and has put the timeless into their hearts, without men's ever discovering, from beginning to end, the work which God has done. I recognized that there is nothing better than to be glad and to do well during life. For every man, moreover, to eat and drink and enjoy the fruit of all his labor is a gift of God. I recognize that whatever God does will endure forever; there is no adding to it, or taking from it. Thus has God done that he may be revered.

— *Ecclesiastes 3:9-14(NAB)*

❖　❖　❖

103
The love and value of work in St. Joseph

Let your soul take time to meditate on the life and death of my spouse Joseph; on his anxieties, tribulations and sufferings; his flights, journeyings and privations; his dedication, renunciation and abnegation; his faith, hope, and charity; his obedience, chastity, and love. Let your heart take the time and reconsider his virtues, and it will know how to appreciate the value of this man, chosen by God to take upon himself such great tasks and arduous responsibilities. ... He was never idle, for "idleness lulls to sleep, and the sluggardly soul will go hungry" *(Prov 19:15).* He knew that work was a source of sanctification, and even though he wore out his body, he lifted up his spirit; for he did not "look to what is seen. For what is seen is transitory, but what is unseen is eternal" *(2 Cor 4:18).*

Martha over-exerted herself for the things of this world, and was obliged to hear these words from the mouth of the Lord, "Martha, Martha, you are anxious and worried about many things. There is need of only one thing. Mary has chosen the better part and it will not be taken away from her" *(Lk 10:41-42).*

I must teach you to combine work with prayer. If you do this, you will have the disposition of Martha and the spirit of Mary, and your work will rise up to God like fragrant incense offered in reparation for your sins and all the sins of men.

Joseph worked throughout his life until he fell gravely ill. Jesus worked from his early childhood, helping his father in the carpenter workshop. I too worked, and we all felt weariness of body, exhaustion and pain. Some will say, "How is it that Christ, being without sin, could experience in his body weariness, fatigue, anguish and solitude?"

Christ "took upon himself the sins of many" *(Heb 9:28).* He made pain, weariness and death his very own. And through his work He taught men the use of an efficacious means of sanctification which is within the grasp of all minds, and which consists in offering to God each morning our works, tasks, and sufferings in expiation for our own sins and those of others. If anyone does not see that work is a source of spiritual richness, it is because he is short-sighted and lacking in good sense. For he will not be able to benefit from the grace which all work, done well and in the presence of God, brings with it. Man gives in to discouragement because he has not yet learned to lift his eyes to heaven and call God Father, Friend, and Master. He does not know how to share his weariness, work and fatigue with Him. Man must learn to speak with his God and to live with Him.

May St. Joseph serve as your model in this life.

— Our Lady to Consuelo

❖   ❖   ❖

104
Let your life on earth be entirely merged in Mine

My daughter, what the soul cannot always do with her immediate acts in Me, she can supply with the attitude of her good will. Then I will be so pleased by her that I will make Myself a vigilant sentinel of her every thought, of her every word, of her every heartbeat, etc. Moreover, I will place them as retinue inside and out of Myself, looking at them with so much love as fruit of the good will of the creature.

When the soul, merging herself in Me, makes her immediate acts with Me, then I feel Myself so greatly attracted to her that I do together with her that which she does; and I change her action into Divine. I keep track of everything and reward everything. Even the smallest things, as well as a single good act of the will, do not remain unrewarded in the creature.

Thus let your life on earth be entirely merged in Mine. Do not do a single act that does not go through Me; and every time that you merge yourself in Me, I will pour into you new grace and new light. Moreover, I will make Myself a vigilant sentinel of your heart in order to keep you distant from any shadow of sin. I will guard you like my own Humanity, and I will command that the Angels form a crown for you, so that you be defended from everyone and everything.

– Luisa Piccarreta

❖   ❖   ❖

105
Repressing first impulses

The point of the whole matter consists in repressing the first impulses, and if the soul pays close attention to this everything will turn out fine. If, however, she does not, at the first unrepressed impulses the passions will break forth and shatter the Divine Fortitude which kept her so pressed in on all sides as to keep her well protected and remove those enemies that always seek to seduce her and do harm to her poor soul. If, however, as soon as she detects these impulses she enters into herself and, humbling herself repenting and laying hold of courage, applies the remedy, Divine Fortitude will once again envelop her soul…

Therefore be attentive to the first impulses, thoughts and words that might not be proper and holy, for should they escape you, however insignificant they may first appear to be, it is no longer the soul that reigns but the passions that dominate. Make it a point, therefore, to surround yourself with this Divine Fortitude. In this you will not remain alone, not even for an instant.

— Luisa Piccarreta

❖ ❖ ❖
106
It is only I who can give you order, union, joy, and true activity

When you hope for something from Me, I never refuse it; but so seldom do I receive what I hope for from you!

I hope that you will leave the passing things that engross you, to come to My Heart that waits — how few there are that do not stop by the way! And yet it is only I who can give you order, union, joy, and true activity...

My little daughter, do not stop along the way!

— Sister Mary of the Holy Trinity

Commentary: This does not mean that you should not do what you are doing. *True activity* means you should allow Me to do it with you so that it becomes Our work, not just yours. My work in you.

— A Servant of God

❖ ❖ ❖
107
Good Works Should Be Nothing But
an Overflow from the Inner Life

"Be ye therefore perfect as your Heavenly Father is perfect" *(Mt. 5:48).* With all due proportion, the way that God acts ought to be the criterion and the rule both of our interior and exterior life.

However, as we already know, it is God's nature to give, and experience teaches us that here below He spreads his benefits in profusion over all creatures and, especially, upon human beings. And so, for thousands and perhaps millions of centuries, the entire universe has been the object of this never failing prodigality, which pours it out in ceaseless gifts.

— Dom Jean-Baptise Chautard, O.C.S.O.

❖

- V -

Devotion and Virtue in Work

❖ ❖ ❖

1

Trust in the Lord with all your heart, and do not rely on your own insight. In all your ways acknowledge Him, and he will direct your paths (Proverbs 3: 5-6)

Our knowledge, artistic and productive skills in thinking and working, are perfections of our faculties, e.g., of our intelligence. But the moral virtues perfect us as human beings. In technical terms, the former are perfections *secundum quid* [in certain respects], and the later perfections *per se* [on the whole]—of our humanity. We need both sets of perfections, but it is the moral virtues, our perfection as human beings, that are the most important, and indispensable. We obtain them through grace, prayer, the sacraments, and the practice of the virtues. We all have this potentiality to grow in these moral virtues and that is what God expects of us… When we remember what we are in ourselves, we give thanks to God for His gifts, and are vigilant against the erring inclinations within us, that we may avoid acting them out.

— *Fr. Raphael Simon, O.C.S.O.*

❖ ❖ ❖

2

The special watchwords of the predestined

Another deceit has spread through the world; many imagine that they are following Christ their Master though they neither suffer affliction nor engage in any exertion or labor. They are content with avoiding boldness in committing sins, and place all their perfection in a certain prudence or hollow self-love, which prevents them from denying anything to their will and from practicing any virtues at the cost of their flesh. They would easily escape this deception if they would consider that my Son was not only the Redeemer, but their Teacher; and that He left in this world the treasures of his Redemption not only as a remedy against its eternal ruin, but as a necessary medicine for the sickness of sin in human nature. No one knew so much as my Son and Lord; no one could better understand the quality of love than the divine Lord, who was and is wisdom and charity itself; and no one was more able to fulfill all his wishes (*I John 4:16*). Nevertheless, although He well could do it, He chose not a life of softness and ease for the flesh, but one full of labors and pains; for He judged his instructions to be incomplete and insufficient to redeem man, if He failed to teach them how to overcome the demon, the flesh and their own selves. He wished to inculcate that this magnificent victory is gained by the Cross, by labors, penances, mortifications, and the acceptance of contempt: all of which are trade-marks and evidences of true love and the special watchwords of the predestined.

-Our Lady to Venerable Mary of Agreda

❖ ❖ ❖

3
Our Blessed Mother's counsel

It is evident that men do not act according to right reason, but according to the impulse of passion, excited by the senses and their objects… Do thou guard thyself against these pernicious efforts, and never resolve on anything, or govern thyself by anything that is merely sensible or arising from sensible impressions, nor pursue the advantages held out through them.

In thy actions take counsel first of all from the interior knowledge and light communicated to thee by God in order that thou mayest not go blindly forward; and He shall always grant thee sufficient guidance. Immediately seek the advice of thy superiors and teachers, if thou canst do so before making thy choice. And if thy superior or teacher is not at hand, seek counsel of others, even inferiors; for this is more secure than to follow thy own will, which may be disturbed and blinded by passion.

This is the rule to be followed specially in the exterior works, pursuing them with recollection, with secrecy, and according to the demands of circumstances and fraternal charity as they occur. In all of them it is necessary not to lose out of sight the north-star of interior light.

– Our Lady to Venerable Mary of Agreda

❖ ❖ ❖

4
The business of the world does not excuse us from prayer without ceasing

This is not a theoretical devotion [Brother Lawrence's practicing the presence of God] that can only be practiced in the cloister. Everyone must adore and love God. It is not possible to carry out these obligations without establishing a heartfelt exchange that makes us appeal to him at every moment, like children who depend on their mother's constant help. This is not difficult; it is easy and necessary for everyone. In fact, the constant prayer Saint Paul enjoins on all Christians consists of this.

Those who fail to do it do not recognize their needs or their incapacity for good. They do not know who they are nor who God is, nor our constant need of Jesus Christ. The business and dealings of the world do not excuse us from this duty. God is everywhere, and we can converse with him anywhere. Our hearts can speak to him in so many ways, and with a little love we will not find this difficult.

— *Joseph de Beaufort*, The Ways of Brother Lawrence

❖   ❖   ❖

5

It made no difference to Brother Lawrence what he did
provided he did it for God

This disposition [to want only what God wanted] left him with such great indifference to all things and in such complete freedom that it resembled the state of the blessed. He took no sides. You could detect no preference or particular inclination in him. Our natural attachments, even for the holiest places or for one's country, did not concern him. He was equally liked by those who held opposite opinions. He wanted the common good without reference to those for whom or by whom it was brought about. Citizen of heaven, nothing held him bound on earth…

He was content with any place, with any task. Brother Lawrence found God everywhere, while repairing sandals or praying with the community. He had no particular desire to go on retreat because he found in his ordinary work the same God to love and adore as can be found in the most remote desert.

His sole approach to God was to do everything for his love, and so it made no difference to him what he did, provided that he did it for God. It was God, not the thing itself, that concerned him. He knew that the more opposed to his natural inclination the work was, the more valuable was the love with which he offered it to God. The smallness of the thing in no way diminished the worth of his offering, because God who needs nothing, considers only the love accompanying our works.

— *Joseph de Beaufort*, The Ways of Brother Lawrence

❖   ❖   ❖

6

*Brother Lawrence was more intent on doing than on
thinking about what he was doing*

Those who conduct themselves in the spiritual life only according to their own inclinations and preferences, who think they have nothing more important to do than determine whether or not they have devotion, this type of person cannot be stable or be on the right path because these things continually change, either due to our own negligence or by the order of God who varies his gifts and his actions over us according to our needs.

Brother Lawrence, on the contrary, steadfast in the way of unchanging faith, was always even-tempered because all his efforts were directed exclusively to carrying our the duties of the place where God put him, considering only the virtues of his state in life as his reward. Instead of paying attention to his dispositions and examining the road he was walking, he looked only at God, at the end of the journey. Therefore he made great strides toward him by practicing justice, charity, and humility, more intent on doing than on thinking about what he was doing.

— *Joseph de Beaufort*, The Ways of Brother Lawrence

❖   ❖   ❖

7

*Whoever walks upon the way of virtue partakes of my own Life; whoever walks
upon the path of vice lives in contradiction of Me*

My Incarnation grafted humanity to the Divinity. Whoever seeks to stay united with Me, through her will, her deeds and her heart, and seeks to live her life in imitation of my Own, grows in my own Life and develops the graft that I made, thereby adding other branches to the tree of my Humanity. If, on the other hand, a soul does not unite herself with Me, then, besides not growing in Me, she will not develop the graft. Whoever chooses not to be with Me, therefore, cannot have Life; and so the graft is lost to perdition.

— *Luisa Piccarreta*

❖   ❖   ❖

8

*The soul's infused participation in the work of Creation,
Redemption and Sanctification*

My daughter, those who use their senses to offend Me, distort my image within them. Sin makes the soul dead: not that she actually died, but she becomes dead to all that is Divine.

If, instead, the soul makes use of her senses to give Me glory, then I can say, "You are my eyes, my ears, my mouth, my hands and my feet." I thereby conserve within this soul my Creative work. If, in addition to giving Me glory, the soul includes suffering, satisfaction and reparation for others, then she conserves within herself my Redemptive Work. By bringing these works of Mine to ever greater perfection in herself, the soul gives rise to my Sanctifying Work, sanctifying everything and conserving it within herself. So all that I have accomplished in Creation, in Redemption and in Sanctification, I infuse a participation of this into the soul; it is all there, if the soul corresponds to my work.

— Luisa Piccarreta

❖ ❖ ❖
9
The Work of Angels and Victim Souls

Whether or not the Angels actually succeed in their guardianship of souls, they always carry out their office and never shrink from this task that has been given to them by God. Even if, despite their care, diligence, assiduousness and continual assistance, they see souls falling into perdition, they are always there at their posts. Nor is it true that by their success or failure they give greater or lesser glory to God, because their will is always fixed upon accomplishing the work given to them.

Victim souls are human angels who must make reparation for, beseech on behalf of, and protect humanity. Whether they succeed or fail, they must not cease from their work, at least not until it is granted to them from on high.

— Luisa Piccarreta

❖ ❖ ❖
10
To enter into the Divine Will, it is enough that
a soul desire It and give up its own will

As I reflected upon the Holy Divine Will, my sweet Jesus said to me: "My daughter, you don't need paths, nor doors, nor keys to enter into my Will because my Will can be found everywhere. It flows under one's feet, to the right, to the left, over one's head—everywhere. To enter, creatures need but remove the pebble of their own will. Although it lies within my Will, their will does not participate nor enjoy its effects. It is alien to my Will because that pebble, a soul's own will, hinders the flow of my Will, just as rocks on a beach keep the ocean water from flowing everywhere.

"But if a soul removes the rock of her own will, in that very instant she flows in Me and I in her; and she finds all My goods at her disposal: power, light, assistance and everything she desires. That is why there are no special paths, nor doors, nor keys to my Will. A soul has but to desire it and all is done. My will assumes all the work, gives the soul what she lacks, and makes her expand into all the limitless boundaries of my Will.

"With virtues it is just the opposite. How many efforts are needed, how many battles, how many long paths… and when it seems that some virtue smiles on a soul, a somewhat violent passion, a temptation, a frustration or an unexpected encounter casts the soul backwards, back to the starting point, where she must start anew at the beginning of the road."

—Luisa Piccarreta

❖ ❖ ❖
11
A courageous soul does more in a day that a timid one does in a year

My daughter, timidity stifles grace and clogs the soul. A timid soul will never be good in working great things—neither for God, nor for its neighbor, nor for itself. It is as if the timid soul has its legs tied. Therefore, not being able to walk freely, it always has one eye on itself and the effort that it takes to walk. Timidity makes the eye always look down, never up.

The strength in its work doesn't derive from God but from oneself. Thus, instead of growing stronger, grace grows weaker. It happens the same as to that poor farmer who planted seeds, and, having seeded and worked his little piece of land, harvests little to nothing. Conversely, a courageous soul does more in a day that a timid one does in a year.

— Luisa Piccarreta

❖ ❖ ❖
12
Humility

Consider everyone to be better than yourself. Without this thought even a worker of miracles is far from God.

— Theophan The Recluse

❖ ❖ ❖
13

He rewarded me because I was just,
repaid me, for my hands were clean,
for I have kept the way of the Lord
and have not fallen away from my God.

. . .

He repaid me because I was just
and my hands were clean in his eyes.
You are loving with those who love you:
you show yourself perfect with the perfect.

With the sincere you show yourself sincere,
but the cunning you outdo in cunning.
For you save a humble people
but humble the eyes that are proud.

You, O Lord, are my lamp,
my God who lightens my darkness.
With you I can break through any barrier,
with my God I can scale any wall.

— Psalm 17 (18):21-30 (Grail)

❖ ❖ ❖
14
*Let no difficulty or hardship disturb thee, nor deter thee from any
virtuous exercise no matter how hard it may be*

Thou knowest well, my dearest, that thou hast been incessantly instructed and exhorted by divine enlightenment to forget the terrestrial and visible and to gird thyself with fortitude (*Prov 31:17*), to raise thyself to the imitation of me, copying in thyself, according to thy capacity, the works and virtues manifested to thee in my life. This is the very first purpose of the knowledge which thou receivest in writing this history: for thou hath in me a perfect model, and by it thou canst arrange and converse the conduct of thy life in the same manner as I arranged mine in imitation of my sweet Son. The dread with which this command to imitate me has inspired thee as being above thy strength, thou must moderate and thou must encourage thyself by the words of my most holy Son in the Gospel of St. Mathew: *"Be ye perfect as my heavenly Father is perfect"* (*Matt 5:8*). This command of the Most High imposed upon his holy Church is not impossible of fulfillment and, if his faithful children on their part dispose themselves properly, He will deny to none of them the grace of attaining this resemblance to the heavenly Father. All this my most holy Son has merited for them. But the degrading forgetfulness and neglect of men hinder them from maturing within themselves the fruits of his Redemption.

Of thee particularly I expect this perfection, and I invite thee to it by the sweet law of love which accompanies my instruction. Ponder and scrutinize, by the divine light, the obligation under which I place thee, and labor to correspond with it like a faithful and anxious child. Let no difficulty or hardship disturb thee, nor deter thee from any virtuous exercise, no matter how hard it may be. Nor be content with striving after the love of God and salvation of thyself alone. If thou wouldst be perfect in imitating me and fulfilling all that the Gospel teaches, thou must work for the salvation of other souls and the exultation of the holy name of my Son, making thyself an instrument in his powerful hands for the accomplishment of mighty works to advance his pleasure and glory.

— Our Lady to Venerable Mary of Agreda

❖   ❖   ❖

15

Gratitude is a special mark of those who are Mine

I do not waste My gifts; when a soul receives My smallest gifts with gratitude and respect, then I can confer more on her. Gratitude is a special mark of those who are Mine.

— Sister Mary of the Holy Trinity

❖   ❖   ❖

16

*The greatest difficulty in practicing virtue consists
in dying to all that is pleasurable in the senses*

I have often repeated to thee this same warning, and I shall continue to do so more often in the future; for the greatest difficulty in practicing virtue consists in dying to all that is pleasurable in the senses. Thou canst not be a fit instrument in the hands of the Lord, such as He desires thee to be, if thou dost not cleanse thy faculties even of the images of all creatures, so that they do not find entrance into thy desires. I wish it to be to thee an inexorable law that all things, except God, his angels and saints, be to thee as if they did not exist. These should be thy sole possession; on this account the Lord has opened to thee his secrets, honors thee with his familiarity and intimacy, and for this purpose also do I honor thee with mine, that thou neither live nor wish to live without the Lord.

— Our Lady to Venerable Mary of Agreda

❖ ❖ ❖

17

The works of the man who possesses God are generosity, dedication, and love;
these are the perfumes which are pleasing to the Lord

From my earliest childhood, my greatest desire was to do always the will of God; all this refined my soul and raised my spirit more and more. For sanctity does not stagnate, nor is it a flower which springs up at a set time or place. Sanctity is there where God is. He is sanctity and He was in my virginal womb in all his plenitude. The works of the man who possesses God are generosity, dedication and love; these are the perfumes which are pleasing to the Lord. In the garden of the Beloved, the flowering is increasingly luxuriant. Be grafted onto Him and the fruits will be copious. Moistened with the water of his grace, they will not lose their charm. He forms in the soul his divine beauty, and it is eternal, as God is eternal.

— Our Lady to Consuelo

❖ ❖ ❖

18

To insist on having our own way is a grave sin, which is in no way
in accord with the spirit of God

Before beginning this painful journey, I want to teach you many things. I desire and I trust that you will assimilate them well, so that you may understand how the soul which is submitted to the virtue of obedience must sometimes endure many interior torments. But even if our hearts may bleed because we must tear ourselves away from our own standard of judgment, never must our weak human nature overstep into that which is forbidden, nor must we ever circumvent that which God has ordained and that which we are obliged to carry out. To insist on having our own way is a grave sin, which is in no way in accord with the spirit of God. But to take a firm position and not to draw back, not even one bit, from that which God has commanded and ordained, is a lofty science and a most sublime gift.

— Our Lady to Consuelo

❖   ❖   ❖

19
Sublime wisdom which is not learned or studied
in the classrooms of this world

And for my part, I say to all people who have not yet learned to familiarize themselves with this holy and divine science of coming to know God, this sublime wisdom which is not learned or studied in the classrooms of this world: the chair of this most lofty science is in heaven and from there it descends into hearts, and all those who have sat down at the school of poverty, of humility and of self-renunciation, have grasped its meaning. Because, "Wisdom is a breath of the power of God, a pure emanation of the glory of the Almighty" *(Wis 7:25)*, which falls like an abundant dew upon humble souls.

— Our Lady to Consuelo

❖   ❖   ❖

20
On leading holy lives

The Jews have a saying that if Israel lived God's law perfectly for just one day, the kingdom would be restored. And though we don't think of it as often as we should, we Christians do hasten the second coming of Christ by leading holy lives.

— Magnificat (missal)

❖   ❖   ❖

21
Vow of perfection

With the grace of God and the help of Mary, my sweet Mother, I make the vow of total perfection in all its breadth, according to the light I believe I have received from Our Lord… I commit myself, then, to total perfection, under pain of sin, constantly and in everything, that is, at each moment, in my thoughts, my desires, my words, my actions, my physical movements, from the most important command to the smallest and optional and intimate detail.

Thus, I undertake not to refuse Our Lord anything, not to think of the past, not to anticipate the future and, in the present, to concern myself only with God: I leave it to Jesus and Mary to make reparation for the past, to pave the way for the future and to ensure perfection in the present. I undertake not to entertain any useless thought and not to allow myself any useless physical movement. I undertake to smile constantly at infinite and merciful Love, to look only on God and not to think voluntarily of myself, annihilated in the Most Blessed Trinity.

I consider the vow of total perfection to be a vow of love and self-abandonment, a vow of self-immolation and self-sacrifice, a vow to forget myself and to keep my attention constantly focused on God. I include in this vow the total gift of myself to the Blessed Virgin in so far as this is in every respect most pleasing to Our Lord. I make the vow of total perfection *freely, and gladly, out of love,* simply to tell God that I love him, that I count on him alone, that I trust him and that I abandon myself to his action.

I have an indescribable sense of my unworthiness: I am convinced of my nothingness; I feel weak, poor, powerless. Because of that, my confidence in Jesus is like a limitless ocean engulfing the torrent of my misery. I cast myself with faith and love into the regions of infinite Mercy. The goodness of God: that is my firm assurance and my sweet peace.

— Blessed Dina Bélanger

❖   ❖   ❖

22

Living in the Divine Will seems a hard thing to do

I understood the holiness, the beauty, and the greatness of living in the Divine Will. Then I thought to myself, "Living in It seems a hard thing to do. How can the creature possibly reach that point?" Human weakness, the often painful circumstances of life, unexpected encounters, the many problems that leave you at a loss—don't they all hold the creature back from living in this holy state that requires the greatest attention?

And my sweet Jesus, resuming his words with an unspeakable tenderness as to make my heart burst, added:

"My little daughter of my Will, my concern and my continuous longing to have the creature live in my Will are so great that when the creature and I have agreed with firm decision that he must live in my FIAT—that is My Will—the first one to make the sacrifice is Myself.

"To attain the goal of having him live in It, I place Myself at his disposal. I give him all the graces, light, love and knowledge of my Will, so that he will feel the need to live in It. When I want something and he quickly accepts to do what I want, I see to everything. And when he doesn't do It because of weakness or circumstances, not through lack of will or through negligence, I will make up for him and do what he was supposed to do. I turn over to him what I've done as though he had done it himself.

"My daughter, living in my Will is Life that I have to form—it is not virtue. And life needs motion and continual acts. If this were not so, there would no longer be life. At best, it could be a work, which does not need continual acts, but not life.

"Therefore, when because of unintentional indisposition or because of weakness the creature does not do what he should, I don't cut off the Life. I continue It. And perhaps in that same indisposition there is also my Will, which permits those weaknesses. Therefore the creature's will continues to mingle with Mine.

"And then, along with everything, I look at the agreement we entered into, the firm decision we made as opposed to any contrary decision. In view of this I continue my commitment to make up for what the creature lacks. In fact, I double the amount of graces. I surround the creature with new love and new stratagems of love, so he may become more attentive. I awaken in his heart the utter need to live in my Will. This need is for his own good, for it may make him aware of his weakness. He will then rush into the arms of my Will and beg Me to hold him close so he may always live with It."

— *Luisa Piccarreta*

❖   ❖   ❖
23
Take courage and don't be afraid

"My good daughter, take courage and don't be afraid. I won't leave you nor can l leave You. The chains of my Will link Me to you inseparably.

And then, why are you afraid that you will leave my Will? When you entered It, there was a firm and decisive act of wanting to live in It. So, too, in order for you to leave It, another firm and decisive act would be needed."

– Luisa Piccarreta

❖

- VI -

The Need for Prayer

❖ ❖ ❖
1
Learn to pray

L earn to pray; you have need of the spirit of prayer. Through prayer you attain a more exact knowledge of the divine reality. The better you get to know God, the more you love Him; and the more you love Him, the less possible it is to live without having an intimate and perfect union with Him; this is attained only through prayer. Jesus teaches you that it is not necessary to say great things; for in the presence of God there are many silences which are more eloquent than words.

As to petitions, do not be too preoccupied, for your Father knows very well what you have need of at each moment. The model of the perfect prayer is the "*Our Father*".

— Our Lady to Consuelo

❖ ❖ ❖
2
The simplicity of the Jesus Prayer

The practice of the Jesus Prayer is simple. Stand before the Lord with the attention of the heart, and call to Him: "Lord Jesus Christ, Son of God, have mercy on me!" The essential part of this is not in the words, but in faith, contrition, and self-surrender to the Lord. With these feelings one can stand before the Lord even without any words, and it will still be prayer.

— Theophan the Recluse

❖ ❖ ❖
3
When prayer becomes difficult

A penitent once came to a Russian starets complaining that his spiritual life had dried up and that he could no longer bring himself to pray. The Russian monk told him that what he had to do was to redouble his efforts at prayer. When I once recounted this exchange to my own spiritual director, a man who loved truth, he smiled and suggested another course. "At such times," he said, "reflect on the truth about yourself, on the things that you might be inclined to do, if the opportunities arose and no one was looking. Look into the hidden recesses of your nature. If the mercy and justice of God were not there to help keep you on the path of purity and truth, what dishonesty, what impurity might not you be capable of? What you would see about yourself would get you praying again. Remember, without God's grace we are lost. Pray for the grace to see that."

– diarist

❖   ❖   ❖
4
Prayer and the university

Although I would never begin an academic lecture with a prayer, because a lecture in a British university is not an act of worship, there is ultimately no separation. I would be horrified if I hadn't, even indirectly, taught my pupils to pray.

– Nicholas Lash

❖   ❖   ❖
5
The example of the Angelic Doctor

Let us follow the example of the Angelic Doctor [St. Thomas Aquinas], who never began to read or to write without seeking for God's help by prayer; and who in simplicity acknowledged that all his learning had come to him, not so much from his own study and toil, as immediately from God.

– Pope Leo XIII

❖   ❖   ❖
6
On seeing the need for prayer

Try an experiment and you will discover a number of useful things along the way. Try to find time to stay alone with yourself: shut the door and settle down in your room at a moment when you have nothing else to do. Say, "I am now with myself," and just sit with yourself. After an amazingly short time you will most likely feel bored… Why is this so? It is because we have so little to offer to our own selves for food for thought, for emotion and for life. If you watch your life carefully you will discover quite soon that we hardly ever live from within outwards; instead we respond to incitement, to excitement. In other words, we live by reflection, by reaction. Something happens and we respond, someone speaks and we answer. But when we are left without anything that stimulates us to think, speak or act, we realize that there is very little in us that will prompt us to action in any direction at all. This is really a very dramatic discovery. We are completely empty, we do not act from within ourselves but accept as our life a life which is actually fed in from outside; we are used to things happening which compel us to do other things. How seldom can we live simply by means of the depth and the richness we assume that there is within ourselves... So first of all you must learn to sit with yourself and to face boredom, drawing all the possible conclusions.

After a while this becomes worse than boredom, because we are not simply bored in a way that allows us to say, "I am an active person and am of use to my neighbor. I always do good, and for me to be in the state of suspense where I am not doing anything for anyone else is a trial." We begin to discover something else. We are bored when we try to get out of this boredom by turning inward to see if there is anything in ourselves that will put an end to it. Quite soon we discover that there is nothing, since all we have to think about we have already thought about dozens of times... We are not in the habit of doing nothing, and so it becomes worrying and can lead us to the point of anguish. If you read the Desert Fathers, who had good experience of this, or the monks who spent their lives in monasteries, you will see that there are moments when they simply ran out of their cells shouting for help, trying to meet something or someone, whatever they could find. The devil himself would have been better than this emptiness of self-contemplation. One of the spiritual writers, Theophan The Recluse, says, "Most people are like a shaving of wood which is curled round its central emptiness." If we are really honest, we must admit that this is a very apt description of the state of practically all of us.

Then we must be able to fight this anguish and to say, "No, I will stick it through, and I will come to the point where the anguish itself will prompt me to do what good will is incapable of doing." Indeed, a moment comes, a moment of despair and anguish and terror, which makes us turn even deeper inward and cry, "Lord, have mercy! I am perishing. Lord, save me!" We discover that there is nothing in us that can give life, or rather is life; that all we called life, imagined life to be, was outside and inside there was nothing.

Then we look into the abyss of nonentity and we feel that the deeper we go into it the less there will be left of us. This is a dangerous moment, this is a moment when we must hesitate.

At this point we have reached the first layer of depth where we begin to knock at a door. For on the layer where we were just resting from our neighbors before we felt bored, on the layer where we are simply bored and feel offended that we should be, on the layer on which we begin to fidget and worry, then feel slightly anguished, we have as yet no reason to cry and shout with a despair that fills all our mind, all our heart, all our will and all our body with a sense that unless God comes I am lost, there is no hope, because I know that if I emerge out of this depth I will simply be back in the realm of delusion, or reflected life, but not real life.

This is the point at which we can begin to knock at a door which is still closed, but beyond which there is hope, a hope which Bartimaeus, the blind man at the gates of Jericho, felt, out of his utmost despair, when Christ was passing.

— Orthodox Archbishop Anthony Bloom

❖ ❖ ❖
7
Contemplata aliis tradere

The work of the Dominican Order is to "give to others the fruits of contemplation." Contemplation was thought of as a bowl which when filled begins to spill over, and this overflow is the activity which contemplation gives rise to. Another image is that of a funnel, where the waters of contemplation are channeled with great force in some particular way. The notion of activity as the consequence of contemplation, and not the other way around, is profoundly Dominican and needs to be appreciated more, for surely it must be the characterizing way of any future Christian society where what we do in the external order of things has its origins in Our Lord's movements within the contemplative soul.

— diarist

❖ ❖ ❖
8
Everything you do can be a prayer

The principle of holy will means that each of you must work for the salvation of souls according to your own situation. Whatever you do in word or deed for the good of your neighbor is a real prayer. (I am assuming that you actually pray as such at the appointed time.) Apart from your prayers of obligation, however, everything you do can be a prayer, whether in itself or in the form of charity to your neighbors, because of the way you use the situation at hand... And this is why I told you that actual prayer can be one with mental prayer in many ways. For when actual prayer is done in the way I described, it is done with loving charity, and this loving charity is continual prayer.

— The Dialogue of St. Catherine of Siena

❖ ❖ ❖
9
Recollection is a gift that takes humility, grace, and prayer

Freedom from distraction is not given to the mind quickly, nor whenever we wish it. It comes when we have first humbled ourselves, and when God chooses to grant this blessing to us. This divine gift does not depend upon the length of time we pray or the number of prayers we recite. What is needed is a humble heart, the grace of Christ, and constant effort.

— Schema Monk Agapii

❖ ❖ ❖
10
In every action, word, and thought remember God and His holy will

When outward surroundings make prayer difficult, or when you have no time to pray, at such times, whatever you may be doing, strive to preserve the spirit of prayer in yourself by all possible means, remembering God and striving in every way to see Him before you with the eyes of your mind, in fear and love. Feeling His presence before you, surrender yourself to His almighty power, all-seeing and omniscient, in such a way that in every action, word, and thought you remember God and His holy will. Such, in brief, is the spirit of prayer.

— Schema Monk Agapii

❖   ❖   ❖
11
On saying grace

You say grace before meals. All right. But I say grace before the concert and the opera, and grace before the play and pantomime, and grace before…swimming, fencing, boxing, walking, playing, dancing, and grace before I dip the pen in the ink.

— *G. K. Chesterton*

❖   ❖   ❖
12

Many times, abiding in our hearts, Jesus makes us feel the need to pray.
Ah, then Jesus wants to pray and have us with Him.

If our life is to correspond to the life of Jesus, it must be in total conformity with His. Our soul must form the intention of remaining in all the Tabernacles of the world to keep Him company continuously and to provide Him with constant relief and reparation. Moreover, it is with this intention that we should perform all our actions throughout the day. The first tabernacle exists within us, in our hearts. So, we should attend closely to everything that good Jesus wants to do in us. Many times, abiding in our hearts, Jesus makes us feel the need to pray. Ah, then Jesus wants to pray and have us with Him. He becomes one with our voice, our affections, and our whole heart, so that our prayer might be one with His! To honor Jesus' prayer, we will be careful to lend Him our entire being, so that loving Jesus, becoming one with His own sacramental Host, may raise his prayer to Heaven to speak to the Father, renewing the effects of his own prayer in the world.

— *St. Annibale di Francia*

❖   ❖   ❖
13
How unnatural it is not to speak to Him

Imagine two men sharing a ship's cabin on a voyage to Australia. It would be unnatural for them not to speak to one another. But suppose one of the men was completely dependent on the other—for his food, to be dressed and undressed, to be moved about; and suppose the other cared for him with the utmost devotion; what would be said of the invalid if he never so much as spoke to his benefactor? That is exactly our position in regard to God if we do not pray. He is not only always with us on the voyage through life, but we are completely dependent upon Him for our very being and even for every breath we breathe. How unnatural it is not to speak to Him, to ask Him to help us, to express our sorrow if we offend Him, to admire His goodness, to thank Him for his benefits.

— *Canon Francis Ripley*

❖   ❖   ❖
14
Gratitude is the key that opens up the divine treasury

Let your memory be like a bell that rings continuously within you, reminding you of all that I have done and suffered for you, and of the many graces I have bestowed upon your soul. Thank Me and be grateful: gratitude is the key that opens up the divine treasury. Allow your intellect to think of nothing else, concern yourself only with God. If you do this, I will find my image within you, and I will receive the satisfaction that I cannot receive from other creatures. And this you must do continuously, because if the offense is continuous, then the satisfaction must be continuous.

— *Luisa Piccarreta*

❖   ❖   ❖
15
The Blessed Mother in prayer

The scene is Elizabeth's house at the time of Mary's visitation. Elizabeth speaks:
"Perhaps my time has come, Mary. Pray for me."
"I will support you with my prayer until your labor ends in joy…"
Elizabeth withdraws to her rooms. Mary, a capable and provident woman, gives the necessary instructions, prepares everything that may be necessary, and at the same time, She comforts Zacharias who is worried.

In the house that is sleepless that night, and where one can hear the strange voices of women called in to help, Mary is watchful like a lighthouse on a stormy night. The whole house rotates around Her, and She sees to everything, smiling sweetly. And She prays. When She is not called for this or that matter, She concentrates in prayer. She is now in the room where they always gather for their meals and to work. Zacharias is with her, and he sighs and walks up and down uneasily. They have already prayed together. Then Mary has continued to pray. Also now that the old man, being tired, has sat down on his big chair near the table, and is quiet and sleepy, She prays. And when She sees him sleeping with his head resting on his arms crossed on the table, She takes Her sandals off … making less noise than a butterfly fluttering around the room. She takes Zacharias' mantle and lays it on him so gently that he continues to sleep in the comfort of the woolen cloth that protects him from the cold air of the night that comes in, in gusts from the door, which is very often opened. Then She starts praying again, and She prays more and more intensely, kneeling down, raising Her arms, when the painful cries of Elizabeth become heart-rending.

— Maria Valtorta

What is noteworthy in this description of Mary at prayer during her visitation is the simple observation: "When She is not called for this or that matter, She concentrates in prayer." This tells us, does it not, that when circumstances warrant, acts of charity take precedence over formal prayer, though in Mary it is clear that interior recollection, a spirit of prayer, underlies them both.

— diarist

❖   ❖   ❖

16
The fruit of silence is prayer; the fruit of prayer is faith;
the fruit of faith is love…

Mother Teresa used to hand out what looked like a business card to people she met, but it wasn't a business card but a message:

"The fruit of silence is prayer; the fruit of prayer is faith; the fruit of faith is love; the fruit of love is service; the fruit of service is peace."

❖   ❖   ❖

17
Whatever you ask in prayer, believe that you have received it

Jesus speaks to the disciples' wonder at the fig tree that Jesus had cursed the day before and that now stands withered:

Have faith in God. Truly, I say to you, whoever says to this mountain, "Be taken up and cast into the sea," and does not doubt in his heart, but believes that what he says will come to pass, it will be done for him. Therefore I tell you, whatever you ask in prayer, believe that you receive it, and you will. *(Mk. 11:22b-23 RSV).*

Chrysostom's commentary on this passage: Prayer is an all-efficient panoply, a treasure undiminished, a mine never exhausted, a sky unobstructed by clouds, a haven unruffled by storm. It is the root, the mountain and the mother of a thousand blessings. It exceeds a monarch's power... I speak not of the prayer which is cold and feeble and devoid of zeal. I speak of that which proceeds from a mind outstretched, the child of a contrite spirit, the offspring of a soul converted — this is the prayer which mounts to heaven... The power of prayer has subdued the strength of fire, bridled the roar of lions, silenced anarchy, extinguished wars, appeased the elements, expelled demons, burst the chains of death, enlarged the gates of heaven, relieved diseases, averted frauds, rescued cities from destruction, stayed the sun in its course and arrested the progress of the thunderbolt. In sum, prayer has power to destroy whatever is at enmity with the good. I speak not of the prayer of the lips but of the prayer which ascends from the inmost recesses of the heart.

— Chrysostom

❖   ❖   ❖

18

Our work can be a prayer

You have heard it said: Pray like everything depends upon God, and work like everything depends upon you. But the saints will tell us that our work itself can be a prayer. How? When we work in a spirit of recollection, bringing the work we do to the Lord, both before, during and after. Work done in remembrance of his presence in company with our work. Work done for him and through him.

This is how work becomes prayer, not so much by what we say in our interior voice, often hardly feasible when we're concentrating on some task, but by how we listen with our interior ears, to what He might be saying to us in and through the task at hand. Prayer then is conversation, and the art of conversation begins with listening. Good workers are good listeners and in the measure we listen as we work, can we not believe that our work is prayer?

— diarist

❖   ❖   ❖

19

If prayer is right, everything is right

Prayer is the test of everything; prayer is also the source of everything; prayer is the driving force of everything; prayer is also the director of everything. If prayer is right, everything is right. For prayer will not allow anything to go wrong.

— Theophan The Recluse

❖   ❖   ❖

20

Having surrendered ourselves entirely to the never-sleeping care of God, we should joyfully and humbly endure the sweat and labor [of our cross]

It is said in the Gospels: *"If any man will come after me, let him deny himself, and take up his cross, and follow me"* (Matt 16:24). When we pray, then, we must first give up our own will and our own ideas, and then take up our cross, which is the labor of body and soul that is unavoidable in this spiritual quest. Having surrendered ourselves entirely to the never-sleeping care of God, we should joyfully and humbly endure the sweat and labor, for the sake of the true reward God will grant to the zealous when the right time comes. Then God, imparting His grace to us, will put an end to the wanderings of our mind and will place it—together with the remembrance of Himself—immovably within the heart…

When this inner order is established, everything in a man passes from the head into the heart. Then a kind of inner light illumines all that is within him, and whatever he does, says, or thinks, is performed with full awareness and attention. He is able to discern clearly the nature of the thoughts, intentions, and desires that come to him; he willingly submits his mind, heart and will to Christ, eagerly obeying every commandment of God and the Fathers… And God, seeing this humility, does not deprive the supplicant of His grace.

— Schema Monk Agapii

❖   ❖   ❖

21

Ante Studium: Prayer of St. Thomas, recited before he sat down to work

Ineffable Creator,
From the treasures of your wisdom, you
     have established three hierarchies of angels,
     have arrayed them in marvelous order
     above the fiery heavens,

and have marshaled the regions
　　of the universe with such artful skill.
You are proclaimed
　　the true font of light and wisdom,
　　and the true origin
　　raised high beyond all things.
Pour forth a ray of your brightness
　　into the darkened places of my mind;
disperse from my soul
　　the twofold darkness
　　into which I was born:
　　sin and ignorance.
You make eloquent the tongues of infants.
　　Refine my speech
　　and pour forth upon my lips
　　the goodness of your blessing.
Grant to me
　　keenness of mind,
　　capacity of remembering,
　　skill in learning,
　　subtlety in interpreting,
　　and eloquence in speaking.
May you
　　guide the beginning of my work,
　　direct its progress,
　　and bring it to completion.
You are true God and true Man, and you
　　live and reign, world without end.
　　　　　　　　　　　　　　　　　　Amen.

❖　❖　❖

22

Prayer of the mind in the heart

Prayer of the mind in the heart comes quickly to some people, while for
others the process is slow. Thus of three people known to me, it entered
into one as soon as he was told about it, in that same hour; to another it
came in six months' time; to a third after ten months, while in the case of

one great staretz it came only after two years. Why this happens so, God alone knows.

– Schema Monk Agapii

❖ ❖ ❖

23

How can we pray without ceasing?

Last night as I was falling asleep or perhaps during the night at some wakeful moment, I received an understanding about prayer that I had never seen before. I knew that prayer includes as a most important component the simple act of listening to God. But I had never connected the notion of prayer-as-listening to the ideal of prayer-without-ceasing, as Paul admonishes us. What I came to understand last night was this: that if we are recollected which means that if we are listening, if our attention is turned to what God wants us to do all through the day, if we are quiet in this recollected way, not even praying for guidance but simply listening for it, then could not prayer be said to be unceasing? Perhaps continual listening in deep recollection is the most perfect form of prayer. It is different from true contemplation to be sure, but I believe closely related to it—perhaps it is contemplation in the active mode, since one can be recollected in this way in the midst of great activity. And when one is so recollected, one's activity achieves a kind of rightness, just because one is listening and being instructed. Here we have the practical context in which is realized more perfectly the truism that God is the primary cause and we are but secondary causes of all the good that we do.

I do not think this recollection, this listening, is necessarily conscious. Rather it is a habit of the soul, a disposition that is simply there, like breathing (but unlike breathing, a disposition that does not come naturally but only as a gift, and perhaps typically only at the end of a long and maybe difficult spiritual journey where one has learned the lesson that the most important one to listen to is not one's self).

The essence of recollection is to do nothing without an interior listening to see if it is right or wrong to do this thing. In such a life there is apt to be a good deal of waiting, of inaction, of something that might strike others as passivity, for such a soul does not want to act out of impulse, or external constraint, or pressure, but only out of a sense of its rightness, as a consequence of some interior conviction that this action, this direction, is now called for and is right to do. And when the individual who has seemed passive now acts under this conviction, the effectiveness of the action is pronounced, its rightness is unmistakable, and much indeed is all of a sudden accomplished, oftentimes with seemingly little effort (or at least wasted effort). Such a person often feels himself or herself to be more a witness to the action rather than its perpetrator, an instrument of the action rather than its author, precisely because the action came about as a reaction, in response to something interior, something the actor himself or herself did not produce but experienced as somehow given, something that the honest person knows did not exactly come from him, all without denying the crucial secondary causality of the actor. Nor should this be seen as something extraordinary. Socrates once told (in *Crito*) how his muse instructed him to desist speaking right in the middle of a sentence. Recollected people are like that; their recollection is a state of unbroken listening to know what is right and what is wrong for them to understand, say, and do.

Many are partial to the playing of Arthur Rubinstein, and feel that there is a quality to his playing, a gracious musicality, that is rare in other pianists even of great stature. This was especially so in his later years when, as he said, he re-learned how to play. There is a remarkable observation by someone who sat beside Rubenstein at the piano in later years, serving as page-turner, an observation which might account for this extraordinary musicality. The page-turner said he felt Rubinstein's fingers somehow hesitated just before striking the note, an infinitesimal, barely discernible pause. We do not know, of course, but perhaps in each pause Rubenstein offered an impulse of his own making to one not entirely his own, that would be given in its place.

— diarist

❖ ❖ ❖

24

Ask ceaselessly, without wearying. It is My joy to answer!

Ask all of Me: ask every day, every morning what is necessary for the day, for yourself and for the human race. Ask ceaselessly, without wearying. It is My joy to answer! I always answer; but My answer is varied. You would understand it better if you knew how to live by faith.

— Sister Mary of the Holy Trinity

❖   ❖   ❖
25
Truths are inscribed in the heart by the finger of God

You write that at times, during prayer, a solution to some problem that perplexes you in your spiritual life comes of itself from an unknown source. This is good. It is the true Christian way of being taught God's truth. Here the promise is fulfilled, "And they shall be taught of God" (*John 6:45*). So indeed it is. Truths are inscribed in the heart by the finger of God, and remain there firm and indelible. Do not neglect these truths which God inscribes, but write them down.

— *Theophan The Recluse*

❖   ❖   ❖
26
Strive to be always in constant remembrance of God

The essence of the whole thing is *to be established in the remembrance of God, and to walk in his presence.* You can say to anyone: "Follow whatever methods you like—recite the Jesus Prayer, perform bows and prostrations, go to Church: do what you wish, only strive to be always in constant remembrance of God." I remember meeting a man in Kiev who said: "I did not use any methods at all, I did not know the *Jesus Prayer*, yet by God's mercy I walk always in His presence. But how this has come to pass, I myself do not know. God gave!"

— *Theophan The Recluse*

❖   ❖   ❖
27
Our prayer begins to be of value only when grace comes

Our task is the art of the Jesus Prayer [*Lord Jesus Christ, Son of God, have mercy on me, a sinner*]. We must try to perform it quite simply, with our attention in the heart, always preserving the remembrance of God. This brings by itself its own natural fruit—collectedness of mind, devoutness and fear of God, recollection of death, stillness of thought, and a certain warmth of the heart. All these are natural fruits of prayer in the heart, and are not the fruit of grace. This fact must be kept well in mind, lest we boast to ourselves and to others and become proud.

Our prayer begins to be of value only when grace comes. As long as we have only the natural fruits of prayer, what we achieve is valueless, both in itself and in the judgment of God. For the coming of grace is the sign that God has looked on us in mercy.

I cannot tell you just how this action of grace will be made manifest, but it is certain that grace cannot come before these natural fruits of inner prayer have made their appearance.

— Theophan The Recluse

❖ ❖ ❖
28
If fulfillment is sometimes delayed, this may be because the petitioner is still not yet ready to receive what he asks

The *Jesus Prayer* is like any other prayer. It is stronger than all other prayers only in virtue of the all-powerful Name of Jesus, Our Lord and Savior. But it is necessary to invoke His Name with a full and unwavering faith—with a deep certainty that He is near, sees and hears, pays whole-hearted attention to our petition, and is ready to fulfill it and to grant what we seek. There is nothing to be ashamed of in such a hope. If fulfillment is sometimes delayed, this may be because the petitioner is still not yet ready to receive what he asks.

— Theophan The Recluse

❖ ❖ ❖
29
He who prays is in touch with the FIRST cause

"Those who pray," says the eminent statesman Donosco Cortes, after his conversion, "do more for the world than those who fight, and if the world is going from bad to worse, it is because there are more battles than prayers."

"Hands uplifted," said Bossuet, "rout more battalions than hands that strike…"

He who *prays is in touch with the FIRST cause*. He acts directly upon it. And by that very fact he has his hand upon all the secondary causes, since they only receive their efficacy from this superior principle. And so the desired effect is obtained both more surely and more promptly.

— Dom Jean-Baptiste Chautard, O.S.C.O

❖   ❖   ❖

30

For He who judges your actions does not sleep or rest

You must train yourself a great deal in prayer and penance for the world has a great need of souls who pray, of spirits who are given to sacrifice, of hearts who are committed, valiant, prudent, and full of love. But from all this commitment, which on your part must be total and sincere, you must not hope for delights, congratulations, or rewards. For if you take faith for your companion, all the rest is subordinate. What is useful and necessary is to possess and love faithfully that which, thanks to faith, we know that we possess, namely, God who is loved by the will, reaffirmed by the mind, and witnessed to by actions.

You must not become too preoccupied with the tribulations, the dryness, or the dark night of the soul. All these are difficult trials through which you will all have to pass. And although they are painful because they break your spirit, you must not think that you are being abandoned by the Lord. For God dwells, though hidden, in the soul as it passes through each of these stages. You will make every effort and you will continue to struggle, with faith and trust. Work tirelessly, not only in the fullness of day, but also in the obscurity of night. Just as every worker or artisan and everyone who works should draw a just salary, you will likewise receive as a reward the wages of your work. For He who judges your actions does not sleep or rest; his Heart keeps watch, is ever attentive to your words, and scrutinizes your works.

— Our Lady to Consuelo

❖   ❖   ❖

31

He made of his work a perfect prayer

The divine Savior was moderate in everything, mortified and austere. He maintained a holy reserve. He prayed constantly, and even when He was working He made of his work a perfect prayer.

— Our Lady to Consuelo

❖   ❖   ❖

32

On the need for both contemplation and action

Just as the love of God is shown by acts of the interior life, so the love of our neighbor manifests itself by the works of the exterior life, and consequently the love of God and of our neighbor cannot be separated, and it follows that these two forms of life cannot exist without one another.

And so, as Suarez points out, there cannot be any state that is properly and normally ordered to bring us to perfection, that does not at the same time share to some extent in both action and contemplation,…

Action relies upon contemplation for its fruitfulness; and contemplation, in its turn, as soon as it has reach a certain degree of intensity, pours out upon our active works some of its overflow. And it is by contemplation that the soul goes to draw directly upon the Heart of God for the graces which it is the duty of the active life to distribute.

And so, in the soul of a saint, action and contemplation merge together in perfect harmony to give perfect unity to his life.

Man, unfortunately, too often separates what has been united by God, and consequently this perfect union [of heart and arm] is rarely found. Besides, it depends for its realization upon a number of precautions that are too often neglected. We must not undertake any thing that is beyond our strength. We must habitually, but simply, see the will of God in everything. We must never get mixed up in works that are not willed for us by God, but only when, and to the extent that, He wants to see us engaged in them…

From the very start, we must offer our work to Him, and during the course of our labors, we must often make use of holy thoughts and ardent aspiratory prayers to stir up our resolution to act only for and by Him. For the rest, no matter how much attention our work may require, we must keep ourselves always at peace, and always remain completely masters of ourselves. We must leave the successful outcome of the work entirely in the hands of God, and desire to see ourselves delivered from all care only in order that we may be, once again, alone with Jesus Christ. Such are the extremely wise counsels of the masters of the spiritual life, to those who want to reach this union.

– Dom Jean-Baptiste Chautard, O.C.S.O.

❖   ❖   ❖

33

Prayer

My sweet Love, I remain in your Heart. I am afraid to go out of it. You will keep me there; is it not true? Our heartbeats will continually touch, so that You will give me life, love, and close and inseparable union with You.

For pity's sake, I beg You, my sweet Jesus, if You see that I am about to flee from You at times, for pity's sake, let your heartbeat accelerate in mine; let your hands press me closer to your Heart; let your eyes look at me and send me darts of fire; so that feeling You, I may immediately let myself be drawn back into union with You.

For pity's sake, oh my Jesus, be on guard so that I may not get the better of You. I supplicate You to watch over me. Oh, give me a kiss, embrace me and bless me and give me your holy hands to do together with me that which I must do.

— Luisa Piccarreta

❖   ❖   ❖

34

At the work bench where he plied his trade together with Jesus, Joseph brought human work closer to the mystery of the Redemption.

— Pope John Paul II

Dear Saint Joseph, Patron of Workers, pray for us!

❖

- VII -

"Our Father"

Inspired Meditation on the Lord's Prayer
from an
Anonymous Servant of God (1960)

"Our Father"

My little children, you must understand that I am a Father who gives Himself and in giving Himself, gives everything—just as I communicate My Being to My Only Begotten Son eternally, so that even as He is true God, He has nothing in Himself but everything from Me— that is why He is the Littlest of the little. *And so I would be a Father to you, communicating Myself totally to you in My Son.* O My little children, see, then, how necessary it is for you to be so small that you are nothing in yourselves, nothing outside of Me—like My Son—*so that you may receive everything from me.*

And now little children, pray to Me, your Father, loving one another in My Son, call on Me, "Our Father Who art in Heaven," realizing now that *this is a Father who asks nothing, absolutely nothing, except that you be willing to accept everything.* And now ask this same Father to show you how much you are closed to Him, how unlike His Son you are, because you seek your peace and your happiness, not in what you receive from the Father, but in what you have in yourself. Do you understand what true holiness is? That it is having nothing except what is from the Father? That is why the poor are blessed in spirit, as Jesus Himself is Blessed; because, having nothing in themselves, everything they have is from the Father, and therefore their only will, as with My Jesus Himself, is to do the Will of the Father.

And now, as you are one with Me in My Son, look into yourselves and see where your happiness truly lies, whether it is in Me, your Father, or in yourself. For "where your treasure is, there your heart is too." See, then, where your mind loves to dwell, in what it delights, for there is your treasure. Think now of the perfect integrity of Jesus, Who said to the person who had called Him "good", "Why do you call me good? God alone is Good." Consider this tremendous jealousy to see every good in the Father. And now ask yourself, "What makes me sad? What makes me happy." That is your treasure, that is what you love, the good that makes you happy is the possession of it, the good that makes you sad in the privation of it, the loss of it.

True, you are not of the world — you do not seek money, or fame, or carnal pleasures, but ask yourself now, in Me, in Your Father — knowing how much you are loved by Me, so that there is nothing to fear — now ask yourself, when you are shown by circumstances that you do not really possess a virtue which you thought you did possess, when you feel that the powers you thought were your own, are no longer yours — you even suspect that perhaps they never were yours — when you see all these deficiencies in yourself, when My very Mercy allows you to see nothing but the misery of your soul, are you not saddened and depressed, even to the point of hopelessness? Where then, is your treasure? And your heart? But now, realizing that I have emptied you of yourself only in order to give Myself to you, cry out to Me — with your brothers and sisters — for they too are being emptied as you are being emptied — cry out with them to Me, "Our Father," "Our Father, Who art in heaven," realizing that *I am not a mere human father, that I am a Father Who would give you Himself, everything, everything that you need.* Realize how far you are from believing in the immensity of My Paternal Love, and ask Me for that realization too — because it is so very necessary for you. And now, in the light of the realization of My Love, you will understand, quietly and firmly in Me, that the reason you do not trust Me is that You do not mistrust yourself. And the reason why you do not mistrust yourself is that you do not believe in my Love for you. And therefore, you live in the thought of your own goodness, and that is why you are not open to Mine. You will say to Me, "But Father, I see nothing but misery in myself! How can You say that I live in my own goodness?" Ah! My child, do you not see that this is the complaint of the "poor proud man," the man who is attached to the wealth he does not have? For if you are prevented by your misery and lack of virtue from coming to Me, from Whom you know that you must receive everything, what does that show if it is not a desire to take repose in your own virtue? The mere fact that you cannot succeed in doing so is only the work of My Mercy in you, which keeps you poor.

And now realize too, that if you are saddened by the lack of these created goods, these virtues you would possess, are you not gladdened in the possession of them? And now, see too, is not your soul closed to Me by such desires—even as you try to convince yourself that you want these things only to please Me? See, then, how far you are from My Son, from the Holiness of My Son Who has nothing of Himself and everything from Me! But do not see this in order to make yourself the more miserable, but know, in My Paternal Heart, that I want you to see this, not to reject you, but only to make your soul the more open to My Love, that I want only to be able to give Myself to you ALL! *No! Do not let yourself be grieved by the realization of this hardness of your heart. For to understand how hard your heart is, is a grace, a great grace that I give you, the grace to see what you truly are outside of Me.* But now, seeing your stony heart, only ask Me, and I will give you a heart of flesh, a heart which will rejoice only in My Goodness. This is the asking that delights My Heart, a turning to Me in the knowledge of your own misery; this is a crying out to Me in the Spirit of My Truth. "And the publican, standing afar off, would not so much as lift up his eyes towards heaven; but struck his breast, saying, 'O God, be merciful to me, a sinner'."

Turn away, therefore, little children, from the illusion of anything good you could do of yourselves without Me, O little brothers and sisters of My Jesus, My Children, and now call on Me realizing that I am truly your Father in heaven, that I ask nothing, absolutely nothing of you, only that you call on Me in truth, in the Spirit of My Son who is Truth.

And now I will teach you the reason why you are so concerned with your own goodness and power. Little children, it is not primarily because you are proud. When you think that way, you are only pushing yourself deeper into the same error, for then you will begin to be concerned how you may overcome this pride, how you can make yourself acceptable to Me. My little children, it is not because you are proud, it is because you do not understand My Goodness—"Father forgive them, for they know not what they do." "You know not." Therefore, now beg My Spirit of Truth to enlighten you, My children, to teach you that all goodness is in Me, and from Me, in My Son, so that, in the knowledge of your weakness, you may come to Me, and not seek comfort in your own perverse thoughts.

See, My little children, how much you are preoccupied with yourselves, because you do not understand My Goodness, because you do not understand that I am a Father Who would give you everything, Whose one desire is to give you everything Myself, that I would be a Father to you as I am the Father of My Jesus, that I would delight in what comes from Me. As you realize this more and more, you will turn in horror from your own self-sufficiency, you will delight in your utter poverty—because then you will know that only in your poverty can you cry out to Me with perfect joy, "Our Father, Who art in Heaven."

"Who Art in Heaven"

Where is this heaven, My children? Where do I exist? I exist in My Son; for Me to be is to be the Father of My Son, as His Being is to be My Son, as together We Breathe forth the Kiss of the Holy Spirit. Therefore I have no being in Myself alone—My Being is to be in My Son in the Love of Our Spirit. Thus when you say "Our Father Who art in heaven," you must understand this "heaven" to be My Son as we are United in Our Holy Spirit, you must understand that I am a Father whose Being is to be in My Son, and He in Me—as My Son Himself has told you: "My Father is in Me, and I am in My Father." I am your Father in Heaven, then, as I am the Father of My Only Begotten One, of the Word, now made Flesh, Who is your Lord, Jesus.

When you understand this exaltation of My Paternity, a Paternity which is in the very Godhead, you will have a better notion of the tremendous dignity to which you were raised when My Son taught you to pray "Our Father Who art in Heaven." For He was doing nothing less than making it known to you that His Father, Myself, am your Father, that as I am in Him, so am I in you. "The kingdom of heaven is within you." And thus when you say "Our Father Who Art in heaven," you are calling on your Father Who is the Father of the Only Begotten Son, of the Word, of the Word made Flesh. Then you will see how great your daring is that, by the bond of Our Love, you dare to say (as the priest sings in the Mass) "Our Father, Who art in heaven," you dare to call this Father Who is the Father of the Son co-eternal with Himself, the Father of your Lord and your God, "Our Father."

And this explains that other meaning of "heaven"—for if I, the very Father of a divine Son, am likewise your Father, I must be in you as I am in My Firstborn. That is why My Firstborn has Himself told you that "the kingdom of heaven is within you." In other words, the Kingdom of heaven is within you as I, Your Father, am within you. For if I were not within you, I would not be a Father to you as I am a Father to Jesus. And that is the difference between human and divine paternity. For although you are, in a sense, in your human father too, and he in you, by a family similitude of nature, and by bonds of human affection, yet your human father is not in you as I am in you. For I am in you as you are mystically one with Me. I am in you as I am in the Son, and as you are in that same Son. And as I am in you, so you are in Me—as you are one with Jesus Who is One with Me, His Father, and your Father.

And what is a father? A father is one who communicates his own nature to his child. But there are degrees of perfection in this paternity, according as the likeness communicated is itself more or less perfect. And proportioned to the perfection of the likeness communicated is the permanence of the indwelling. And thus it is that because I communicate Myself perfectly to My Son, My Son is in Me, and I am in Him as He has told you. Indeed it is impossible that I should not be in Him, and He in Me, since We are One identical Substance. And that is why, since you are One Mystical Body with My Son, One Mystical Substance with Him, it is impossible for you not to be in Me Who am the Father of that Son, or for Me not to be in you who are one with Him. For in My Son I communicate My very Nature and Substance to you, as far as a creature can receive It— and what you can receive, what you can receive of My Nature, is incomparably beyond what you can conceive—even as the consummation and reward of the life which I communicate to you is, as My Paul has told you, beyond your conceiving.

For as St. Thomas teaches, nature is the principle or source of operation in a thing, so that, if I communicate My Nature, *I give you the power of operating as I operate.* And how do I operate? Since God is a Spiritual Substance, I have only the two spiritual operations, of knowing and loving. And therefore, just as I know Myself, in My Son, so you will know Me in Him, in My Word; and as We love One Another in Our Holy Spirit, so you will love Us in Our Spirit. For this is the distinction between God and all created spiritual substances, that in God there is no distinction between the concept by which He knows Himself and the Self that He knows. In God, to know and to be are the One Identical Thing.

You are aware in yourself of acts of knowing and loving — but you know that, for you, to be is one thing, to know or to love is something else. For you realize that you are the same person before you think, while you are thinking and after you have thought; and likewise for loving. But for God there is no distinction between to be, to know and to love. That is why whatever God does is eternal. And thus what I give you in communicating My Nature to you is this, that you have within yourself the germ of knowing Me in My Son, of loving Me in My Spirit, My Son and My Spirit being the very same God Whom you know and love in knowing and loving Me.

But even in this life the operation of the nature I have communicated to you is substantially My operation. That is why Paul teaches you that "faith is the substance of things to be hoped for." For you hope for the eternal possession of Myself, the vision of Me in My Son. But by faith you are already united with Me in My Son, you already see Me, true, "darkly, as in a mirror," yet substantially — for what you know of Me now in My Son, will be verified perfectly in the next life. It is true that now you do not see Me in Myself, you do not see Me in My Son — that is why St. Paul compares your present knowledge to a mirror, because in a mirror you see, not the object in itself, but in an image. Yet the two are in a way one, since what you see in the image, you recognize in the object when you see it, so that it is as though you saw the object. For by faith you know things of Us that only We Ourselves know, that no other being, no creature, not even the highest of the Angels, could know by his natural knowledge.

But even more, through love, the supernatural love which is in Our Spirit, you become progressively more and more assimilated to Our Being in the Unity of that Spirit. For "God is Love," and the reflection of Our Love for One Another is in your love of one another. "God is Love," and the actuality of love is union; and therefore, you belong to Me in the measure of your union with one another in My Son. And it is in the measure of this union with one another in My Son that you will realize the mysterious depths of tenderness which is My love of you. Loving one another in My Son, you will cry out to Me with the tenderness of My Own Love of you, a tenderness which is now yours, the tenderness of My Love for My Son and of His Love for Me, so that, loving one another in

My Son, loving one another as I love My Son, you will cry out to Me, in My Son, "Our Father Who art in Heaven." Heavenly Father, now Our Father, Father of the Word made Flesh, now in Him become Our Father, "Hallowed be Thy Name!"

"Hallowed be Thy Name"

My dear children, this is how you know My Love of you, in your desire that My Name be sanctified in you. For knowing that you are My very Own children, in the knowledge of this, knowing how very much I love you, do you not feel within yourselves an overwhelming desire to be conformed to Me perfectly in My Son? Now that you understand how you are one with Me in Jesus, My Son, do you not begin to see how far, in yourselves, you are from Jesus, the Holy One? Do you not sense, in the very joy of your sublime elevation in Him, from what depths you have been raised? Even now, even as you are united with Me in Jesus, and as you cry out to Me, "Our Father Who art in heaven," does not this very intimacy with Me cause you to feel how very far I am from being sanctified in you?

For when you do not know that you are supported by My Infinite Love, you do not dare to look and see how miserable you are in yourself—if you did, you would sink into utter despair. But now, held up by the Power of My Merciful Love, there arises in you an irresistible desire to remove everything in yourself that closes you, however little, to Me. Now there is nothing to fear in Me—"His left hand is under my head, and his right hand shall embrace me"—and because you do not fear Me you begin to fear yourself, you begin to see the horror and misery of your own soul. Knowing that I give Myself to you, blind, so to speak, to all your wretchedness, you desire to give yourself to Me—for all true love is a giving of self. And then you ask, from the depths of your souls, that My Name be sanctified in you. That is the expression of your desire, in Me, to give yourself totally to Me, the desire that whatever impedes My Gift of Myself to you might be removed: "Our Father Who art in Heaven, hallowed be Thy Name."

But why "Hallowed be Thy Name?" My dearest child, do you know what My Name is? The name of anything, as the philosophers teach, is a kind of sign enabling one to understand what the thing is. And therefore, to Jesus alone and preeminently belongs this title, that He is My Name, the very Name of the Father, since He alone makes Me known adequately—as He says of Himself in this regard: "No one knows the Father but the Son, and those to whom the Son reveals Him."

But it is to you, My children, that Jesus has revealed Me, so that now you know Me through My Word. But not merely through Him, but in Him. For that is the difference between a human word, or name, and My Word. For a human word is a sensible sign, itself standing for a human concept or idea, through which it signifies what a thing is. But this, My Word, now made Flesh, that is, made (as a human word) into a sensible sign—for whatever I do for you, I do conforming it to the needs of the nature I have given you—My Word, then, now made Flesh, signifies What I am, not by a mere human concept (it would be impossible to signify the divine Essence by a human idea) but by the Concept Who is My very Word, eternally generated by Me, My Perfect Likeness, Himself true God. And then you know Me in Him, not through the medium of your created concept; you know Me in My Son as He Himself knows Me, as coming out of Me and Being One Nature and Substance with Me. So that you too, when you say to Me, "Our Father Who art in heaven," you too come out of Me, that very same Father. For I communicate My very Substance to you mystically as you are mystically One with My Only Begotten Son.

And thus you know Me, your Father, not as you know other things by a merely human concept or idea, but in Him—as the priest says at the minor elevation of the Mass, *"per ipsum, et cum ipso, et in ipso,"* through Jesus, and with Jesus and in Jesus, *"est tibi Deo Patri Omnipotenti"*—be unto Thee, O God the Father Almighty—that is to say, the offering is made to Me, the Father, not only by virtue of Jesus, and together with Him, but as you are in Him, as you are one in Him. For note carefully that this prayer goes on to say *"in unitate Spiritus Sancti, omnis honor et gloria"*—that is to say, as you are united with My Son in that same Spirit of Love in Whom He and I are united, you offer up to Me, the Father, all honor and glory. For Jesus alone, in Himself, honors Me, and likewise He glorifies Me, as He has told you. For only He Who knows Me glorifies Me, and honors Me. And thus it is that you, My children, honor and glorify Me, not in your own understanding, however elevated, but in My Son, My Word, the very Living Concept of Me, The Father, the Concept of your God Who is Himself very God. Do you see, then, My Children, how you are really and truly My children to whom I communicate Myself as to My Only Begotten One, and do you see, even as you see this, this further truth, that it is only in My Son, My Word, only in Jesus that I give Myself to you—so that you are, mystically, One Generation? And thus it is that, knowing Me in Jesus, you know that you are not conformed to Me in yourselves as He is conformed to Me. For He is My Son by an eternal Generation, so that there is no comparison of any creature, however exalted, to this Son, "being made so much better than the angels as He hath inherited a more excellent name than they." So it is, as Paul says too, that you are co-heirs with My Son; but yet there is only One Son of the Father, His Only Begotten One. And so it is too, that, knowing your lowliness as you are in My Son, and how far in yourselves you are from manifesting My Essence, from being My very Name, you are moved to cry out in your very joy, a joy which is one with the spirit of filial fear, "Hallowed be Thy Name!" let Thy Name be sanctified, Let Thy Name which is ourselves as we are one with Thy Son, become perfect in us, so that we too, in Jesus, and with Him and Through Him, may be the perfect manifestation of Yourself, Our Father in heaven.

"Sanctificetur Nomen Tuum!" In Jesus Your Name is Sanctified as it must become sanctified, so that the Holiness, the Goodness, the Purity of Our Father may be perfectly known outside Himself, in us, His children. Our Father! That Your Name may be sanctified in us, that we may become, in Your Son, the perfect image of Your Holiness! Our Father! we are Your children, Your Name, in Your Son. Make us, Your Name, Holy.

"Thy Kingdom come"

And now your very desire that My Name, Your Father's Name, be sanctified, is, as I have shown you, a desire for your perfect unity in My Son, Who is at once the Head of Your Mystical Body and your King. And so, in desiring that you be sanctified in Him, you are desiring the perfection of His Kingdom, a Kingdom in which both the Ruler and the ruled are perfect, the Ruler because He is true God as well as true man, the ruled because they are perfectly conformed to their perfect Ruler—not merely as in a human kingdom, but as having mystically, one Nature with their Ruler.

For in any human kingdom, in any merely human states the perfection of the whole, as a whole, the common good, is not anything more than a kind of activity in which the ruled act in conformity with their just ruler, but in this heavenly kingdom, heavenly even as it is still on earth, because it is not of this world, in this Mystical City of Jerusalem which is the very Body of its Ruler and Head, the end and purpose, the common good, is not merely a kind of moral conformity of the subjects to their ruler—the perfect activity and operation of this Kingdom does not consist in this merely, that the subjects act as their ruler commands. *No! The common good of this Kingdom which is the Mystical Body of Christ, is nothing less than the activity of this same Christ in His members. For Jesus is in truth your King, and He rules over you as He acts in you, being One with you.*

And now you can see this the more clearly in the wonderful effect of the Holy Eucharist. For just as, in the natural order, the subjects of a good king are nourished, so to speak, by the just laws he gives them, so that they are assimilated, spiritually, to his wisdom in a certain way, yet not to his very substance; so in this heavenly kingdom your King gives you, not merely the just decrees which proceed from His Wisdom, but My Son gives you His very Wisdom, which is Himself. For in God there is no distinction between His Wisdom and His Substance. And thus, as you are nurtured by My Jesus, Your King, nurtured by His very Substance, so you are assimilated to His very Substance and Wisdom.

Loving Me, then, as your Father, and realizing that as you are one with My Son, you, like him, have become My Name, you realize in the contemplation of this very truth that My Name is not sanctified in you as it should be. Then you ask Me that My Name in you might become sanctified. And then it becomes clear too how this sanctification of My Name in you is the coming of My Kingdom, in your mystical oneness with My Son, your Ruler, in the realization of that supernatural common good which is the perfect and unimpeded activity which is perfect in them because their being in Him is perfect. *As you are perfectly one with Him, you act as He acts—even as He does My Will perfectly because He is One Being with Me.*

And now observe this too, that as you are one with My Son, so you are one each with the other, together with Jesus as He is One with Me. Do you see, then, how everything in the prayer My Son has taught you is contained in its first two words—"Our Father!" For it is as you are together when you call on Me that My Jesus acts perfectly in you, and this is expressed when You say, not merely "Father" but "Our Father." *And as Jesus acts perfectly in you, My Name is sanctified in you, and My Kingdom has come because you are perfectly subject to your King, having become One Mysti-*

cal Substance with Him. And now your loving cry, "Our Father!" is heard by Me as you are lost, each in the other in Jesus, My Son. And this same cry, "Our Father," expresses your longing for your perfection, your perfection in Jesus, a longing for the very thing He longed for when He instituted the Holy Eucharist, the consummation of His Life and Priesthood, the longing to be One in Him as He is One in Me.

"Thy Will be done, on earth as it is in Heaven!"

My little Children, now you can see and understand the great lesson I would teach you, how to ascend from the multiplicity of created things to My Simplicity. For is it not clear already, without my having to tell you, that this petition, "Thy will be done, on earth as it is in heaven!" is contained in what has preceded? For the very meaning of My Kingdom in you is that you are ruled perfectly by My Son, and therefore My Will is done in you as it is in Him, that is, in Heaven, because you are one with My Son. It is true that according to the natural human mode of knowing and understanding, these are distinct petitions, and that is why My Son taught you to pray in a multiplicity which conforms to your nature. But, just as I am pleased when My philosophers and theologians, beginning with the multiplicity of the creatures which I have given them as the means to come to Me, bring everything back to Me, Your Father—so that the multiplicity of My creation becomes the means of adoring My Simplicity with My Son and through Him in our Holy Spirit; so I would have you understand this prayer My Son has taught you, to understand it in such a way that you see and love everything in it, in Me, and not as each of you is alone and isolated, but as you are united, each to the other even as My Son and I are united in the Holy Spirit. And thus you are now able to call Me, "Our Father" realizing that in this, in the very Beginning of this prayer in Me, everything else is contained, just as in Our Life, the Life of the Blessed Trinity, everything proceeds from Me, the Father, and as the whole created universe proceeds from Our Divinity and is pre-contained in Our Perfection. So it is I would have you meditate on the Our Father, in such a way, that is, that you may be brought more and more to the realization of all Goodness in Me, *of My Principality*, so that, like My Son, you will delight in My Goodness as your All, and so that I, then, will delight in you, because I will see nothing in you but My Image, that is to say, My Son.

"Give us this day our daily bread!"

A nd now, if you will consider this prayer as a whole, you will see, quite easily, that its second part, beginning with the present petition, is concerned with the means by which the end, the coming of My Kingdom for which you have been praying in the first part, is to be brought about. For the end is, as I have explained, the perfect conformity of all My children to My Jesus and, in Him, to Me, and this not merely as something potential, something which is able to operate but is not actually operating, but *in the actuality of the operation*—just as We, your God, are not merely able to operate perfectly, but Our very Ability is the Actuality of Our Act and Actuality. For in God there is no becoming, only Being. And that is why the former petitions, concerning the end are consummated with the petitions, "Thy kingdom come, Thy will be done!" because *the end and perfection which you desire in Me is the actuality of doing everything as I would have you do it*—just as the philosophers teach that the common good is not merely a state of potentiality, but a perfect operation, a perfect actuality. For as God is perfect Actuality, so the end of each thing, which imitates the Perfection of God, consists, not in the ability to act, but in the actual operation, in the actuality which participates in Our Infinite Actuality, in the measure to which it is given to each creature to imitate Us.

So now knowing My Goodness and My Love of You, a Love that seeks only to give you all that you need to do My Will. what is more natural than that you should ask Me, Your Father, for all that you need to bring about My Kingdom on earth? And is it not true that these petitions for what you need to do My Will are already pre-contained in those first two words you cried out to Me, "Our Father!"? If I am a Father, your Father, and such a Father, a Father Who is in Heaven, can I refuse My Children what they need to do My Will? "If some son among you should ask his father for bread, will he hand him a stone? Or if he asks for a fish, will he hand him a serpent? If, then, you, evil as you are, know how to give good things to your children how much more will your Father in heaven give good things to those who ask Him?"

Do you begin to see, then, how this whole prayer is an unfolding of My Paternal Heart, of My Benevolence to you? Do you see how it expresses the infinitely tender Love and Appreciation of My First Born for Me, as well as His solicitude for you? It is thus that you are moved to ask Me for what you need by this tender, childlike realization of Who I am and of what I want. For now like My Jesus, and in Him, you seek no good outside of Me. With Him, now, all that you have is from the Father, and so you ask Me, not for what, in yourselves, you want, but for what I want in you.

But though you are My Children, you are human, and you live in time, and so your needs, like your being, are likewise in time. And time is past, present and future. And thus, if you will examine the three petitions, "give us our daily bread," "forgive us our trespasses," and "lead us not into temptation," you will see that the "daily bread" is for the present, forgiveness is for the past, and the avoidance of temptation and deliverance from evil relate to the future—so that in these three petitions you ask for all that you need, in the order of time, to bring about My Kingdom.

But now notice that the very first of these petitions relates to the present, not to the past, even though it is true that the past precedes the present in the order of time. The reason for this is that the Life of Your God, the Life of Our Blessed Trinity, is an eternal Life, a Life in which there is neither before nor after—that is why My Son did not say to the Pharisees, "Before Abraham was, I was," but "Before Abraham was, I Am." And so, My children, as Our Life is an Eternal Present, I want your life together with one another in My Son and Me, to be only in the present. For it is only by living in the present that you can live in Us. For you will notice, if you stop to observe it, that as soon as your mind moves to the past and to the future—it can hardly do one without the other—you leave the infallible Security of My Providence for you, and then you are all preoccupied with taking care of yourselves.

That is why My Son reminded you again and again not to be solicitous about providing for yourselves what you shall eat and what you shall wear. That is why He asked you to consider flowers and the brute animals, beings who are without reason. For being without reason, they cannot be tempted to be excessively concerned with taking care of themselves. But men, having reason, are moved by nature itself to take care of themselves, to provide for themselves, which in itself is a good. But possessing not only a rational nature, but a fallen nature as well, they are inclined to an excessive solicitude about the future, so that they are irrational in their use of reason—irrational because they do not trust Me, their Father, to provide everything they need, even to seeing that they make a right use of the reason I have given them. For, like Martha, all My children, with the exception of My Son and His Mother, are excessively solicitous about many things. For multiplicity is the domain of human reason, the multiplicity of past, present and future, too, so that anxiety always accompanies the human providence which is not in My Providence, and which, therefore, moving in time, is forever remorseful about the past and worried about the future—and therefore never living in the present, in the Eternal Present of Our Love and Providence for you.

And now, you can see why the first of these petitions should be in the present—because the temporal things here are ordered by Our Eternity, not by the order of human prudence. And so, as this whole prayer is contained in its first petition, "Our Father!" so the last two of these three petitions are pre-contained in the first, "Give us this day our daily bread!" For notice, in this petition you ask not only in the present, "Give us this day," but you ask for the present, "our daily bread." In the present, in Me, you desire only what I provide for you now, knowing that not only am I your Father, but that I am an Eternal Father, Who knows better than yourself, infinitely better, what you need. And in the spirit of filial fear, the fear of your own proud providence, you desire and ask for only what you need now, realizing that you must live by every word that comes out of My Mouth, that is, by what I give you now; and loving Me in what I give you now, grateful for it because you know that what I give comes only from My Infinite Love of you and from My Infinite Wisdom. "Give us this day our daily bread!" Give us the substance that nourishes us, our bodies by material bread, our minds by the light to know and to seek all goodness in You, Our Father, give us the Body, the Blood, the Soul and Divinity of Your Son in the Holy Eucharist, that by this Bread we may each day be conformed more perfectly to You in Him, loving one another as we are One in Him!

My Little Children, do you see now the meaning and depth of this petition, "Give us this day our daily bread!"? Give us this, Our Father in Heaven, the things we need to become perfectly conformed to You in Your Son. We ask You, Heavenly Father, not because You do not know our needs, infinitely better than ourselves, but because the measure of Your giving is in our receptivity to Your Gift. For You have made us to Your image and likeness, and therefore it is in ourselves to be disposed to what You would give, since the appetite You have given us is a free appetite, an appetite moved by our own reason and not, as in the brutes, moved only by Your Wisdom. And therefore You have made Yourself, in a way, dependent on ourselves since You can give Yourself to us only in the measure that we, by our own free choice, make ourselves receptive to You, open our souls to Your Goodness.

And now, Dear Children, do you see the meaning of sin as I have permitted it in My Merciful Love and Providence? Do you see that I have permitted sin only as a means of showing you, by your own experience, how utterly without hope you are in yourselves? For I permitted sin in the knowledge and intention of sending My Son, so that all souls open to the Truth, to the knowledge of My goodness and of their misery in themselves, would embrace My Son as their loving Redeemer. But the liars, those who not only sinned (all men sin), but who, having sinned, cover up their corruption with the whitewash of lies and hypocrisy, and go about accusing others in order to hide their own wretchedness, from themselves and from everyone else, these liars cannot embrace My Truth. That was what My Son meant when He said: "I know my Sheep, and My Sheep know Me." Those who are of the truth, recognize the truth, those who know that they are lost in themselves are saved by My Son Who came to save what was lost. But the liars and hypocrites hate My Son and they hate Me too, and they hate all those who are Ours, because liars feel themselves accused in the presence of the truthful, even though Our Sheep judge and accuse no one—for charity sees no evil. But those who are without charity see evil where it does not exist, and unwilling to cast the beam out of their own eye, unwilling to face the evil in themselves, they go about ever fearful that the good see and judge the evil in them which they know is there but which they refuse to face in themselves. And so, in the end, they crucify all My Little Children with My First-Born, even as Herod perfected praise out of the infants and sucklings he massacred in pursuit of the Infant Jesus.

But even then, even as they are crucified by those who hate Me, what do My children think and say? Even then they do not accuse their murderers—as the holy infants did not accuse them. Because My children know that those who persecute them are weak, ignorant men, ignorant of My Merciful Love. For if they knew that they were loved and forgiven, that their sins were as nothing in comparison with My Love, they would indeed come to Me, as the prodigal son returned to his father, in order to be forgiven by Me, and loved. And therefore, My Only-Begotten One cried out to Me for those who crucified Him: "Father, forgive them, for they know not what they do!" "Father, forgive them, for they know not what Our Love for them is, they do not know that this Love is dying on this Cross in order that they might know Your Love, the Love of the Father! Father, do not let this agony be in vain but through it, show Your children Your Love, show them that they are justified in Me, that they may not seek the perverse justification of themselves, by sinning against the Spirit of Truth, Our Spirit, Who testifies within their own souls that they are unjust!"

O My Little Children, consider with Me how important it is to cast the beam of your own justification out of your eye, that you might see that your neighbor, even he who persecutes you, needs what you need, that he needs to know My Merciful Love, to know that I love My children, not because they are good, but because I am Good. My little children, look into yourselves and see how all your transgressions arise from this, that you do not believe in My Love for you... And now see that I am so anxious to persuade you of My Love that I have given you My Only-Begotten Son, to be murdered by you in order to prove My Love. Realize now how much your heart is hardened, because you do not believe in My Love. Realize how sad and depressed you are because you cannot, by the Spirit of My Truth, live the lie of your own virtue; yet you cannot turn away from that illusion and allow the dead to bury the dead. Realize that, because of this, you are neither hot nor cold. Realize that the one thing I want, the one thing necessary, is for you to be open to Me, because then I can give Myself to you as I give Myself to My Son, then I can take My delight in you because I see only Myself in You.

This, then, is why My Son taught you to pray to Me in order that, by your own free choice, you might become totally open to Me. And this is why He taught you to ask Me, "Give us this day our daily bread!" because He would have you in the same relation to Me as He Himself is. Do you not, as you ask Me to give you this day your daily bread, hear the echo of the eternal words I spoke to My Son, "Thou art My Son, this day have I begotten Thee."? My Son is begotten in this eternal day, and to the likeness of the eternal day, you ask Me now, "Give us this day our daily bread!" Give us Yourself, dearest of Fathers, as You give Yourself to Your Son, for we too are Your little children, we too are the lilies of the field, who toil not, neither do we spin, for we take no delight in our own works, in our own hopes outside of You. Therefore we ask you for what we need, only now, only this day, only in the Day of Your Son.

Dearest of Fathers, give us Your Love, in the full measure of Your Desire, for now by that very Love, in Jesus and Mary, we are opened to Your Love. Dearest of Fathers, give us Your Love, and know that by Your very Love, we understand how much You Love us, that You have loved us first, in Your Son, that You have been waiting for us to come of age, to realize the depth of Your Paternal Heart, to be freed of the foolish fears of our own unworthiness, knowing that it is only Your Word that makes us worthy.

Our Father, give us this day our daily bread, give us the actuality of Your Being which is out of time and only Now. Our Father, kiss me now with the kiss of Your Mouth, the Kiss which is Your Holy Spirit, the Mouth which is Your Son, through Whom and in Whom You speak Your Word. Kiss me with the kiss of Your Mouth, for the Blood Which flows from the breast of Jesus is better than wine. For wine indeed takes me out of myself, but only to make me less than a man. But the Blood of Your Son takes me out of Myself into Your Bosom—Our Father Who art in heaven! My beloved to me, and I to him who feedeth among the lilies! My little children, consider the lilies of the fields how they grow; they labor not, neither do they spin. My little children, as you ask Me for this bread, be not solicitous saying, "What shall we eat?" for I am your Father, and I know what bread you need. My little children, permit Me, your Father in Heaven, to love you. Only ask Me, that I may give you Myself! "Give us this Day our daily bread!"

"And forgive us our trespasses, as we forgive those who trespass against us!"

My children, see how well I understand your little heart, how fearful you are, even in this loving embrace, as you ask Me for My Love and as I love you, how fearful you are lest your sins keep you from Me. And indeed they would! But what are you to do? To whom should you go if not to Me in My Son? Do you think to make yourself worthy of Me by your own sufferings and penance? Do you not see that it was through Judas, poor, unhappy Judas, that I would teach you this lesson, the lesson of the futility of withdrawing into yourself after sin in order to make yourself worthy of Me and of My Son? And now do you see that that is why My Son taught you to ask, as you are one with Me in My giving you this Eternal bread, "Forgive us our trespasses!" And now you know that in the very asking of Me to forgive, you are forgiven, so that now there is no need of any fear or misgiving that perhaps I am not pleased with you because of your past sins. For now you are one with Me, now you are become My Son.

Only think, if you have any misgivings still, that perhaps even now I have not forgiven you totally, ask yourself, "Have I forgiven those who have offended me?" My beloved little child, look into your heart as your head rests against My Bosom and ask yourself that question. Is it not true that, not only do you forgive those who have hurt you, you no longer remember that they have hurt you. That is the testimony of My Spirit within your heart, the testimony that I have forgiven you your trespasses, and that they no longer even exist for Me. And now, My beloved little child, rest peacefully in Me, and whisper once again to Me, "Our Father!" My beloved little child!

"And Lead us not into temptation!"

Do you see, dearest children, how even yet you fear? And it is good that you should fear, for this is not the servile fear of those who do not know their Father, this is the filial fear of My little children who, in the very depth of their love of Me, know their own weakness, know how easy it would be, in themselves, to fall into temptation. For My Word is truly a two-edged sword cleaving between the soul and the spirit, cleaving between you as you are in yourselves, your soul, and your spirit, what you are in Me, in My Son. So it is that in My Son you know your own soul for what it is, and hate it—because whatever is not in Me is hateful. And you, even as you are in Me, know your soul for the weak and hateful thing it is. For in Me, you are not afraid of the truth, for now you are one with My Truth, and you know that the Truth is your Friend. And so now you cry out to Me, Your Father, "Do not let us fall into temptation, dearest of fathers. For we are creatures of time, and even though at this moment we are united with You in Your Son, in the Love of Your Spirit, yet this is no assurance that, even in the very next moment, we may not fall into temptation. For our strength is not in ourselves, and of ourselves we are prone to fall at any moment."

Do you see, dearest children, how this petition is the proof and reward of the purity of your love? For now, even as I embrace you, and you know My Infinite Love of you, you know, by the very purity of your love, the Purity of My Love in you, that this union with Me, your Father, comes totally from Me—so that My very Love of you annihilates you in the knowledge of your own corruption.

O dearest children, if you could but know how this holy misgiving of yourselves as you say, "and lead us not into temptation," if you could but know how this holy fear rejoices My Heart, how it overwhelms Me in the realization that you are totally Mine, now and forever!

"But deliver us from evil!"

My children, you can see how this petition is hardly distinct from the preceding one. Temptations, as you have learned, are indeed necessary, for without them you would never learn how to depend on Me, in My Son, totally. And the weakness in yourself which I show you is only intended to teach you to rely on My Strength, the Fortitude of My Spirit. And thus it is necessary for you to experience the desolation of apparent separation from Me, so that you may cry out to Me with My Son, "My God, my God, why hast Thou forsaken me?" But this cry of weakness and abandonment is the seal of your strength. It is then that your strength has become Mine, so that there is no deliverance for you except in Me.

This is indeed a great mystery, and the consummation of your happiness in Me. It is indeed your mystical death with My Son, the consummation of your victory, His victory in you and yours in Him, in which you become the deliverer of many souls as you yourself are abandoned. Until now it seemed as though there was something you could do to help yourself in the battle with evil. But now, nailed to the Cross with My Son, there is nothing you can do—you can only cry out to Me, "Why hast Thou forsaken Me?" Dearest of children, know that I have no more forsaken you than I have forsaken My Own Beloved Son. Know, then, that this day, with Him, is the day of your joy, the day when you bring to Me all the souls I have given you. Blessed are you when they shall revile you, and persecute you, and speak all that is evil against you, for my sake. Be glad and rejoice for your reward is very great in heaven.

And now, My Little children, see how disturbed you become when you hear these words? It is because you are afraid to think that you suffer persecution for My sake. The reason is that you are not yet purified perfectly, so that the movement of self-love rushes to your defense, persuades you that you are not worthy of this My blessing. Little children, it is true that you have not yet learned to depend utterly and totally on Me. But do not be afraid, for it is only by loving Me and trusting Me as I have shown you, that you will, in My time, have nothing of yourself of which to be afraid—because your trust will be totally in Me. Then you will know that this, My blessing, is indeed for you, and you will rejoice and be glad. But already, dearest children, know that it is for you as in a prophecy. For this ultimate blessing of persecution for Me is already fulfilled for you in Me, as you are My very little child. "Our sister is little, and hath no breasts. What shall we do to our sister in the day that she is to be spoken to? If she be a wall, let us build upon it bulwarks of silver; if she be a door, let us join it together with boards of cedar. I am a wall; and my breasts are as a tower since I am become in his presence as one finding peace."

My dearest little children, these words were spoken first of Mary, and then of My children in her. My dearest little children, permit Me to love you in Jesus, My Son, and in Mary, My daughter and His Mother: that is everything.

(Abridged slightly, emphases added)

❖

Addendum

❖

A Case in Point

Learn to perceive and encounter God in all things;
because all that is created is his work,
and bears his seal and his divine breath.
— Mary to Consuelo

❖   ❖   ❖

An Unlikely Story

As told in 1997

The following account tells the true story of an improbable business venture un-
dertaken in the spirit of the Psalmist's bold declaration, "Unless the Lord builds
the house, those who build it labor in vain"(Ps 127:1).

- I -

This is a story about a small, multinational company, the Logos Corporation, that was interiorly dedicated to God at the moment of its conception 27 years ago, in 1970. Its history since then has been so unusual it caused a knowledgeable investment banker to say of it recently "Logos is not a business, it's a mystery." As you will see shortly, the many unlikelihoods involved in its formation, its product, and its financial history do indeed seem to defy natural explanation. First and foremost there is the unlikelihood that any commercial enterprise begun by penniless people and with 50-100 well-paid employees could survive on its own for 27 years without ever once realizing a single dollar in profit, in fact, while incurring annual losses often in excess of two million dollars. Yet this is the case with this little company. This circumstance is not because the business was ill-conceived or had nothing worthwhile to sell or was poorly managed.

Rather it is because the product—a computer system that translates between natural languages—was so difficult to build, involved such advanced and problematic technology, that it took virtually all those years to develop it and then get the marketplace to accept it. This situation is still going on—technical work still needs to be done, the marketplace is still half asleep, the balance sheet is still awry—but *mirabile dictu*, the company is still going strong. The picture isn't all negative of course: today the Logos translation system is being used profitably (for its users) by well-known multinational companies in a dozen nations of the world. But while this shows that the company has already given something of demonstrable value to the world, it must also be said that from a financial perspective this Logos Corporation should have sunk into oblivion many years ago. So this is a story about a company that has all its life mysteriously contravened the economic laws of gravity, a company as it were that has come to walk on water, by the grace of God and some graced individuals.

❖   ❖   ❖

The second unlikelihood relating to Logos Corporation concerns the fact that the product this company aimed at developing and bringing to market—a computerized translation system—was considered by the best scientific and technological minds of this country to be unbuildable. Let me explain. In the earliest days of the computer, back in the 50's, computer pioneer Alan Turing proposed that these new electronic super-calculators should not only be able to crunch numbers but also be able to do things like play chess and translate languages. Turing was prescient about computers and chess, but the case with language translation turned out to be quite otherwise. To be sure, right after his seminal remarks, numerous attempts were indeed begun worldwide to build just such computer translation systems (known as machine translation systems—MT for short). Government funding flowed freely into university-based research projects for ten years until 1967 when a devastating evaluation by the National Science Foundation (published in a document known as the ALPAC Report) almost overnight brought all these efforts to a halt. This famous report, in assessing the achievements of these projects to date, found them unacceptable and unpromising, and concluded that translation by computer was in all probability not feasible. It appeared that natural language is too complex, too ambiguous, too fuzzy to lend itself to logical, numerical treatment by any method then known to the state of the art. By the late 60's the received wisdom was that MT could not be done and, as a consequence, virtually everyone abandoned the field.

The dust had barely settled on this debacle when Logos Corporation was formed (in 1970), to pick up this task and attempt the impossible. It is said that necessity is the mother of invention and so it was in this case—a unique national need had suddenly arisen just then that made another attempt at MT worth considering on the part of the government. And here was a tiny new company, Logos, claiming it could do what Oxford, MIT, Harvard and IBM and many other powerful organizations around the world had tried and failed to carry off.

The opportunity had to do with the Vietnamese war and President Nixon's intention late in the war to turn the fighting over to the South Vietnamese and bring our soldiers home. It was called the Vietnamization Policy. This was in the late 60's when the U.S. public had grown restless and unsupportive of the long drawn-out conflict. It seemed like a good idea but there was a major problem—to turn the war over to the South Vietnamese forces meant the U.S. had to supply them with advanced military equipment, equipment that they had to learn to use and maintain. This in turn meant that they either had to acquire a good command of English or be given thousands of military training and maintenance manuals translated into Vietnamese for this purpose. Neither solution seemed realistic. Teaching the South Vietnamese forces English so that it could fight our kind of war would take years. And someone calculated that it would take at least seven years to translate the manuals needed. The problem was so serious that an emergency meeting of the President's Scientific Advisory Council was convened at the White House to see what could be done. One of the participants at that meeting, Evrett Pyatt (later to become Under Secretary of the U.S. Navy), suggested using computers to do the translation. Everyone present knew of the negative ALPAC conclusions regarding prospects for this sort of thing, but Pyatt said he had heard tell of a little company that claimed it had a solution. It was worth looking into at least. And so this is where I came in. The little company was Logos Corporation which I had formed just weeks before in anticipation of this very need. I was contacted and brought to Washington at once to make my case.

❖   ❖   ❖

In retrospect it seems unlikely that a tiny fledgling company of just a few people, with no track record and no money, barely a month old, should be called upon to address a crisis of this importance. The qualification that made Logos unique and that brought us to the government's attention seemed pure happenstance — I happened to be the only person in the United States in 1969 who (1) knew some Vietnamese, (2) knew something about computers, (3) knew something about machine translation, and (4) believed he could do the job. I was the farthest thing from an expert in any of these areas, but the combination was unique and did indeed give me an advantage over companies like IBM when they inevitably tried to muscle in on the opportunity. I went to Washington and made my case to a room full of anxious officials who, for all their skepticism, knew they had little choice but to give me a try, assuming I was real. To test this last qualification, they asked me one question about the system I proposed to build for them — how good will it be? I answered, "Not very good strictly speaking, but good enough to do this job." I was told later that had I said anything else I would not have carried the day. That day is still very vivid in my mind. Our company, only just born, could now take its first breath of life.

Logos Corporation soon received a small contract to demonstrate a prototype capability of English-Vietnamese translation. We were given a long list of English technical terms concerning helicopters and were told that on the day of demonstration our system would be asked to translate into Vietnamese twenty pages from a previously unseen Army helicopter manual employing those terms. We had all of three months to build this prototype. Now all we had to do was pull it off. Given the history of this technology, our own lack of genuine expertise, the short amount of time granted us, the fact that we were virtually starting from scratch, our prospects understandably were not considered good. Evrett Pyatt admitted to us later that government experts had chided him for chasing after "fools' gold."

❖   ❖   ❖

Had those officials in Washington asked me how I was going to pull this off, I would not have known how to answer. The truth is I didn't know. I just felt I could do it, and somehow my confidence must have come across. Happily the officials at that Washington meeting never asked. I had some rather vague ideas of an approach, not yet really worked out in my mind, but underneath was this bedrock conviction that any difficulties arising along the way would get solved as we went along. Looking back I see that there really was nothing in my academic or professional background that should have allowed me to feel that way, nothing in terms of my conventional secular preparation. As it turns out there was a reason for such boldness, one I did not become aware of until later, and of which I will speak in a moment.

I am by nature a somewhat retiring person. My academic background was in philosophy and theology. At one point in my youth I was trained in several languages by Air Force Intelligence. One of them was Vietnamese. This was before the war and there seemed absolutely no point in learning Vietnamese at the time, as far as I was concerned personally, and my study of the language was halfhearted at best. After military service I studied theology and for several years served as a Protestant minister engaged in ministry to the bohemian community of New York's Greenwich Village, until my conversion to the Catholic Church in 1960. Following my conversion, I made a living as a contributing editor for the Columbia Encyclopedia, writing and editing articles on the lives of the saints. I eventually drifted into the computer field in the early 60's at the age of 33, initially as a technical writer. Up to this point in my life, my chief bent was literary. I was always good at languages but they never much interested me and I positively detested grammar and things like parsing. Nor did I ever exhibit any talent for technology or science. Yet at some point early in my new computer career I began to read about the difficult machine translation problem and almost at once conceived the idea that, hey, I could build a machine translation system that really worked. It was this pure naked conviction alone that brought me to the attention of the government at that moment of crisis.

Well before I ever thought of forming my own company, I had gone to see the government's leading expert on machine translation, a man by the name of Zbigniew Pankowicz, to talk about my interest in this area. He was a Polish nobleman who came to the U.S. after having been incarcerated in Buchenwald and Auschwicz during World War II. By this point in my life I was a VP in a small software company and on my own initiative had begun to look more seriously into this problem of machine translation. I had dinner with Pankowicz on that first encounter and we talked about the possibilities of a Vietnamese system. I remember at one point leaning over the table and saying to him, with the deepest conviction, "I just want you to understand that I can do this." He must have believed me for he spoke of me later to Evrett Pyatt. The rest is history.

The fact that Logos was small, green and virtually penniless wasn't the main reason we were such an unlikely candidate for this undertaking. What made our selection and subsequent accomplishments most unlikely was the kind of people who made up Logos in those days and who would eventually pull this off. It is here in the people that we get to the heart and soul of this story.

- II -

By the time this opportunity arose in 1970, I was living as a member of a Catholic lay community of over 100 adults plus scores of children of all ages, on a two hundred acre farm in the foothills of the Catskills north of New York City. The community had been formed some years earlier by a man we call here simply H. He was a brilliant individual, gifted in extraordinary ways both intellectually and spiritually. Above all he was a staretz, a spiritual father in the classic sense (and my spiritual father), a man chosen by God to prepare souls for Him. A book could be written about this man but it is God's will that he remain hidden.

Despite his intellectual gifts, H published nothing, cared little for the limelight, and remained virtually unknown until his death in 1980. He functioned rather as a director of souls to any and all who came to him for help and guidance. Eventually a community of some two hundred men, women, and children formed around him, and many hundreds of others — priests, nuns, and laity — came for counsel and spiritual help. The community operated with the blessing of the diocesan auxiliary bishop and had a common economy, rather like a kibbutz. Its members were drawn from every walk of life: teachers, social workers, nuns (who left their orders to join this community), several priests, a lawyer, a cab driver from Israel, some computer specialists, a farmer, a few medical doctors, some engineers, mechanics, a steady stream of fresh graduates from Catholic colleges, dozens of mothers and scores of kids of all ages — all living under obedience as spiritual sons and daughters of this spiritual father. Except for our Vietnamese linguists, all the early workers at Logos Corporation came from this Catholic kibbutz.

I too lived under obedience to my spiritual father and so it was natural that I would approach him first about this idea of forming a company. I told him of the opportunities I foresaw and of my conviction that I could solve this problem. He seemed genuinely interested, if a little cautious. "To do something like this you will need Ph.D.'s from Harvard," he said. I said if we need them we'll get them. He looked at me for a while and then said, "Well then, do it." That was all I needed. When Logos was formed shortly thereafter, H became its first Chairman of the Board.

❖   ❖   ❖

It takes money to start a company and our little Catholic kibbutz lived from hand to mouth and could never have undertaken something like this. We made a few feeble efforts to raise it on Wall Street and from some individual private investors all without success and then, unexpectedly, we received our funding from the most unlikely source of all—a loan from a nun. This sister was a spiritual child of H's who came to be with him from time to time. Like all religious she had taken a vow of poverty, but her circumstance was rather unusual. Her wealthy father had given considerable sums of money to her order under the proviso that should his daughter ever need funds at some point or other, she should be allowed to draw from a special account in her name. For this nun, Logos became such an occasion. The loan was not especially large but it was all she had and enough to get us started. A year later we were able to repay it down to the last penny—the only financier ever to be so favored in the long history of this company.

The company got its precious name from H in what always seemed to me to be a favor from heaven. As we were getting ready to form this company, we needed to decide on a name. I asked H if he would name it for us and he came up on the spot with some kind of playful acronym. I forget what it was but my instant reaction was to reject it. "No," I said, "we ought to have a serious name, a name that really means something." He looked at me quizzically for a moment and then closed his eyes and sank into what seemed like the deepest contemplation. This went on for many long minutes. When he came to, he said simply, "Call it Logos."

❖   ❖   ❖

Logos began its life in the bitter cold winter of 1969-1970 in a small unheated milk house on the community farm. At first there were just two of us, my partner and spiritual brother from the community, Charlie B. and myself. We painted the walls and installed a Teletype machine that enabled us to communicate with a timesharing computer in Stamford, Connecticut. Charlie was a gifted mathematician who could take my half articulated notions and program them into cogent software. Working day and night, we began to program the pieces of this system. Sometimes, late at night, it was so cold in the unheated structure that the ink on the Teletype ribbon would be frozen, and nothing would appear when the machine printed—not until the incessant pounding melted the ink. When that first government contract finally came in, we moved to a larger single-room building in town, installed more modern equipment and added more staff from the members of our community. Among these were several teaching sisters who had left their orders in the post Vatican II chaos, a few students just out of high school or junior college, later augmented by a few college graduates, and finally a handful of mothers from the community, mostly with liberal arts degrees. And we found a gentle Vietnamese scholar by the name of Binh who agreed to join our little enterprise. All of these Charlie and I had to train from scratch to use computers and to work with language in the particular way needed.

Three months later, when the time came for our demonstration, a plane load of some twenty-five government officials, experts, and military types jammed into our little facility, among them a Vietnamese army colonel. There were vocal naysayers among them too, one an expert from Rand Corporation who seemed only too eager to spot all our shortcomings. But the angels were with us. We ran the test text through the system and gave the output to the Vietnamese colonel. Our own Vietnamese linguist poured over the results with him. At one point our linguist Binh put his finger on something and said, "Well, that's not right." The Vietnamese colonel peered closer and then stood up and announced. "No, the machine translated that correctly." That was the turning point. Smiles crept over bureaucratic faces all around and, naysayers notwithstanding, we were on our way. Not long after that, Logos got a seven figure contract to build a real, full blown working translation system capable of translating warehouses full of manuals.

Our little company built that system in a year, completing it on time and within budget. The system was tested by the South Vietnamese in Saigon and was judged capable of producing translations that, with post-editing, were found to be of from "good to excellent" quality. Before long, the U.S.

Army, Navy and Air Force began sending us crates full of manuals. We enlarged our staff and set up a full-scale production line. We had already translated about five million words into Vietnamese when one morning we got a telephone call from the Pentagon telling us to stop everything — the war was about to end.

In official reviews after the Vietnamese war was over, Evrett Pyatt cited our project as having constituted one of the outstanding technology success stories of the entire war effort. Indeed, the Pentagon formally acknowledged that the feasibility of large-scale machine translation had now been demonstrated. Zbigniew Pankowicz, who had been the government's technical administrator of the Vietnamese contract, received the Pentagon's second highest civilian award for his role in this project. Our little band of nuns, students, and mothers had indeed chalked up an outstanding success and we were proud as punch. But the original reason for Logos was over. Now we had to find new reasons for being.

❖   ❖   ❖

That was in 1973 and somehow we survived and so has machine translation as a technology. Slowly, painfully, from that point on, Logos, and machine translation in general, began its long crawl back into respectability and technical viability, not only in the U.S. but around the world. Today there are scores of commercial systems and hundreds of Ph.D.'s being awarded every year for research in this field, a few of them even about the Logos system. Not all these systems are successful, not all the brainy ideas being proposed will ever work very well. In fact, most never do. As someone once said, natural language is the most complex event in the universe. Getting a computer to cope with it will always involve an unlikely stretch. Yet the Logos approach continues to be in a class by itself and to have by far the best track record, more than any other commercial or university-based system in the world.

The outgrowths of that original system nowadays translate between English, French, German, Italian and Spanish and are generally viewed by big multinationals as the only real game in town. And these Logos systems keep getting better year after year. Of course Logos is not the same Company today as it was in the early days. The company has nearly one hundred people today, only five of whom originally lived in that lay community. The company is scattered over facilities in Germany, Italy, Canada,

California's Silicon Valley and New Jersey. Almost everyone in the Company has an advanced degree, including those Ph.D.'s from places like Harvard that H said we would need. As you walk through the modern facilities of our Company nowadays, you will hear any number of languages being spoken.

From all appearances, then, the Company is thriving. And that surely is a hopeful sign in light of yet another situation that is brewing. We live in an age of information explosion, increasingly so now with the Internet. Information is surging around the globe like tidal waves, most of it in English. People on the other side of language borders would prefer that information be in their own language. For many it is inaccessible unless it is. Much of this information is trivial of course, and worse in some cases, but much of it is vital too, to commerce, education, culture, science, technology, and even to the Vatican (which now has a Web site on the Internet). As in the days of the Vietnamese conflict, the task of translating all this information far exceeds human resources. And even were there enough translators (which there aren't) and people could afford their services (which they can't), much of this information could not get translated fast enough for it to be useful. As this issue heats up, as it surely will, little Logos Corporation expects to be there in the middle of it all, offering translation that will be near instantaneous, affordably cheap and eminently useful even if still far from perfect. And who knows, perhaps someday in the distant future this technology will become a bridge over the Babel of more than 3000 languages that have divided peoples since time immemorial. Far-fetched perhaps, but at least it's now feasible, technologically speaking. The story of this little company, then, seems far from finished.

OK, that's Logos Corporation, more or less, from the outside looking in. Now let me tell you something about this Company from another angle, more from the inside looking out.

- III -

There is a joke that used to be passed around the Logos Board of Directors whenever the Company's periodic financial difficulties seemed about to bury us—*nothing matters so long as we retain the movie rights to the story.* There's not a little truth in that, for the most extraordinary things have happened to this company, particularly in the area of finance. The following is a typical example of what I mean. One day in the late 70's the company was down to its last few dollars and could not make its payroll. At the bleakest point, a loose acquaintance of our financial VP walked in one afternoon to chat, learned of our difficulties, and wrote a check on the spot for 100,000 dollars. That sort of thing has happened time and time again where someone or some group would show up and pull the firm back from the brink. This company has almost expired so many times that, after a while, one becomes inured.

One of those individuals who came and saved the day was James A. Linen, a man who had been President of Time, Inc. and publisher of *Time* Magazine. When he retired from that vast publishing responsibility he took an interest in little Logos, made some timely investments in the Company, got us a big contract with the pre-revolutionary government of Iran for a Farsi (Persian) system, and shortly (after H died) became our Chairman of the Board. (This was in the late 70's, early 80's. We had just completed the Iranian contract when the revolution occurred; it took us eight years to get paid for our work, in a courtroom of The Hague). Then for a few years we were actively represented in the marketplace by the famous sports management company, IMG, that was built by Mark McCormick and Arnold Palmer and that handles many of the premier sports figures of our time. We were even championed for a time by Charles Van Doren and the Encyclopedia Britannica. George Steinbrener, present owner of the Yankees, played a critical financial role in Logos at one point. (Each of these is an interesting story in its own right.) We have had investments by some of the most outstanding investment banks, companies and venture capitalists in the world including the super wealthy French Schlumberger family, one of the Wall Street Lerner brothers, Bessemer (the great granddaddy of American venture capitalists), American Research and Development (original investor of the computer company DEC), Houghton Mifflin, Germany's auto giant BMW, and so on.

The list of organizations and financiers who have become intrigued with Logos is long indeed. Almost always they first sent skeptical experts to investigate our technology, and invariably the experts' recommendations were positive. Several even likened what we were doing to the sort of thing that wins Nobel prizes. A computer scientist from Poland after listening to a detailed explanation of our approach, exclaimed that the system "blew his mind." One analyst from Wall Street, a foreign-born gentleman particularly sensitive to the value of language, said he ranked what we were doing on the first rung of technological achievements of the 20th century. Obviously, excessive as these statements must seem, there had to be something analogous taking place in the minds of investors who continued to pour money into the Company year after year without return. Whenever an investor had had enough, and naturally many did after a time, others would always appear to take their place. On average, this infusion of capital has amounted to two million dollars per year for 27 years. And this is still going on. In the last few years the infusion has been closer to twice that sum.

Clearly these investors have all had visions of gold at the end of the rainbow. But the reasons for their investment are more complex than that. The most important backers over the years have always said they were attracted to Logos partly because of its religious background. They felt that the Company and its technology somehow seemed "destined" to contribute to the welfare of mankind (in their own words) and that this sense added a dimension to their investment that made their subsequent losses a bit less troublesome. No one likes to lose money, of course, but losing it for a worthy cause can reduce the pain. The Company's latest round of investors from Europe is no exception in this regard. This particular group had been following the company for a number of years, and on the occasion of their investment they alluded to the company's religious origins as relevant to their investment decision. They did not try to understand that origin, or probe it, but they were well aware of it and said they made their investment in part because of it.

❖   ❖   ❖

In what way can it be said that this company has a spiritual aspect? Well, nowadays probably nothing would directly suggest such a thing except for the on-going miracle of its survival. But for the first fifteen years of the Company's life, a full size picture of Our Lady of Guadalupe hung in the Company's main conference room for all to see, investors, prospective customers, visiting experts, whomever. But more tellingly it was the people who worked for this company. H once said the real genius of Logos lay in the spirit of cooperation of its workers. And it was true. We were able to accomplish what we did because we worked as if with one mind. There were no real ego problems, no criticism of each other, no dragging of feet, no withholding of information to gain advantage, only willing cooperation. The common good was everything (after God). As the technological leader, I felt as though I had fifty minds and pairs of hands as extensions of my own. And they were good minds and capable hands. There seemed nothing we could not do, could not solve, working in that spirit. In later years, when the original workers from the lay community became a small minority in Logos, the culture of cooperation nevertheless survived, perhaps not without its flaws, but enough to make Logos a different kind of company in the estimation of virtually all who know it or work for it.

Truly, this way of working must have been pleasing to God for very quickly in those early days we got into extremely deep waters, technologically speaking, and had to feel our way and make technological decisions on a daily basis that could easily have ruined us down the road if they were wrong. But, strange as this may seem, they never were. There is something truly remarkable about that fact, given the difficulty of the undertaking, the modest educational level of those doing all this work, and the fact that we really didn't know what we were doing before we had to do it. We worked as one, sometimes as long as 16 hours a day, and always, it seemed, the result in the end had a beautiful rightness about it. A senior project engineer from Apple Computer, a technical wizard with two advanced degrees, who now works for us, after studying the innards of our system, said he's never seen any system in his life quite so elegant. Some facets of the system, he said, made him want to "leap out of his chair."

Probably it was an advantage that none of us had ever been formally trained for this work, for it allowed us to do our jobs with completely open minds, minds that could be moved to see and do the right thing. I myself have always felt that the myriad little lights or inspirations that enabled us to solve each problem as it arose, and that in the aggregate went to make up the Company's technology, were given to us as gifts. There's no other explanation for it in my mind. I say this with some authority since I am the so-called intellectual father of this system and ought to know. What I know is that, speaking for myself, I was never more than an instrument.

❖ ❖ ❖

My spiritual formation at the hands of H taught me to believe that God has a great deal to do with our daily work, that if we ask him He blesses the work of our hands, and even more, that He does it with us. There is nothing extraordinary in this actually. As St. Thomas taught, it's in the nature of things for God to be the primary cause, and for us to be but secondary causes, of all the good that we do. As Jesus said, "Without Me you can do nothing." It's true that not many people work this way, not consciously, particularly when it comes to technical work. But H most certainly did, as did eventually those of us who lived under his direction. He made working in this spirit an intrinsic and necessary part of our formation.

H liked to build things, mechanical devices made of Mecanno, high-fi assembly kits put together transistor by transistor, wire by wire, and so on. He had me work with him this way for the first five years that I lived with him, at night after coming home from my job, or in the early morning and on weekends. We worked as monks, keeping recollected even as we focused completely on the task at hand. No anxiety about the work was ever allowed to mar the peace of these hours, sometimes almost through the night. If a difficulty arose, which it often did, the routine was to quietly review the work up to that point, go over the steps, break the problem down, whatever, always believing that it would turn out right, never allowing the imagination to cloud a relentless objectivity, never allowing anything to destroy the peace.

Once, I recall, we were making a model gearbox with three forward speeds and one reverse speed. Some problem arose in getting it to shift gears smoothly that seemed to stump us. We were working early in the morning and as it became time for Mass, we put our tools down and went off to church. After communion H went into contemplation as was his custom. This time, when he came out of it, he looked at me and announced that Mary had given him the solution to our gearbox problem. We went straight home and indeed the problem was taken care of. Now, that sort of thing just amazed me at the time, that Our Blessed Mother would take an interest in something so trivial as a model gearbox, and that she even knew anything about gearboxes (though of course that's silly, but I was a recent convert and Mary was new to me).

This is not just a "cute" story because a real formation was taking place in connection with this work. H believed that God is involved in the rightness of everything we do. I lived and worked along side of him for a number of years and came to believe the same thing, that whenever I undertook some piece of work, I was never on my own, never doing it alone. Any task given to me to do, however trivial, held God's interest every bit as much as my own, and could be done with his help, or to put it more accurately, would be done with me as his instrument. My job was to keep myself open and recollected. That was how all of us worked in the early days of Logos when all the employees were products of this spiritual formation. To be sure, it didn't mean you became passive—we had to apply ourselves to do the work much as anyone, but we believed we were never doing it alone, working out of our own resources. It was not that you necessarily thought about God when you worked or consciously prayed. Generally you couldn't, not if the work was intricate or demanding, which it usually was. But when a difficulty arose, it made all the difference in the world what you did next. You could get quiet and turn to God expecting the answer, or you could become anxious and try to force one by yourself. It made all the difference in the world which.

I don't mean to suggest here that little lights were always popping off in our heads. Sometimes, perhaps, but most of the time it had to do with the way you went about a task. In my own personal experience, whenever a problem arose, my first reaction would be to try to force a solution. It would usually take the direction of increased complication and usually was never really satisfactory. When this happened, sometimes a red light would go on in your head, causing you to back off and open your mind to other possibilities. That's when you'd get a little light, an instinct to do it another way. The answers God gave like that were always simple and worked just right. You didn't come to this way of working first off. You generally had to be driven to it by your own mistakes. Mistakes taught you what not to do. In once sense mistakes were your friend. But after a while, as you learned the right way to work, the mistakes didn't have to be so egregious, although they were always there and always useful. A professor of industrial management science was brought in by an investment group once to study the way we went about our work. In the end he expressed amazement at the extent to which the company's work was driven by what he called "counter-factual evidence." He said this was unique in his experience. He said the disposition of most people when they work is to see where what they are doing is right. At Logos, he said we had almost a lust to see where it was wrong, so that we could make it better. That way of working came directly from H.

Some years before Logos came along, H and I, working in this spirit, built an electrically driven power train for a model automobile that comprised

a three-speed gear box, an operable clutch and a working rear-wheel dif-
ferential that did all the things that real automobiles do when they turned
tight corners. It was rather neat, actually, and H suggested I take it to my
place of work and show it around, which I did. I happened to be em-
ployed at that time as a systems analyst for a nonprofit think tank that
was designing command and control systems for the Strategic Air Command (SAC). I showed the model around, including to some of the higher
ups. In a way it seemed like a naive thing to do at the time, and I would
never have done it on my own initiative. But as it happened, some years
later one of those higher-ups who had been impressed with this model far
more than I realized, became the catalyst to a major investment in the
early days of Logos, just in time to take over when that first loan by the
nun was running out.

❖   ❖   ❖

I do not mean to suggest that secondary causes do not have a vital role
to play in the God-man nexus. I said earlier that I was never
particularly interested in languages, but I was good at them and
doubtless Logos would never have been formed had this not been the
case. Once while I was studying Greek at Hunter College one summer,
the professor put a long Greek sentence on the blackboard and proceeded
to lecture us about its grammatical properties for twenty minutes. When
she was through, she asked if there were any questions. I raised my hand
from the last row and said that I was unable to explain why, but I felt that
the sentence was ungrammatical. Naturally all eyes turned to look at this
weird character in the back of the room, but the professor, bless her,
turned to the sentence and studied it. It happened that I was right, and
for the rest of the summer this professor (she was chairperson of the
Classics department) never ceased thanking me and encouraging me to
study language. There was another incident like that at Logos. We had
just finished translating our first military manual, an Air Force
instructional book on instrument flying. It had been translated by
machine, post-edited by one of our Vietnamese engineers, and finally
reviewed by our top linguist, Binh. It was all set to be delivered to the Air
Force and I was just browsing through it when something struck my eye.
I could not understand the Vietnamese actually but a sentence, rather
long, in the middle of this thick manual jumped out at me as
ungrammatical. I showed it to Binh and I was right. So there's some kind

of curious gift I was born with that allows me to tune into languages at a structural level, a gift that probably has no conceivable utility outside of the use I would eventually put it to. I was flying with a friend once on a Lufthansa flight and had spent the last half hour absorbed in a German newspaper. "What's it say?" my friend wanted to know. "I have no idea," I replied. "I've been reading the syntax."

❖   ❖   ❖

Although I was subsequently trained in Vietnamese, my original language training in the Air Force was in Russian. For a short time in my Air Force career I used to listen to Russian pilots converse over their radios and would try to glean intelligence from their chatter. It required a solid foundation in Russian to be able to do something like that, and to this end the Air Force conducted an intense Russian language training program that went on six hours a day for 18 months, where the students heard and spoke nothing but Russian. I heard about the program before getting into the Air Force and conceived the notion that this was for me. This was at a time when the Korean War had just started and young American youth were being drafted and sent as green troops into Korea. That prospect didn't particularly appeal and so when my draft notice arrived, I enlisted in the Air Force, hoping against hope that I might get into this language school. I loved Russian literature with a deep passion and the prospect of reading these authors in their own language seemed too good to be true. During Air Force basic training I found out that there was indeed a slight possibility of getting into that school, but the odds were not especially good. By now I wanted this schooling so badly that I made a deal with God. If he would get me into that school, I promised I would use these language skills for his honor and glory. That prayer was uttered from the heart, for I faced the prospect of spending my four-year enlistment doing something I cared nothing about. But my prayer was heard and soon I received word of my assignment to language school. I thanked God from my heart and worked hard at mastering the language. After completing the Russian program and working for a while listening to these pilots, I received another assignment, this time to study Vietnamese, which I undertook with considerably less passion. But a deal is a deal (I doubt that I would be writing this story today were it not for that prayer) and God held me to it, or so it seems to me now. At the time this story begins, though, the deal was surely more in his mind than in mine.

❖   ❖   ❖

Now I must tell you something that occurred to me when I was only four or five years old when the seed of this technology was planted in my mind, when (as I believe) the finger of God touched my mind in a special way and prepared me for this undertaking later in my life. I do not expect all my readers to accept this, but as far as I am concerned I have no doubts that this is the true beginning of the Logos story as told above. It is this childhood event that accounts for the fact that I could appear before a government board in a moment of crisis and announce, with deepest conviction, that I could solve the seemingly unsolvable problem facing the government, even while not yet knowing quite how I was going to be able to do that. And also for that fact that someone such as I could convince so many financiers through the years that Logos had something very special indeed.

For a period of perhaps a month, when I was four or five years old, before starting kindergarten, every morning after my father had dressed, had breakfast and then disappeared down the cellar stairs to the garage for the trip to his office, I would go straight to my parents' bedroom and look in the wastepaper basket for something I urgently needed. The Pilgrim laundry service that did my father's shirts in those days had the practice of folding up its ironed, starchy white handiwork around a piece of cardboard and of holding it all together with a light blue paper band. Every morning my father would take out a fresh shirt, break open the band, and dump it and this all-important piece of cardboard into the wastepaper basket by his bureau. There, unbeknownst to anyone else, I would come on my mission to rescue this critical item the moment the path was clear. This all took place at the height of the depression in 1933 or 1934. I still can see the dark blue and white Pilgrim delivery wagon that once a week delivered my father's freshly laundered white shirts. The wagon had an electric motor and tires of solid rubber and would creep up to our curb without a sound like some huge feline animal. To me the wagon was de-livering raw material vital to my first real undertaking in life.

One side of the cardboard was glossy white, and very inviting to the eye of a little boy. I had been collecting these cardboard pieces every day for some weeks until by now I had a pile of about twenty of them all neatly stacked. Then began an unusual project that in retrospect seems unlikely for a boy that age. I took these cardboards and proceeded to design an abstract system with about 20 interacting components, each cardboard piece representing an important part of the whole. On one cardboard I would draw a graph (an actual two-dimensional matrix of some sort, with a suggestion of plots), on another something that looked like a complex tic-tac-toe construction, with certain boxes blackened and others left white. On other charts I drew what to memory seems like strings of number groupings with boxes drawn around them. On still others I drew networks of lines and circles. Each of these cardboards had a unique, specific function in my mind, but a function that was entirely abstract, unrelated to anything real.

I still vividly recall sitting against the wall in my parents' bedroom one morning in particular, the sun streaming in on me through the windows, making some new entry on one of the cardboards, perhaps a new number, or a new line somewhere, and then having to adjust two or three other cardboards to reflect this change elsewhere in this system. It was serious work and I would sit this way, morning after morning, shuffling through this stack of cardboards as if I were maintaining a system of real importance. It was a purely formal work in the sense that the system did not relate to anything real, not even in my mind. The system was entirely self-referencing where each chart seemed to have intricate connections with one or more of the others, but where the system as a whole had nothing to do with anything beyond it in the real world. What held my fascination was simply these interrelationships and interdependencies among the various components, the fact that what happened on one chart had implications for other charts. This activity forms one of the most vivid experiences of my childhood. Everything was done with great deliberation and intensity. I still recall the pleasure and deep satisfaction over what I had done, and this sense that I had discovered something very special, something no one else knew, something terribly important though I could never have explained why it was important or even what it was exactly. I don't recall how it ended. Probably I ran out of ideas as to how to make those components interact. At any rate I soon lost interest in it.

I never thought again about that childhood adventure until years later during the early days of the Vietnamese project. We were trying to raise some money at a point where the funds from that nun were running out. I had been in contact with one of the higher ups at that think tank I had worked for ten years previously, a person who had been especially impressed by the power train I had shown around the office, the one H and I had built together. This individual liked what he heard about Logos and put together a group of thirty financiers each of whom was asked to throw in $10,000 as a "crap shoot." But first there had to be a technical evaluation. They sent a computer specialist and I proceeded to demonstrate our system. I put in an English sentence and moments later out came the Vietnamese. I could see at once that the translation was wrong. This computer specialist would never have known the difference, of course, and I could have passed it off as perfect. But it isn't in my nature to do that, so I told him it was wrong, but that I knew why and could fix it. I went into a table in the computer memory and changed a single number and then ran the sentence again. This time it came out quite different, and quite correct. The individual was stunned that a single change in a single table could produce such a different effect and he reported back that we had something at Logos that looked very good. Shortly after we got the funds. It was then that I myself realized the connection between the system we were building and that childhood game I used to play where a single change in one table affected all the other tables in my set of cardboards. In subsequent years I often reflected on this connection—and the feeling I have today about the present Logos system is exactly that feeling I had when I was five, of something special, of something given.

❖ ❖ ❖

My reader, the account of Logos Corporation that I've given here may seem rather odd and perhaps greatly overblown to you; but as you know by now, I am given to seeing God's hand in everything that happens. And if I have seemed to toot a human horn in this account, it was never my intent. It is God's work I wish to celebrate. The Tower of Babel and the multiplication of languages arose as a consequence of mankind tooting its own horn, of man thinking he could do great things on his own, without God. The Tower of Babel was to reach to the high heavens as a monument to human greatness. God saw it as an act of pride and prevented them from completing it by confusing their language, leading to the so-called Babel of languages that we have today. It's interesting, though, that God was not against the Tower as such, only against their wanting to build it without Him. The 18th Century German mystic, Anne Catherine Emmerich, received a revelation to that very effect:

> "The building of the Tower of Babel was the work of pride. The builders aimed at constructing something according to their own ideas, and thus resisted the guidance of God... They thought not of God, they sought only their own glory. Had it been otherwise, as I was distinctly told, God would have allowed their undertaking to succeed." (From *The Visions of the Venerable Anne Catherine Emmerich, as recorded in the journals of Clemens Brentano.*)

I do not know if Logos will ever one day become a great oak tree of a company or whether instead it will be cut up into lumber boards and used by others. Whatever the case regarding the company itself, the fact remains that its technology is gifted. God brought it into being and has never ceased to bless it. Just the other day we received two visitors from France. One was a professor in the field of "artificial intelligence" at the premier French *École polytechnique*, the other the president of a small Paris-based firm specializing in natural language processing, an individual with a Ph.D. in both computer science and linguistics. After being presented with an overview of the Logos technology, the professor commented it was rather remarkable that a system begun so many years ago should have such a contemporary look about it. To which the other visitor replied, "Yes, and truly, this approach ought to become the standard for the whole world."

So it seems that what was begun so long ago belongs as yet to a future time, and that only then can the full Logos story be told. I expect it will always remain an interesting story, given the hands in which this future rests.

❖ ❖ ❖

Postscript 2007

The foregoing account was written in 1997, three years before the sudden demise of Logos Corporation in 2000. After 30 years this little company was obliged to close its doors. Although many large companies here and abroad used this technology to advantage, and some continue to do so to this day, profitability and financial promise never materialized and eventually the investment monies needed to keep this enterprise going dried up. That the promise of financial reward had seemed very real to these investors may be gleaned from the fact that over 85 million investment dollars had been poured into the company by the time it had to cease operations.

In light of its moorings in Divine Providence, the demise of this company is doubly mysterious because a second investment motive for many had been the prospect that this technology might do good in the world. More than one investor said as much. Now this prospect seems unlikely, although this part of the story is not quite finished. When Logos closed it doors in 2000, German interests acquired the Logos translation system and associated technology, and recently, in 2005, a prestigious German technology institute (DFKI), recognizing its value, has undertaken to offer the Logos system and associated technology over the Internet to universities and translators free-of-charge, especially to those interested in exploiting the system for third-world languages. This so-called "open-source" Logos system is called OpenLogos, and several universities in India are currently using components of OpenLogos to develop an English-Hindi machine translation system. It remains to be seen whether exploitation of Logos technology will increase in the future.

Given its history, we can believe that God's reason for bringing Logos into being and sustaining it all these years had nothing to do with returns on investment. The reason then must have had to do with the people who became involved with Logos, particularly the workers, most of whom in the earlier days of Logos came out of the Catholic kibbutz described earlier. These people, many of them young and right out of college, came to this kibbutz out of a hunger to find God and to be with the like-minded. The community that was formed proved immensely satisfying in both these respects, and among the young more than thirty marriages eventuated, producing large, happy families. Many took jobs at the company that had emerged from their midst, and the salaries this produced provided essential support to the on-going, common life of the community. And then, when the community eventually disbanded, the technological training that these men and women had received at Logos equipped them, by God's Providence, to pursue successful technical careers in situations all over the country.

But there may have been a hidden, deeper benefit for the individuals involved in this work, a benefit that in God's eyes may have been the most important reason for Logos. Many of the workers connected with this undertaking (only the Lord knows for how many this was true) learned to work in a new and more fruitful way, coming to know and rely on a power beyond their own to help accomplish tasks they were asked to do. With that help, a band of fairly ordinary people without special qualifications was able to accomplish what the best universities and most powerful companies around the world tried but could not bring off, at least not nearly as well. Some, even perhaps many, of the workers who achieved this success knew it had not come from their own hands alone. That understanding, that concrete, actual experience of God as the true author of the good that we do, must be the real inner story of this little enterprise and the deepest reason why it happened in the first place.

— Contributed by the founder (secondary cause) of Logos Corporation

❖

Epilogue

❖

If God calls me to apply my activity not only to my own sanctification, but also to good works, I must establish this firm conviction, before everything else, in my mind: Jesus has got to be, and wishes to be, the life of these works.

My efforts, by themselves, are *nothing*, absolutely nothing. "Without me you can do nothing." They will only be useful, and blessed by God, if by means of a genuine interior life I unite them constantly to the lifegiving action of Jesus. But then they will become *all-powerful*: "I can do *all things* in Him who strengtheneth me" *(Phil 4:13)*. But should they spring from pride and self-satisfaction, from confidence in my own talents, from the desire to shine, they will be rejected by God: for would it not be a sacrilegious madness for me to steal, from God, a little of His glory in order to decorate and beautify myself?

This conviction, far from robbing my will of all initiative, will be my strength. And it will make me really feel the need to pray that I may obtain humility, which is such a treasure for my soul, since it is a guarantee of God's help and of success in my labors.

Once I am really convinced of the importance of this principle, I will make a serious examination of myself, when I am on retreat, to find out: 1, if my conviction of the nothingness of my own activity, left to myself, and of its power when united to that of Jesus, is not getting a little tarnished; 2, if I am ruthless in stamping out all self-satisfaction and vanity, all self-admiration in my apostolate; 3, if I continue unwaveringly to distrust myself; 4, and if I am praying to God to preserve me from pride, which is the first and foremost obstacle to His assistance.

The Credo of the interior life, once it has become for my soul the whole foundation of its existence, guarantees to it, even here below, a participation in the joys of heaven.

The interior life is the life of the elect. It fits in with the end God has in view when He created us.

– Dom Jean-Baptiste Chautard, O.C.S.O.

❖

Holiness is formed of Little Acts

My child, holiness is formed of little things; so, whoever disregards little things cannot be holy. It would be like someone who neglects the little grains of wheat which, taken together, form the pile of wheat. By failing to gather them he would lack the necessary and daily nourishment of human life.

Similarly, whoever does not apply himself to gathering together so many little acts, would lack the nourishment of holiness. And just as one cannot live without nourishment, so, too, without the nourishment of the little acts, he would lack the true form of holiness, and the sufficient mass to form holiness.

— Our Lord to Luisa Piccarreta

❖

A single act done in God's Will

If you knew all the good that one word of my Will contains, as well as a single act done in It by the creature, you would be stupefied. In one act one takes as in his fist, Heaven and earth. My Volition is the life of everything, and flows everywhere; and she who lives in my Will, together with my Volition, flows in each affection, in each heartbeat, in each thought and in each thing that creatures do. She flows in each act of her Creator, in each good that I do, in the light that I send to the intelligence, in the pardon I lavish, in the love that I send, in the love that I arouse, in the comprehensors that I beatify, and in everything. There is no good that I do, nor a point of Eternity in which she does not have her little place. Oh, how dear she is to Me. I feel we are inseparable. She is the true and faithful one of my Will whom I never leave alone. Therefore, run in It and you will experience what I say to you.

— Our Lord to Luisa Piccarreta

❖

Examination of Conscience

To conform completely to Jesus, the soul must enter into herself and apply the following reflections: In everything I do, can I say that a continuous stream of love flows between God and me? Our life is a continuous cascade of love that we receive from God: if we think, it is a stream of love; if we work, it is a breath of love; if we speak, it is love; our heartbeat is love. Everything we receive is from God. But do all of our actions run toward God with love? Does Jesus find in us the sweet enchantment of his Love that runs to meet Him, so that, ravished by this enchantment, He may inundate us with even more abundant love?...

Do I allow myself to be formed by the divine hands as the Humanity of Jesus did? We should consider whatever happens within us that is not sinful to be a divine operation. Otherwise, the soul deprives the Father of his glory, permits the divine life to leave it, and loses sanctity. All that we experience within ourselves—inspirations, mortifications, and graces— are nothing other than the operations of love. Do we accept them as God wills them? Do we give Jesus the freedom to work, or do we instead reject the divine operation and compel Jesus to interrupt the work He has begun because we consider everything from a human perspective or as a merely casual event? Do we cause Him to fold his hands because what He sees in us is not the fruit of his Love? Do we abandon ourselves in his arms as though we were dead, receiving all the blows which the Lord disposes for our sanctification?

— *St. Annibale di Francia*

❖

❖   *Prayer*   ❖

I THANK YOU, O MY JESUS, for having shrunk your Divinity into your Humanity, hiding all the grandeur of a God behind the most ordinary actions. O my Jesus, I offer You all my steps, actions, and movements in reparation for everything and for everyone. I ask pardon for those who do not act with right intention. I unite my actions to Yours to divinize them. United to all the works that You did with your most Holy Humanity, I offer them to You — to give You all the glory that creatures would have given You, if they had worked in a holy way with right intention.

— *Luisa Piccarreta*

❖

Endnotes

I - Inspiration, Grace, Free Will

I-1   *Unpublished ms.*

I-2   *Book of Heaven.* Vol. 12, p. 57.

I-3   *Autobiography*, p. 108.

I-4   *The Sacrament of the Present Moment, p. 59.*

I-5   *The Sacrament of the Present Moment,* p. 60-61.

I-6   *The Mystical City of God*, p. 372-373.

I-7   *The Mystical City of God*, p. 681.

I-8   *Unpublished ms.*

I-9   *The Mystical City of God*, p. 283.

I-10   *The Mystical City of God*, p. 301-302.

I-11   *Unpublished ms.*

I-12   *Unpublished ms.*

I-13   *God and the World*, p.18.

I-14   Timothy Ware, ed., *The Art of Prayer*, p. 134.

I-15   Timothy Ware, ed., *The Art of Prayer*, p. 134.

I-18   *Book of Glory*, p. 52.

I-19   *Unpublished ms.;* quotes are from "Anne Sullivan's Letters and Reports," in Helen Keller, *The Story of My Life,* p. 138, 143, 159.

I-20   See Endnote for *Chapter VII.*

I-21   *Unpublished ms.*

I-22   See Endnote for *Chapter VII.*

I-23   *Unpublished ms.*

I-24   *Book of Heaven*, vol. 8, p. 11.

I-25   *Book of Heaven*, vol. 14, p. 114.

I-26   *Book of Heaven*, vol. 1, p. 15.

I-27   *Book of Heaven*, vol. 5, p. 13.

I-28   *Book of Heaven*, vol. 5, p. 42.

I-29   Gerald Bray, ed., *Ancient Christian Commentary on Scripture*, vol. vii, p. 153. Augustine and Basil quoted from *The Fathers of the Church, 86 Volumes.* Catholic University of America Press. 1947.

I-30   *Unpublished ms.*

I-31   *The Spiritual Legacy of Sister Mary of the Holy Trinity*, para. 231, p. 161.

I-32   Gerald Bray, ed., *Ancient Christian Commentary on Scripture*, vol. vii, p. 17. Quoted from P. Schaff et al., eds. *A Select Library of the Nicene and Post-Nicene Fathers of the Christian Church, 2 Series*, New York: Christian Literature, 1887-1895. Reprint, Grand Rapids, Mich.: Eerdmans, 1952-1956. Reprint, Peabody, Mass.: Hendrickson, 1994.

I-34   Thomas C. Oden and Christopher A. Hall, eds., *Ancient Christian Commentary on Scripture*, vol. ii, p. 141. Quoted from *The Fathers of the Church, 86 Volumes*. Catholic University of America Press, 1947.

I-35   *Dogmatic Constitution on the Church*, 4.

I-36   *The Soul of the Apostolate*, p. 12f.

I-37   *Christ, The Life of the Soul*, p. 21f.

II − Faith and Understanding about God and Self

II−1   *The Spiritual Legacy of Sister Mary of the Holy Trinity*, para. 161, p. 136.

II-2   *Book of Heaven*, vol. 14, p. 113-114.

II-4   *Book of Heaven*, vol. 8, p. 71-72.

II-5   *The Spiritual Legacy of Sister Mary of the Holy Trinity*, para. 441, p. 256.

II-6   *Unpublished ms.*

II-7   *Unpublished ms.*; quotes from JPII's encyclical *Ratio et Fides*, which quotes from *Dei Verbum* (2nd Vatican Council document)

II-8   *Unpublished ms.*; quote is from *Einstein in Berlin*, p. 262.

II-9   *Book of Heaven*, vol. 15, pp. 45,49.

II-10   "*The Ways of Brother Lawrence*" in *On the Practice of the Presence of God*, p. 115.

II-11   "*The Ways of Brother Lawrence*" in *On the Practice of the Presence of God*, p. 117.

II-12   "*The Ways of Brother Lawrence*" in *On the Practice of the Presence of God*, p. 116.

II-13   "*The Ways of Brother Lawrence*" in *On the Practice of the Presence of God*, p. 118.

II-14   *Unpublished ms.*

II-15   *The Sacrament of the Present Moment*, p. 51.

II-16   *Unpublished ms.*

II-17   *Unpublished ms.*

II-19   Timothy Ware, ed., *The Art of Prayer*, p. 137.

II-20   *Jesus Appeals to the World*, 15th ed., p. 152.

II-21   *Jesus Appeals to the World*, 15th ed., p. 152-153 ; for *Commentary* see

II-22   *Jesus Appeals to the World*, 15th ed., p. 153.

II-23   *Jesus Appeals to the World*, 15th ed., p. 153-155.

II-24   *Collected Works of St. John of the Cross*, p. 85.

II-25   Gerald Bray, ed., *Ancient Christian Commentary on Scripture*, vol. vii, p. 15. Citation is from Origin, "Fragments on the Pauline Epistles", *Journal of Theological Studies*.

II-26   *Book of Heaven*, vol. 8, p. 64.

II-27   *Book of Heaven*, vol. 7, p. 32.

II-28   *Unpublished ms.*

II-29   *Book of Heaven*, vol. 1, p. 19.

II-31   See Endnote for *Chapter VII*.

II-32   *The Redeemer's Call to Consecrated Souls*, p. 27.

II-33   *Unpublished ms.*

II-34   *Unpublished ms.*

II-35   *Book of Heaven*, vol. 5, p. 4.

II-36   "Sayings on Light and Love," in *Collected Works of St. John of the Cross*, p. 85f.

II-38   Gerald Bray, ed., *Ancient Christian Commentary on Scripture*, vol. vii, p. 121f. Quoted from J. Baille et al, ed., *The Library of Christian Classics*, *26 vols.* Philadelphia: Westminster Press, 1953-1966.

II-40   *Unpublished ms.*

II-41   *Unpublished ms.*

II-42   *Unpublished ms.*

II-43   *For God's Greater Glory*, p. 167.

II-44   *Unpublished ms.*

II-46   *The Mystical City of God*, p. 596-597.

II-47   *From unpublished retreat notes.*

II-48   *The Dialogue*, p. 25; *Unpublished ms.*

II-49   Plato's *Apology*.

II-50   *The Dialogue*, p. 357.

II-51   *Unpublished ms.*

II-52   See Endnote for *Chapter VII*.

II-53   *On the Way to Jesus Christ*, p. 86-87.

II-54   *The Divine Office, Office of Reading*, Friday, 18th Week of Ordinary Time, vol. iv, p. 80-81.

II-56   *Unpublished ms.*

II-57   *Mary, Gate of Heaven*, p. 68-69.

II-58   *Unpublished ms.*

II-59   *Dogmatic Constitution on the Church*, 34.

III - *Theology of Primary and Secondary Causes*

III-1   *The Divine Office, Office of Reading*, June 28th, Feast of St. Irenaeus, Bishop and Martyr, vol. iii, p. 1498.

III-2   *Mary, Gate of Heaven*, p. 44.

III-3   *Book of Heaven*, vol. 18, p. 72-73.

III-4   *Summa Contra Gentiles*, Bk III, Part I (pp. 218-220).

III-5   *Zenit*, April 8th (first day of the conclave to elect successor to Pope JPII).

III-6   *Book of Heaven*, vol. 8, p. 79.

III-7   *Unpublished ms.*

III-8   *Unpublished ms.*

III-9   *Book of Heaven*, vol. 18, p. 81ff.

III-10   *When the Divine Will Reigns in Souls : A Selection of Passages from the Book of Heaven*, p. xix.

III-11 *When the Divine Will Reigns in Souls : A Selection of Passages from the Book of Heaven*, p. 18.

III-12 *When the Divine Will Reigns in Souls : A Selection of Passages from the Book of Heaven*, p. 19-20.

III-13 *When the Divine Will Reigns in Souls : A Selection of Passages from the Book of Heaven*, p. 21.

III-14 *When the Divine Will Reigns in Souls : A Selection of Passages from the Book of Heaven*, p. 21.

III-15 See Endnote for *Chapter VII.*

III-16 *The City of God*, Bk 12, Chap. 26, p. 266.

III-17 *Unpublished ms.*

III-18 *Book of Heaven*, vol. 7, p. 48.

III-19 *Unpublished ms.*

III-21 *Unpublished ms.*

III-22 *Diary of St. Maria Faustina Kowalska: Divine Mercy in My Soul* , #824.

III-25 *Unpublished ms.*

III-26 *Unpublished ms.*

III-28 Commentary from *Unpublished ms.*

III-29 Commentary from *Unpublished ms.*

III-30 Commentary from Gerald Bray, ed., *Commentary on Scripture*, vol. vii, p. 117f. Quoted from P. Schaff et al., eds. *A Select Library of the Nicene and Post-Nicene Fathers of the Christian Church,* New York: Christian Literature, 1887-1895. Reprint, Grand Rapids, Mich.: Eerdmans, 1952-1956. Reprint, Peabody, Mass.: Hendrickson, 1994.

III-31 *Diary of St. Maria Faustina Kowalska: Divine Mercy in My Soul* , #822.

III-32 Commentary from Gerald Bray, ed., *Commentary on Scripture*, vol. vii, p. 30

III-33 *Book of Heaven*, vol. 14 p. 86.

III-34 *Unpublished ms.*

III-36 1st paragraph: *Book of Heaven: Selected Passages #2*, p. 9.
2nd paragraph: *Book of Heaven*, vol. 12 p. 4.
3rd paragraph: *Book of Heaven*, vol. 14 p. 86.

III-37 *Art of Prayer*, p. 278.

III-38 *Art of Prayer*, p. 138.

III-39 *The Spiritual Legacy of Sister Mary of the Holy Trinity*, para. 518, p. 286.

III-41 *The Spiritual Legacy of Sister Mary of the Holy Trinity*, para. 31, p. 89.

III-42 See Endnote for *Chapter VII.*

III-43 *Art of Prayer*, p. 236.

III-44 *Unpublished ms.*

III-46 *Unpublished ms.*

III-47 *Unpublished ms.*

III-48 *Art of Prayer*, p. 236.

III-50 *Book of Heaven*, vol. 5, p. 39.

III-51   Commentary on *Mk 14:66-72*, in Thomas C. Oden and Christopher A. Hall, eds., *Ancient Christian Commentary on Scripture*, vol. ii, p. 222. Quoted from *The Sunday Sermons of the Great Fathers*. Trans. and ed. M. F. Toal. Cistercian Publications. 1991.

III-52   *Book of Heaven*, vol. 15, p. 47.

III-53   *Book of Heaven*, vol. 14, p. 42.

III-55   *The Dialogue*, p. 280.

III-56   *Diary of St. Maria Faustina Kowalska: Divine Mercy in My Soul* , para. 1576.

III-57   *Book of Heaven*, vol. 14, p. 43, 45.

III-58   *The Redeemer's Call to Consecrated Souls*, p. 52.

III-60   *Unpublished ms.*

III-61   *Book of Heaven*, vol. 1, p. 123.

III-62   *New and Divine: The Holiness of the Third Millenium*, p. 113-114.

III-63   *The Life of Jesus Christ and Biblical Revelations*, vol. 1, p 49.

III-64   *Book of Heaven*, vol. 8, p. 66-67.

III-65   *Book of Heaven*, vol. 12, p. 55*ff.*

III-66   *The Spiritual Legacy of Sister Mary of the Holy Trinity*, p. 278, paras. 497, 498.

III-67   *Unpublished ms.*

III-68   *Book of Heaven*, vol. 1, p. 9.

III-69   *The Spiritual Legacy of Sister Mary of the Holy Trinity*, p. 228, para. 385.

III-70   *Unpublished ms.*

III-72   *The Spiritual Legacy of Sister Mary of the Holy Trinity*, p. 262, para. 458.

III-74   *The Divine Office*, Tuesday, Week II of Ordinary Time, vol. iv.

III-75   *Book of Heaven*, vol. 14, p. 28-29.

III-76   *Unpublished ms.*

III-77   *Book of Heaven*, vol. 5, p. 18-19.

III-78   *Fire of Love! Understanding Purgatory*, p. 67.

III-79   *Jesus Appeals to the World*, 15th ed., p. 152*ff.*

III-80   See Endnote for *Chapter VII*.

III-81   *Book of Heaven*, vol. 14, p. 57-58.

III-82   *The Divine Office, Office of Reading*, Friday, 1st Week of Ordinary Time, vol. III, p. 71.

III-83   *Unpublished ms.*

III-84   *Book of Heaven*, vol. 8, p. 29-30.

III-85   *Unpublished ms.*

III-86   *Mary, Gate of Heaven*, p. 253-254.

III-87   *The Mystical City of God*, p. 238-239.

III-88   *Unpublished ms.*

III-89   *Summa Theologica*, vol. 1, Q 19, A 5. Ave Maria Press, South Bend, IN.

III-91   *The Dialogue*, p. 305; *Unpublished ms.*

III-92   From personal correspondence. Fr. Simon is a psychiatrist.

III-93   *Summa Theologica*, vol. I, Q 23, A 8. Ave Maria Press, South Bend, IN.

III-94   *Summa Theologica*, vol. I, Q 23, A 5. Ave Maria Press, South Bend, IN.

III-95   See Endnote for *Chapter VII.*
III-97   *The Divine Office, Office of Readings*, 22nd Sunday in Ordinary Time, vol. IV, p 188-189.
III-98   *Unpublished ms.*
III-99   *Book of Heaven*, vol. 18, pp. 66, 69-70.
III-100   *Book of Heaven*, vol. 14, p. 81.
III-101   *Book of Heaven*, vol. 15, p. 44.
III-102   *Book of Heaven*, vol. 18 p. 68*ff.*
III-103   *Book of Heaven*, vol. 15, p. 18*ff.*
III-105   *The Soul of the Apostolate*, p. 3.

IV - *Work, What We Do*

IV-1   *Mary, Gate of Heaven*, p. 76-78.
IV-2   *Unpublished ms.*
IV-3   *Unpublished ms.*
IV-4   *The Mystical City of God*, p. 365-366.
IV-5   *Unpublished ms.*
IV-6   *"The Ways of Brother Lawrence"* in *On the Practice of the Presence of God*, p. 116, para. 10.
IV-7   *Book of Heaven*, vol. 9, p. 42.
IV-8   *Unpublished ms.*
IV-9   Translated from the French version of this Encyclical, as quoted by Jules Lebreton, S.J. in *The Redeemer's Call to Consecrated Souls,* a book which he edited that records locutions to an anonymous French contemplative woman religious.
IV-10   *Zenit*, Feb. 12, 2003, from Pope JPII's Wednesday Address, quoting St. Ambrose.
IV-11   *Book of Heaven*, vol. 15, p. 5.
IV-12   *Book of Heaven*, vol. 7, p. 48.
IV-13   *Book of Heaven*, vol. 1, p. 19.
IV-14   *Book of Heaven*, vol. 5, p. 5.
IV-15   Quoted in Tugwell, *Albert and Thomas*, p. 612.
IV-16   *Book of Heaven*, vol. 5, p. 14.
IV-17   *The Redeemer's Call to Consecrated Souls*, p. 101.
IV-18   St. Annibale di Francia, *Collection of Letters,* Appendix (no page number).
IV-19   *Unpublished ms.*
IV-21   Book III, Chap. 38, p. 177*f.*
IV-23   Timothy Ware, ed., *The Art of Prayer*, p. 134.
IV-24   Timothy Ware, ed., *The Art of Prayer*, p. 235; commentary from *Unpublished ms.*
IV-25   *Unpublished ms.*

IV-26   *Unpublished ms.*

IV-27   *Unpublished ms.*

IV-28   *The Sacrament of the Present Moment*, p. 51-52.

IV-29   *The Sacrament of the Present Moment*, p. 52-53.

IV-30   *The Sacrament of the Present Moment*, p. 53.

IV-31   *Unknown source.*

IV-33   *The Glories of Divine Grace*, p. 14-15.

IV-34   *Book of Heaven*, vol. 1, p. 123-124.

IV-35   *When the Divine Will Reigns in Souls: A Selection from the Book of Heaven*, p. 61.

IV-36   *Autobiography*, p. 108.

IV-37   Quoted from *The New Year*. Internet site *Mary's Maternity:* www.traces-cl.com/gen02/thenew.htm.

IV-38   *Unpublished ms.*

IV-40   *Fire of Love*, p. 67.

IV-41   *New and Divine: The Holiness of the Third Millennium*, p. 113.

IV-42   *New and Divine: The Holiness of the Third Millennium*, p. 113-114.

IV-43   Book I, Chap. 4, para. 2, p. 35.

IV-44   *Unpublished ms.*

IV-45   *Unpublished ms.*

IV-46   *Unpublished ms.*

IV-49   *Autobiography*, p. 97.

IV-50   *Autobiography*, p. 132.

IV-51   Timothy Ware, ed., *The Art of Prayer*, p. 54.

IV-52   *Unpublished ms.*

IV-53   *The Living God*, p. 29-30.

IV-54   *Unpublished ms.*

IV-55   *Father Joe: The Man Who Saved My Soul*, p. 202-204.

IV-59   *Autobiography*, October 3, 1924, p. 135.

IV-61   *Life in Christ*, p. 190.

IV-64   *Book of Heaven*, vol. 1, p. 16.

IV-65   *Unpublished ms.*

IV-66   Timothy Ware, ed., *The Art of Prayer*, p. 233.

IV-67   Timothy Ware, ed., *The Art of Prayer*, p. 238-239.

IV-68   *The Sacrament of the Present Moment*, p. 54-55.

IV-69   *Beginning to Pray*, p. 33-34.

IV-70   *Book of Heaven*, vol. 7, p. 2.

IV-71   *Diary of St. Maria Faustina Kowalska: Divine Mercy in My Soul*, #1567.

IV-72   *Book of Heaven*, vol. 1, p. 11.

IV-73   Martinez quotations from Joseph G. Trevino, M.Sp.S., *The Spiritual Life of Archbishop Martinez,* trans. by Sister Mary St. Daniel Tarrant, B.V.M. St. Louis: B. Herder, 1966; quoted in Hugh Owen, *New and Divine Holiness: The Holiness of the Third Millennium*, pp. 157-158.

IV-74   *The Spiritual Legacy of Sister Mary of the Holy Trinity*, **para.**15, p. 84-85.

IV-75   *The Soul of the Apostolate*, p. 14-15.

IV-76   Pope John Paul II. *Marian Prayer for World Day of Prayer for Vocations (May 11, 2003).*

IV-77   *The Virgin Mary in the Kingdom of the Divine Will*, p. 157.

IV-78   *Book of Heaven*, vol. 14, p. 47.

IV-79   *Book of Heaven*, vol. 1, p. 14-15.

IV-80   *Summa Theologica*, vol. I, Q 63, A 1. Ave Maria Press, South Bend, IN.

IV-81   *The Mystical City of God*, p. 357.

IV-82   *Practice of the Presence of God*, p. 36-37, in Conrad D. Meester, ed., *On the Practice of the Presence of God.*

IV-83   Quoted by *Zenit* from a meditation of Pope JPII on *Psalm 117(118)*, Feb. 12, 2003.

IV-84   *Einstein in Berlin*, p. 217.

IV-85   *Diary of St. Maria Faustina Kowalska: Divine Mercy in My Sou* , #952.

IV-86   Timothy Ware, ed., *The Art of Prayer*, p. 134.

IV-87   *The Dialogue*, p. 53.

IV-88   *Unpublished ms.*

IV-89   *Book of Heaven*, vol. 7, p. 42.

IV-90   Gerald Bray ed., *Ancient Christian Commentary on Scripture,* vol. vii, p. 18.

IV-91   Timothy Ware, ed., *The Art of Prayer*, p. 136-137.

IV-92   *The Mystical City of God*, p. 411-412.

IV-93   *Unpublished ms.*

IV-94   *The Spiritual Legacy of Sister Mary of the Holy Trinity*, **para.** 386, p. 228.

IV-96   *The Spiritual Legacy of Sister Mary of the Holy Trinity*, **paras.** 455-456, p. 261-262.

IV-97   *The Spiritual Legacy of Sister Mary of the Holy Trinity*, **para.** 519, p. 287.

IV-98   *The Spiritual Legacy of Sister Mary of the Holy Trinity*, **para.** 522, p. 288.

IV-99   "Sayings of Light and Love." *Collected Works of St. John of the Cross,* paras. 20, 21, p. 86-87.

IV-100   Timothy Ware, ed., *The Art of Prayer*, p. 239.

IV-103   *Mary, Gate of Heaven*, p. 226-227.

IV-104   *Book of Heaven*, vol. 12, p. 4*ff.*

IV-105   *Book of Heaven*, vol. 4, April 16, 1902.

IV-106   *The Spiritual Legacy of Sister Mary of the Holy Trinity*, **para.** 59, p. 100. For **Commentary,** see Endnotes for *Chap. VII.*

IV-107   *The Soul of the Apostolate*, p. 50.

V – Devotion and Virtue in Work

V-1   *Spiritual Formation of the Priest*, p. 47. Unpublished ms. of conference for priests, San Alfonso Retreat Center, West End, NJ, July 5-10, 1999.

V-2   *The Mystical City of God*, p. 549-550.

V-3   *The Mystical City of God*, p. 640.
V-4   "The Ways of Brother Lawrence" in *The Practice pf the Presence of God*, p. 124.
V-5   "The Ways of Brother Lawrence" in *The Practice pf the Presence of God*, p. 118.
V-6   "The Ways of Brother Lawrence" in *The Practice pf the Presence of God*, p. 119.
V-7   *Book of Heaven*, vol. 5, p. 24-25.
V-8   *Book of Heaven*, vol. 5, p. 18-19.
V-9   *Book of Heaven*, vol. 5, p. 28.
V-10   *When the Divine Will Reigns in Souls*, p. 123.
V-11   *Book of Heaven*, vol. 8 p. 31.
V-12   Timothy Ware, ed., *The Art of Prayer,* p. 129.
V-14   *The Mystical City of God*, p. 301-302.
V-15   *The Spiritual Legacy of Sister Mary of the Holy Trinity*, **para.** 391, p. 230.
V-16   *The Mystical City of God*, p. 369.
V-17   *Mary, Gate of Heaven*, p. 77-78.
V-18   *Mary, Gate of Heaven*, p. 134.
V-19   *Mary, Gate of Heaven*, p. 142-143.
V-21   *Autobiography*, August 15th, 1922, p. 262-263.
V-22   *Book of Heaven*, vol. 36, Sept. 5, 1938, last paragraph.
V-23   *Book of Heaven*, vol. 236, Oct. 16th, 1938.

VI – The Need for Prayer

VI-1   *Mary, Gate of Heaven*, p. 80.
VI-2   Timothy Ware, ed., *The Art of Prayer*, p. 89.
VI-3   *Unpublished ms.*
VI-4   Quoted by Richard Neuhaus in "The Public Square," *First Things*, Feb. 2005. Nicholas Lash is a Cambridge University professor.
VI-5   From the encyclical *Aeternis Patris* (*On the Restoration of Christian Philosophy*), para. 33.
VI-6   *Beginning to Pray*, p. 67*ff.*
VI-7   *Unpublished ms.*
VI-8   *The Dialogue*, p. 127.
VI-9   Timothy Ware, ed., *The Art of Prayer*, p. 275.
VI-10   Timothy Ware, ed., *The Art of Prayer*, p. 277.
VI-11   Quoted in *Chesterton: A Biography"* by Dudley Barker, p. 65.
VI-12   *The Hours of the Passion of Our Lord Jesus Christ. From* "Reflection for 8:00 PM Hour," p. 28-29.
VI-13   *This is the Faith*, p. 36.
VI-14   *Book of Heaven*, vol. 5, p. 16-17.
VI-15   *The Poem of the Man-God*, vol. 1, p. 112-113.
VI-17   Thomas C. Oden and Christopher A. Hall, eds., *Ancient Christian Commentary on Scripture*, vol. ii, p. 162. Quoted from *The Fathers of the Church, 86 Volumes.* Catholic University of America Press. 1947.

VI-18   *Unpublished ms.*

VI-19   Timothy Ware, ed., *The Art of Prayer*, p. 51.

VI-20   Timothy Ware, ed., *The Art of Prayer*, p. 276.

VI-21   St. Thomas' *Prayer Before Study (ante stadium), published in* the Raccolta #764, Pius XI *Studiorum Ducem*, 1923.

VI-22   Timothy Ware, ed., *The Art of Prayer*, p. 277.

VI-23   *Unpublished ms.*

VI-24   *The Spiritual Legacy of Sister Mary of the Holy Trinity*, para. 29 (excerpt), p. 88.

VI-25   Timothy Ware, ed., *The Art of Prayer*, p. 138.

VI-26   Timothy Ware, ed., *The Art of Prayer*, p. 98.

VI-27   Timothy Ware, ed., *The Art of Prayer*, p. 125-126.

VI-28   Timothy Ware, ed., *The Art of Prayer*, p. 99.

VI-29   *The Soul of the Apostolate*, p. 35.

VI-30   *Mary, Gate of Heaven*, p. 203-204 .

VI-31   *Mary, Gate of Heaven*, p. 232.

VI-33   *The Soul of the Apostolate*, pp. 58-81.

VI-33   *The Hours of the Passion of Our Lord Jesus Christ*, p. 151.

VI-34   Apostolic Exhortation, *Redemptoris custos*, 15 August 1989, 22. Quoted in Francis Fernandez, *In Conversation with God*, vol. 5, p. 488.

VII — Meditation on the Our Father

Unpublished meditation written in 1960 by a servant of God. Under ecclesiastical auspices this servant of God taught priests and served as spiritual director to a convent of religious women. By Our Lord's ordination his identity shall remain hidden.

BIBLIOGRAPHY

St. Annibale di Francia. *Collection of Letters.* Jacksonville, FL: The Center for the Divine Will (Association Luisa Piccarreta), 1997.

St. Thomas Aquinas. *Summa Contra Gentiles.* Trans. Anton C. Pegis, F.R.S.C. London: University of Notre Dame Press, 1975.

—-. *Summa Theologica. Christian Classics.* Trans. Fathers of the English Dominican Province. South Bend, IN: Ave Maria Press.

St. Augustine. *The City of God.* Abridged. Garden City: Image Books. 1958.

Barker, Dudley. *Chesterton: A Biography.* New York: Stein and Day.

Bloom, Archbishop Anthony. *Beginning to Pray.* New York: Paulist Press, 1970.

de Beaufort, Joseph. "The Ways of Brother Lawrence." In *On the Practice of the Presence of God.* Ed. Conrad D. Meester, OCD. Trans. Salvatore Scuriba, OCD. Washington, DC: ICS Publications, 1994.

Blessed Dina Bélanger (Marie Saint Cecilia of Rome). *Autobiography.* Quebec, Canada: Religious of Jesus and Mary, 1995.

Bray, Gerald, ed., *1-2 Corrinthians.* Vol. VII *of Ancient Christian Commentary on Scripture.* Downers Grove, IL: InterVarsity Press, 1999.

Cantalamessa, Raniero. *Life in Christ.* Collegeville, MN: Liturgical Press, 2002.

St. Catherine of Genoa. *Fire of Love! Understanding Puragory.* Manchester, NH: Sophia Institute Press, 1996.

St. Catherine of Siena. *The Dialogue.* Trans. Suzanne Noffke, O.P. Mahwah: Paulist Press, 1980.

Chautard, Dom Jean-Baptiste. *The Soul of the Apostolate.* Trans. A Monk of Our Lady of Gethsemani. Rockford, IL: Tan Books and Publishers, 1946.

Consuelo. *Mary, Gate of Heaven.* Barcelona, Spain: Ediciones Consuelo, 2003.

Blessed Anne Catherine Emmerich. *The Life of Jesus Christ and Biblical Revelations..* Rockford, IL: Tan Books and Publishers, 1986.

de Caussade, Jean-Pierre. *The Sacrament of the Present Moment.* Trans. Kitty Muggeridge. Paperback Edition. HarperSanFrancisco, 1989.

Guardinai, Romano. *The Living God.* Trans. Stanley Goodman. Manchester, NH: The Sophia Institute Press, 1991.

Fahy, Thomas. *Book of Glory: Questions and Answers about the Third Fiat of God.* Jacksonville, FL: Center for the Divine Will: Association Luisa Piccarreta, (no date).

Fernandez, Francis. *In Conversation with God.* London. Sceptor, 2000.

Hendra, Tony. *Father Joe: The Man Who Saved My Soul.* New York: Random House, 2004.

Holmes, Michael, ed. *The Apostiolic Fathers. Second Edition.* Trans. J. B. Lightfoot and J. R. Harmer. Grand Rapids, MI: Baker Book House, 2000.

Iannuzze, Joseph, O.S.J. *The Triumph of God's Kingdom in the Millennium and End Times.* Havertown, PA: St. John the Evangelist Press, 1999.

St. John of the Cross. "Sayings of Light and Love." *Collected Works of St. John of the Cross.* Trans. Kieran Kavanaugh, OCD and Otilio Rodriguez, OCD. Washington, DC: ICS, 1991.

Pope John Paul II. *The Encyclicals of John Paul II.* Ed. J. Michael Miller, C.S.B. Huntington, Indiana: Our Sunday Visitor Publishing Division, 1996.

Keller, Helen. *The Story of My Life.* New York: W.W. Norton and Co., 2003.

à Kempis, Thomas. *The Imitation of Christ.* Trans. Joseph N. Tylenda, S.J. Wilmington: Michael Glazier, Inc., 1984.

St. Maria Faustina Kowalska. *Diary of St. Maria Faustina Kowalszka:: Divine Mercy in My Soul.* Stockbridge, MA: Marians of the Immaculate Conception, 2003.

Lafouge, Jean-Pierre, ed. *For God's Greater Glory.* Bloomington, IN: World Wisdom Books, 2006.

Brother Lawrence of the Resurrection, OCD. *Writings and Conversations On the Practice of the Presence of God.* Ed. De Meester, OCD. Trans. Salvatore Sciurba, OCD. Washington: ICS , 1994.

Levenson, Thomas. *Einstein in Berlin.* New York: Bantam Books, 2004.

Marmion, Blessed Columba. *Christ, the Life of the Soul.* Trans. Alan Bancroft. Bethesda, MD: Zaccheus Press, 2005.

Mary of Agreda. *The Mystical City of God: Popular Abridgement.* Trans. Rev. George J. Blatter. Rockford, IL: Tan Books and Publishers, 1978.

Monier-Vinard, S.J., ed. *The Redeemer's Call to Consecrated Souls.* Tarpon Springs, FL: Logos Institute Press, 2012.

Sister Mary of the Holy Trinity. *The Spiritual Legacy of Sister Mary of the Holy Trinity.* Ed. Fr. Silvere van den Broek, O.F.M. Rockford, IL: Tan Books and Publishers, 1981.

Oden, Thomas C. and Christopher A. Hall, eds., Mark. Vol. II of *Ancient Christian Commentary on Scripture*, Downers Grove, IL: InterVarsity Press, 1998.

Owen, Hugh. *"New and Divine:" The Holiness of the Third Christian Millennium.* John Paul Institute of Christian Spirituality, (no date).

Piccarreta, Luisa. *Book of Heaven.* 19 vols. Carryville, TN: The Luisa Piccarreta Center for the Divine Will, 1995.

—-. *Book of Heaven: Selected Passages #2.* Carryville, TN: The Luisa Piccarreta Center for the Divine Will, 1995.

—-. *When the Divine Will Reigns in Souls: A Selection of Passages from the Book of Heaven.* Carryville, TN: The Luisa Piccarreta Center for the Divine Will, 1995.

—-. *The Hours of the Passion of Our Lord Jesus Christ.* Carryville, TN: The Luisa Piccarreta Center for the Divine Will, 2006.

Pope Pius XII. *Encyclical Mystici Corporis Christi.* http://www.vatican.va 1943.

Ratzinger, Joseph Cardinal (Pope Benedict XVI). *On the Way to Jesus Christ.* San Francisco: Ignatius Press, 2005.

—-. *God and the World: Believing and Living in Our Time. A Conversation with Peter Seewald.* Trans. Henry Taylor. San Francisco: Ignatius Press, 2000.

Ripley, Canon Francis. *This Is the Faith.* Rockford, IL: Tan Books and Publishers, 2002.

Sales, Lorenzo, I.M.C, ed. *Jesus Appeals to the World.* Trans. A.J.M. Mausolff. 15th ed. Staten Island, New York: Alba House, 2004.

Simon, Raphael, O.C.S.O. *Spiritual Formation of the Priest.* Unpublished conference ms. 1999.

Scheeben, Matthias J. *The Glories of Divine Grace.* Trans. Patrick Shaughnessy, O.S.B. Rockford, IL: Tan Books and Publishers, 2000.

Ste. Thérèse of Lisieux. *Autobiography.* Trans. John Beevers. New York: Image Books/Doubleday a division of Random House, Inc., 1957. Reissued 2001.

Tugwell, Simon, O.P., ed. *Albert and Thomas: Selected Writings.* Classics of Western Spirituality. New York: Paulist Press, 1988.

Valtorta, Maria. *Poem of the Man-God.* Trans. Nicandro Picozzi. Rev. Patrick McLaughlin. Centro Editoriale Valtortiano. Sherbooke, Québec Libraire Éditions Paulines, 1987.

Ware, Timothy, ed. *The Art of Prayer: An Orthodox Anthology.* Trans. E. Kadloubovsky and E. M. Palmer. London: Faber and Faber, 1966.

❖

Excerpts from (1) St. John of the Cross (II-54), (2) St. Irenaeus (III-1), (3) St. Athanasius (III-82) and (4) St. Augustine (III-97) are from the *The Divine Office: The Liturgy of the Hours.* Catholic Book Publishing Co. New York. 1975. Copyright owned by International Commission on English in the Liturgy (ICEL). Excerpts are taken from, respectively, (1) Vol. iv: Friday, 18th Week of Ordinary Time; (2) Vol. iii: Feast of St. Irenaeus, June 28th; (3)

Vol. iii, Friday, 1st Week of Ordinary Time; and (4) Vol. iv: 22nd Sunday of Ordinary Time.

Quotations from Early Church Fathers (except where otherwise noted) are from the InterVarsity Press's multivolume *Ancient Christian Commentary on Scripture*, cited above.

 Quotations from Fr. Raphael Simon, Eileen George, A Servant of God, and diarist are from unpublished sources.

❖

Publications by and about Luisa Piccarreta may be obtained from the Luisa Piccarreta Center for the Divine Will, P.O. Box 340, Caryville, TN 37714 (Tel 423-566-5178)

❖

Copyright Credits and Acknowledgments

*The Publisher wishes to thank copyright holders
or other responsible parties for the following permissions:*

Jean-Pierre de Caussade excerpts from pp 51-55, 59, 60 of *The Sacrament of the Present Moment*. English translation copyright © 1981 by William Collins Sons & Co. Ltd. Introduction copyright © 1982 Harper & Row, Publishers, Inc. Reprinted by permission of HarperCollins Publishers. First published in France as *L'Abandon à la Providence divine* by Desciee de Brouwer, © Desciee de Brouwer 1966.

Dom Jean-Baptiste Chauitard, O.C.S.O. excerpts from *The Soul of the Apostolate*, used with permission of Tan Books, Rockford, IL. Copyright © 1946 by the Abbey of Gethsemani, Inc. Trappist, KY.

St. Claude de La Columbière excerpt from *For God's Greater Glory*, used with permission of Ignatius Press, San Francisco.

Sister Mary Consolata and *Fr. Lorenzo Sales, IMC* excerpts from *Jesus Appeals to the World*, Fifteen Edition, used with permission of Alba House Book Publishing, Staten Island, NY.

Consuelo excerpts from *Mary, Gate of Heaven*, used by permission of Fr. Joaquin de Castellfort, Spiritual Director of Consuelo, Barcelona, Spain.

Albert Einstein excerpt IV-84 from *Einstein in Berlin* by Thomas Leverson. Copyright © 2004 by Banton Books, a division of Random House, Inc. Used with permission.

St. Maria Faustina Kowalska excerpts from *Diary of St, Maria Faustina Kowalska: Divine Mercy in My Soul*, used with permission of Copyright Administrator, Marians of the Immaculate Conception, Stockbridge, MA.

Romano Guardini excerpt from *The Living God*, used with permission of Sophia Institute Press, Manchester, NH.

Tony Hendra excerpt from *Father Joe: The Man Who Saved My Soul*. Copyright © by Tony Hendra. Used by permission of Random House, Inc.

St. Irenaeus excerpt from *The Liturgy of the Hours Office of Readings*, used with permission of ICEL.

St. John of the Cross excerpts II-24, II-36, IV-99 from *The Collected Works of St. John of the Cross*, used with permission of ICS Publications, 2131 Lincoln Road, N.E., Washington, D.C. 20002-1199. www.icspublications.org. Excerpt II-54 from *The Liturgy of the Hours Office of Readings*, used with permission of ICEL.

Pope John Paul II excerpts on pp 1-4 from *Laborem Exercens*, and excerpts IV-10, IV-76, VI-33, used with permission of Libreria Editrice Vaticana.

Helen Keller excerpts from *The Story of My Life*, (quotes from Anne Sullivan), used with permission of W. W. Norton & Company, New York, London.

Excerpts from *Lumen Gentium* of the Second Vatican Council, used with permission of Libreria Editrice Vaticana.

Blessed Columba Marmion excerpt from *Christ, The Life of the Soul*, used with permission of Zaccheus Press, Bethesda, MD.

Excerpts from *The Spiritual Legacy of Sr. Mary of the Holy Trinity*, published by Tan Books, Rockford, IL, used without objection.

Excerpts from *The Redeemer's Call to Consecrated Souls*, used with permission of Logos Institute Press.

Hugh Owen excerpt from *The Holiness of the Third Christian Millennium*, used with permission of John Paul II Institute of Christian Spirituality, Woodstock, VA.

Luisa Piccarreta excerpts from *The Book of Heaven* are included per correspondence with The Secretariat of the Cause of Beatification of Luisa Piccarreta, Corato, Italy, expressing no objection to the reprint of the excerpts in this book. All translations used are faithful to the original Italian version of Luisa's writings.

Pope Pius XII excerpts from the encyclical *Mystici Corporis Christi*, used with permission of Libreria Editrice Vaticana.

Joseph Ratzinger (Pope Benedict XVI) excerpts from *God and the World* and from *On the Way to Jesus Christ*, used with permission of Ignatius Press, San Francisco, CA.

Canon Francis Ripley excerpt from *This is the Faith*, used with permission of Tan Books, Rockford, IL.

Matthias Scheeben excerpt from *The Glories of Divine Grace* used with permission of Tan Books, Rockford, IL.

Theophan the Recluse excerpts from *The Art of Prayer*, Timothy Ware, ed., used with permission of Farrar, Straus and Giroux, Inc., New York.

Maria Valtorta excerpt from *The Poem of the Man-God*, used with permission of Centro Editoriale Valtortiano, Isola del Liri, Italy.

Ste. Thérèse of Lisieux excerpts from *The Autobiography of Saint Therese of Lisieux*, used with permission of Doubleday, a division of Random House, Inc., New York.

Scriptural Passages

Note

❖   ❖   ❖

Finally, the editor compiler wishes to thank Arlene Scott without whose help this book could never have been made. Thanks also to Cecilia Mellet, Marian O'Meara, Thomas Fahy, and Fr. Gregory Ogbenika, each of whom in various ways has provided important help in the making of this book.

❖

❖

❖   ❖   ❖   ❖   ❖

I am the vine, you are the branches. Whoever remains in me and
I in him will bear much fruit, because without me you can do
nothing. Anyone who does not remain in me will be
thrown out like a branch and wither; and
the branches will be gathered,
thrown into the fire
and burned.

— John 15: 5-6

❖

298

www.ingramcontent.com/pod-product-compliance
Lightning Source LLC
LaVergne TN
LVHW061222060426
835509LV00012B/1379